TINY

ONE WOMAN'S TRUE LIFE STORY OF SURVIVAL AND SELFLESS LOVE

Emily,
May the Lord richly
bless you with health,
joy, and love.

Very truly,
Jamie
B.

KIMI ← — the Hawiian
My Pen NAME   Name
     — ONLY —   for

                    JAMIE

outskirtspress
DENVER, COLORADO

Author's Note

The information regarding my biological parents was given to me first-hand by various biological family members. The events during my childhood and beyond have been recorded accurately, to the best of my memory. All names, cities, and states have been changed to protect the privacy of all referenced individuals.

Various comments are the sole opinion of the author.

Table of Contents

Introduction

The story of Tiny began before I was born, and has been in the making for 50+ years. As God formed me inside my mother's womb, he knew she would reject me, but HE had a plan and a purpose for the child HE was creating. HE knew the strengths I would need in order to survive not only as an unwanted child but also through the violence I would encounter as an adult.

Adoptions were not as prevalent in the early 1960's, as they are in today's society. My records were sealed by the state, and such information was not available to my new adoptive parents. I was left to dream any dream I chose, as to who my birth mother might be. I chose to dream of her as a glamorous movie star, who would show up one day and tell me how sorry she was for letting me go. Dreaming lessened the pain of rejection, which lurked within my heart.

We all want to know we are loved, and have a purpose for being. People who choose to adopt a child, have a huge responsibility to nurture and swaddle the child in unconditional love. The child needs to know they are accepted as part of the family, by each and every relative. It is a cruel statement to hear someone tell you, "Well you are not really related...you're not a blood relative." Unfortunately, I have heard these words from first cousins and immediate family members. I am sure most adopted children would sadly say they have encountered similar uncaring statements.

Perhaps it is jealousy or pride that makes a person try to undermine the family ties of an adopted child. One such instance happened when I was grown. I took a suitcase of old family photographs to a first cousin's home; I was invited to stay at her house for a few days, and she asked me if I could bring the photos. I considered the invitation as a wonderful bonding time for us, as cousins, and happily agreed to make the four-hour drive.

I thought it odd that my mom told me to be sure and bring the suitcase back with me, and all the photos. I assured her I wouldn't forget to bring it back. I didn't realize, at the time, her concern was not about me being absent minded and forgetting the suitcase. The revelation came after a couple hours of sitting on my cousin's sofa and looking through hundreds of photographs. As we finished looking at the last few, I began to place stacks of pictures back into the suitcase, when my cousin said, "I want that suitcase with the photographs!" Unsure of her abrupt statement, I asked, "What do you mean? Do you want to get some of them copied?" With a stern tone, she replied, "That suitcase should belong to me!" I could tell she was becoming indignant and somewhat angry, but I had no idea what was wrong with her. She knew I was not sure what to say back to her, so she quickly blurted out, "Look, those photographs are of *MY* grandmother and relatives, and Grandmother would want me to have them, not you!" Unsure of what she was getting at, I said, "Well, she was my grandmother too, and she left them to my Mom." That is when she let her true feelings out, and said, "No! She was my Grandmother! You're not even really related! You're not a blood relative, and you are not getting these pictures back; I am keeping this suitcase!" I couldn't help the tears that began to roll down my face, as I realized she never really thought of me as her cousin, or even any part of the family tree. It was a crushing moment that made me wonder how many other "cousins" really didn't think I *belonged*.

From the moment my "cousin" spoke those hateful words to me, I wondered what kind of "relatives" my brother and I would have once our parents were deceased. Would any of them still consider us a niece, nephew, or cousin? As I pondered on the delicate nature of *"family"* to an adopted child, I couldn't help but feel sorry for not only myself, but all the other adopted children in the world who are left feeling they don't really belong anywhere. As I sunk deeper into sadness, a small internal voice said, "You were chosen!" I thought about what it meant to be chosen by my parents, and then I thought about the long process involved in a particular child being placed with a particular family. This was the revelation that was of the greatest importance: I was not an accident, but rather a child created and loved by God, to be placed with a family and set on a course for a life that HE planned for me.

God had a family waiting for me, and I was given my gift of a Mom and Dad, with the bonus of a big brother, when I was three-and-a-half years of age. My personality was already formed, and my tiny (22 pound) stature was full of independence and strong will. This nature was formed in me because the circumstances of my life would demand it. The first three-and-a-half years of my life were spent being lonely; and were void of being held and loved by a Mom or Dad. From an incubator at birth, to a boarding home during my early childhood years, a strength was formed within me, by the hand of God.

There is no other way to explain the personality that developed within me, except to say that God gave me a confidence and strong will despite the circumstances of being alone, unloved, and hungry. Each step had a purpose, and was preparing me for my future.

It is good that we cannot see ahead, to know the threads of life we must weave, as God forms His plan and purpose for our lives, and works to complete our coat of many colors. Sometimes the threads are straight and the path ahead is clear to see; however, there are times the threads become a tangled mess, and we have no idea how we can go on, or how to fix the mess we are in.

People want to believe they are in total control of their circumstances and decisions, but as I look back on my life, I believe I was predestined and placed where God needed me to be. From my birth mother's womb, He directed my path, formed a strong will inside me, and pre-planned my name and family.

My story does not end with a happily ever after; it ends with something far more important - the value of faith. I pray that you come to realize that God's grace is sufficient to see you through the most difficult of circumstances.

TINY was not only birthed as a person, but also in the form of a book, to tell the world that God is real! He shows up to help his children when we cry out to Him. No matter the pain another human inflicts on you, physically or mentally, God is stronger. No one can take your faith from you, or separate you from the Love of God.

My faith has been my anchor as I faced loneliness and uncertainty as a child, and violent bi-polar outbursts from my husband, throughout 18 years of marriage. I witnessed the power of God many times throughout my life. I have seen him show up in a mighty way, for my protection and guidance. I would not want anyone to go through the horrific experiences I have survived; however, I wish the world could know without doubt, that God is real and ready to help, if they would seek him and ask.

The Christian faith is often hard to put into words. We know that we know, but the feeling and peace God gives, is impossible to verbalize. Whether you believe in Jesus Christ or not, you will face difficult circumstances in life. How much greater it is, to have a friend like Jesus, who will carry you through the difficulties and trials of life.

TINY begins with a back-story of how I came to be. The information I received regarding my birth mother, was given to me from first hand accounts, by biological family members.

The chapters regarding my 18 years of marriage describe true and actual events, as they took place. My hope in writing about these experiences is not only to tell how the Lord sustained me, but also to bring awareness to the seriousness of Bi-polar Disorder and how potentially dangerous it can be.

This is my story.

CHAPTER ONE

BECKY

The story of TINY begins in a small Tennessee town, back in the early 1960's. Life was simpler then, and folks knew each other by name. Privacy was hard to come by, which could be good when you were down on your luck and needed help; however, in a small town, revealing a hidden secret could ruin a reputation forever.

Becky McBride was about to find out how quickly her secret life could be made public throughout her small hometown community. Friends and neighbors will often overlook indiscretions, until they become too heart wrenching to bear. Becky would see a shift in attitudes, as her carefree lifestyle evolved into a life of pure selfish indulgences.

There wasn't an abundance of employment opportunities for women in the small town of Gentry, back in the early 60's. After graduating high school, most girls applied for a job as a waitress at the local diner or as a cashier at the Piggly Wiggly Grocery; very few young people in the town had enough money to go to college. Most folks just grew up and got enough work to get by on; they started their families, and basically lived and died in the small town.

Becky had always been able to pick up odd jobs since she was a child. She didn't work because she wanted to; it wasn't an option. The children all had to work to help support the family. Her mother was strict, and hard on all of her children. No matter how much they did, it was never enough... at least not for Becky. Becky's half-sister, Anna, never worked very hard, but always seemed to get recognition and approval. Becky's mother was so cold-hearted that she called Becky "the ugly one" and called Anna "the pretty one."

Becky could feel that her mother loved Anna more. Maybe it was because her mother, Lois, was forced to get married when she was only thirteen years old. Becky had heard the story many times as her mother bitterly told how there was no work for her parents; being in bad health, they made an arrangement with a local farmer, who was 20 years older than Lois, but had money and wanted a wife. Becky's mother had been *given* to this man when she was only thirteen and was forced to be a wife to him, in exchange for saving her family's farm. Lois gritted her teeth and cried as she told how she hated him more and more every time he touched her. Becky and her older brother were products of this tragedy. After his death, Lois married a man of her choosing, and had another son and daughter. Becky knew in her heart that her mother could hardly stand the sight of her, because it brought back memories of a thirteen-year-old girl forced to be a wife rather than getting to enjoy her childhood.

Becky may not have seemed "pretty" to her mother, but she was spunky, energetic, and had no trouble getting a boyfriend. Her long dark hair, deep brown eyes, and cute little figure not only turned the heads of the teenage boys in her school, but turned the heads of many local (married) men, as well.

Lois' diagnosis of diabetes became a financial hardship. Becky had to drop out of school and find work. The owner of the local Piggly Wiggly knew about the family struggles, and offered Becky a job. Her high school years weren't filled with ballgames and proms, but with hard work and harsh realities. The money may have helped buy medicine and food, but it cost Becky her innocence. It doesn't take long for a girl to figure out how to use her "looks" to get by on, and get favors from men.

Becky's sister, Anna Sue, married a great guy who was several years older than her. He had a steady job and had saved a lot of money. A man like Billy was hard to come by in their little town. Anna and Billy purchased an old, run-down motel at the edge of town, from an elderly couple that decided to move to Florida. Anna offered Becky a cleaning job at the motel. Becky was ready for a change; with all the truckers who came and went from the motel, maybe "Mr. Right" would show up and give her the life she had dreamed of.

Anna told Becky stories that the elderly couple had shared with her about Florida. The two sisters began to dream of getting to see the ocean one day, walk on the beach, and feel the warm breeze rush across their faces. But they knew a dream is all it would probably ever be, because a trip like that would cost a lot of money. Money was certainly in short supply for them, and most people in their town.

The motel was good employment for a few years, but the money and raises her sister had promised, never came. However, the cleaning job did offer other opportunities. Becky learned to flirt and tease the truckers in exchange for whiskey and extra tip money. Maybe "Mr. Right" would pull into the parking lot one day, but so far all the men had been a big disappointment. Some of them said they loved her, and would even promise a lot in the beginning, but then they always left her behind. It was looking like the proverbial little house with a white picket fence would never be hers, and her dream of going to Florida was slowly becoming an impossibility. There would never be enough money to cover her dream trip to the ocean.

Before Becky knew it, ten years had passed since she had dropped out of school. She now had two children and a couple marriages behind her. Her hands were calloused from the years of cleaning at her sister's motel, and she needed an easier job. She returned to her job at the Piggly Wiggly during the day, and began waitressing at a saloon four nights a week.

Lois kept Becky's kids, Robert and Dana, most of the time. Between Becky's day job at the Piggly Wiggly and night shift at the Black Cat Saloon, how was she supposed to raise two kids? She had every Friday and Saturday night off, which she used as her "date" nights. Becky decided that with two jobs, some "me" time, and the constant search for "Mr. Right," it was best that her kids live with her Mom for now; at least until she could get her life straightened out.

Lois did the best she could with the children, but with arthritis and diabetes, some days were difficult for her. Becky dropped off money every week, but there was never enough. Lois lived on her monthly social security check and it was barely enough for her to get by on, much less provide food and clothing for two grandchildren. Becky's additional money made the situation manageable, but sometimes Lois just wished for alone time so she could rest.

Becky came by regularly each week to see her children. On a rare occasion, she offered to take them to her place for the night. The months turned to years, as Lois raised her grandchildren and visits from Becky became fewer and far between. Various friends began dropping off the money each week, as Becky began to care less about checking on her mother and seeing her children.

One day, Lois had been feeling more tired than usual, so she called Becky and told her that she needed a few days by herself. Lois told Becky to pick up her children Friday afternoon so she could rest over the weekend. Becky said she would take them for the weekend, but would need to bring them back to Lois on Sunday. Lois was hoping for a longer break from her grandchildren, but she knew Becky would pawn them off on a friend or a practical stranger, to get out of being a mother to her children for more than a day or two.

Surprisingly, Becky actually showed up Friday afternoon to take Robert and Dana for the weekend. Lois kissed her grandchildren good-bye, and told them she would see them Sunday. The children were in tears, begging not to leave. Becky was like a stranger to them; they had begun to call Lois, "Mom." It broke Lois' heart to make them leave with Becky, but she needed a couple days rest, and Becky needed to spend time with her children and show them some attention and love.

It didn't take long for that weekend of rest to come to an end, when a phone call came that evening. The caller told Lois that her grandchildren were locked in a car outside the Black Cat Saloon, and that Becky had already been in there for a couple of hours. Lois quickly called a neighbor, who was also a dear friend, and asked for his help. Lois asked Tom if he would drive to the Black Cat and drag Becky out, if necessary, and tell her to get those children home, or else Lois would be calling the police.

Lois waited frantically. The phone finally rang a little before midnight; it was Tom.

"Ms. Lois, I've got to tell you, that daughter of yours is quite the hellcat," he said. "I literally had to pick Becky up, carry her outside, stand her beside the car, and make her look down at her kids, asleep in the back seat."

Tom went on to explain the cussing Becky had given him, and how she didn't feel any remorse.

"See, those kids are fine!" Becky yelled. "They're sleeping, and I even cracked a window so they would have fresh air. You just ruined my evening for nothing, Tom Buckley!"

Lois held the phone, as her tears hit the floor; she listened while Tom told a story she knew all too well. Lois thought Becky had changed. Seven years had passed since she took Becky to court, and was granted temporary custody of her grandson, Robert.

Lois had received a phone call that dreadful day, in the early morning hours, from a lady who lived in Becky's apartment building. The lady had called asking Lois if she knew where Becky was. Lois told her that Becky should be there in her apartment, because she had picked up Robert the day before. The lady explained to Lois that she heard a baby crying off and on throughout the night, but she never heard any other sounds, just the baby.

Lois grabbed her coat and rushed to Becky's apartment. When Lois opened the door, it was a moment of shock and horror, as the overwhelming stench of warm urine and feces flooded her nostrils. There lay little Robert, all alone in the apartment. He was lying in his crib, wearing a t-shirt and diaper, with a heating pad underneath him. He had no bottle, and there was no way to tell how many hours he had been laying in this condition. The heating pad had literally baked the feces to his skin. One thing was certain; Becky could not be trusted to be a mother. Lois called the town doctor, and he rushed to meet them at his office.

The doctor examined little Robert, and he and Lois both cried as the baby screamed in pain from the diaper being removed. The baked on feces had actually burned his skin and the poor baby was not only hurting, but was hungry as well. Lois told Dr. Smith what she planned to do, and he agreed. The baby could not go back to Becky.

It wasn't difficult for Lois to gain temporary custody of her grandson after that incident. There are advantages to small town "connections." Unfortunately, the story had spread not only through their town, but had reached into several surrounding counties. Becky had promised the judge that she would visit Robert regularly at her mother's, and provide money for his care. It seemed Becky had actually been shamed into behaving herself for a while. Now it was happening again; Lois would have to fight for two grandchildren this time, and her health issues were more complicated than they were seven years ago.

The reality was clear; Becky didn't know how to be a mother, and something had to be done. Becky had once again demonstrated her selfishness and total disregard for her children. She needed to be stopped before something terrible happened to one of the children.

Lois gave her daughter an ultimatum; Becky could either willingly allow the children to live with Lois or she would be taken back to court. This time Lois would accuse her daughter of abandonment and neglect, and tell the court how Becky left the children in a locked car, for hours, outside a saloon. Becky argued that she had not harmed her children and didn't understand what the big deal was. She didn't see the harm in leaving them locked in her car while she was in the saloon having a couple drinks. After several hours of arguing, Becky finally agreed to the arrangement.

"Fine. The kids can live with you," she said. "But I'm not admitting that I did anything wrong!"

Lois made sure Becky understood she had to provide money for the children, or Lois would take her to court and tell the entire story to the judge. It wasn't that Lois wanted to be paid for taking care of her grandchildren, but with extra mouths to feed, school supplies to buy, and additional expenses, Becky would have to help. This was going to be permanent for the children, and they wouldn't be "going home" with Becky ever again.

Becky's two jobs provided plenty of money, and she sent it regularly by mail. She was hurt by her mother's demands, and didn't want to visit for fear of Lois insulting her in front of her children. At least she was sending the money, even though she wasn't able to spend time with Robert and Dana.

Becky was working at the Piggly Wiggly one day, when she noticed some of the cashiers giggling and pointing down one of the aisles. Becky asked what was going on.

"Didn't you see him? Doug Glenwright just walked in!" they said.

"Is that the man who owns the lumberyard?" Becky asked.

"Yes," they replied excitedly, "he's a millionaire!"

Much to Becky's surprise, Mr. Glenwright chose her checkout lane. She felt her heart beating faster as it came his turn to checkout. He was very tall and handsome, just the type of man she dreamed about. Mr. Glenwright broke the ice.

"I see your name tag says, Becky. That's a very pretty name. What is your husband's name?" he asked.

Becky giggled as she answered, "Oh, I'm not married."

Mr. Glenwright smiled.

"Well, that may turn out to be very interesting."

Getting ready for work the next day was pure excitement. Becky made sure to put on a little more eyeliner and blush, just in case Mr. Glenwright came back through her checkout lane again.

It was getting late in the day, when Becky looked up and there he was.

"Well hello again," Mr. Glenwright said. "I forgot to get a few things yesterday."

Becky smiled.

"That happens to me once in a while," she said as she handed him his change.

Then it happened. Mr. Glenwright started to walk out, stopped, and came back to the end of the counter.

"I was wondering if I could buy you a cup of coffee when you get off work?" he asked.

Becky felt her heart pounding, and although she knew Mr. Glenwright had a wife and two children, she couldn't help but say, "Yes!"

Mr. Glenwright (Doug) became a regular visitor at the Piggly Wiggly, and he and Becky went out for coffee every chance they could. They usually parted after about an hour of talking and laughing at the diner. Becky would leave from the diner and go to her evening job at the Black Cat Saloon, while Doug returned home to his family and pretended he was happy to be there. One day, the coffee offer turned into a "drink" offer, and that's when the relationship changed.

Becky was just about finished with her shift at the saloon one evening, when she felt a hand on her shoulder. She turned around to find Doug standing behind her. He had a serious look in his eyes.

"Can I buy you a drink?" he asked.

Becky wasn't sure why or how he had managed to slip away from his wife so late at night, but whatever the reason, he was there.

"Sure," she replied, "I was about to leave, but I'm in no hurry."

She and Doug sat at a table back in the darkest corner they could find, and Doug started to explain how unhappy he was in his marriage. He said that he felt vibrant and alive when he and Becky were together, and he wanted to keep seeing her.

"I have to meet some business associates in Florida next week," Doug said, "and I was wondering if you would accompany me."

Becky was speechless. All sorts of thoughts were racing through her mind, but there was one word she really fixated on - Florida. She thought, *did he really just ask me to go to the one place I've spent years dreaming of?* When she could finally speak, she asked,

"Are you asking me to Florida as a friendly companion, or are you wanting our relationship to be more than friends?"

Doug looked at her silently for what seemed like five minutes, and she was beginning to wish she had just said a simple, "Yes, I'll go."

Doug took Becky's hand and looked deeply into her eyes.

"I think of you night and day," he began. "I think you are a beautiful woman, and I love our time together. I'm going to let you make the decision of friends or lovers. After all, you know I'm married, and you know what that will make you look like to people in this town."

"All I know right now is that I would love to go to Florida," Becky replied. "Can I make my decision about our relationship after the trip?"

Doug was always a gentleman, and he was proving to be that yet again. He leaned forward, giving her a light kiss on her cheek, and said,

"I would love to walk on the beach with you, and see the breeze blow through your hair. Whether you are there as my friend, or if I am lucky enough for you to become my lover… Either way, the trip is yours, if you want it. I'll pick you up at 5am Monday morning, if that is okay with you."

Becky's head was spinning as she heard herself say, "Yes, that sounds great. I will see you Monday."

Becky could hardly sleep all weekend, in anticipation of her trip to Florida. Her dream of seeing the ocean was about to come true, but there were strings attached. What was she going to tell Doug on their first night in Florida? She had a feeling he would be hard to refuse, especially after a moonlit walk on the beach.

CHAPTER TWO

FLORIDA BOUND

Monday morning had finally arrived and Doug was not only true to his word, but he was very prompt. At exactly 5am, there was a knock at Becky's door. As she ran to get the door, she wasn't sure how she should greet him. She could hardly contain her excitement of the trip, so she thought a hug would be appropriate.

Becky opened the door, and there he stood. He looked so handsome, and he seemed genuinely happy to see her. For a split second she felt like she was in love, but how could that be? He never said that he loved her; he just said he wanted to take her to Florida. Becky had been used before, so she wasn't expecting much to become of the relationship once they got back home from the trip. Whether or not she slept with him probably wouldn't change the outcome. In her experiences, they all want you until they get you, and then they move on. Doug was at least giving her the opportunity to have one dream come true - she was headed to the ocean. She would be walking in the sand and taking in all the beauty of the seashore, that very night.

Becky gave Doug a friendly hug, but he held on a little longer than she thought he would. She could tell he was going to pull out all the stops, to help influence her decision about their relationship. Doug loaded her bags into the back seat of his Cadillac and off they headed, south to Florida.

Perhaps it was the excitement, or all the talking they did, but twelve hours of driving only felt like a couple. The day just seemed to fly by. To Becky, every stop they made was exciting. She had never been out of her small hometown and had only heard stories of southern states like Georgia and, of course, her dream state of Florida. It seemed like Doug picked the most beautiful rest stops, and he was taking her to nice restaurants; Becky was feeling like a queen. She wondered how Doug's wife could want to miss sharing such a wonderful day with him. For a moment, Becky wanted to ask if his wife knew she was traveling with him, but decided that was a talk they could have during their long walk on the beach.

They pulled into a beautiful hotel, called a Hilton. Becky had seen pictures of hotels like this in magazines, but she never thought she would get to stay in such a grand place. It was truly becoming a fairy tale trip for her. Doug checked them in, and Becky was look-ing around the lobby when she heard him say, "I prefer a King Bed, please." Becky pretended she didn't hear the conversation; in fact, the thought of getting to live like *this* sounded wonderful, no matter what she had to do to get it. After all, what was one more guy? She had already been with several and whether she married them or not, they were all losers that never offered her anything. This guy was handsome, successful, and treated her like she was a queen... Who wouldn't want to be with this guy?

A man escorted them to their room and put their luggage away; to her, it was like watching a movie. Doug asked Becky if she wanted to freshen up, because he had made dinner reservations for them at the hotel, and after dinner they would take their walk on the beach. Becky suddenly became concerned that her clothes would embarrass him. She had brought the best dresses she owned, but even her best were just simple cotton dresses that suddenly felt like rags, in such beautiful surroundings. Becky asked him what she should wear.

"Oh, I almost forgot," he said. "I took the liberty of buying you a few new things. Since you have never been to Florida, I wanted you to have some bright, tropical things to wear."

Becky was stunned. This man seemed to think of everything. *He even bought me clothes,* she thought. *Wow… now this is a man worth keeping.*

Becky chose a beautiful, white, strapless dress that had a simple, hot pink banding around the hemline; it was stunning. As they were walking out the door, Doug said,

"I hope you don't mind, but I thought you might like a set of pearls. May I put them on you?"

As his hands reached to lift her hair, she could hardly contain her desire to kiss him. He slowly pushed her hair off to one shoulder, as he placed the pearls around her neck. Just as he clasped the pearls, he gently kissed the back of her neck. The decision was made - this was the life Becky had always dreamed of, and she was going to keep it, even if that meant she had to share Doug with his wife.

Doug offered to order dinner, since Becky wasn't familiar with seafood. He ordered her a wonderful trio of scallops, lobster, and baked flounder. Becky had never tasted food so delicious, nor had she been treated to fine wine. Doug explained that he had ordered a nice Chardonnay because white wine goes better with fish, and red wine goes better with heavier dishes, such as steak and other red meats. Becky was learning so much; every moment with Doug was exciting and new. If the trip never came to an end, it would be fine with her.

The dinner lasted over an hour, which was an experience in itself; back home, if you took that long to eat a meal, you were either very ill, or so old that you couldn't chew your food anymore. Nonetheless, the dinner was one she would always remember, and would hopefully get to experience again.

After dinner, Doug asked, "Are you ready for that walk?"

Becky couldn't wait. She was afraid to ask because she didn't want to seem like a child, but she had really wanted to run out and see the ocean the minute they arrived. It was now past eight. What if it was too dark to see anything? Becky quickly answered, "I would love to."

As they exited the back of the hotel, the scenery was gorgeous. There was a beautiful pool with tropical plants all around it, and at least fifty lounge chairs. Becky could just picture herself lounging back in one of those chairs, while Doug was in his meeting the next day.

They walked down a pathway lined with lush plants and flowers, which led to a long boardwalk. Finally, there it was; the beach scene she never thought she would actually see in person. The sun glowed beautiful shades of red and orange, and it was breathtaking. The scenery was more majestic than anything she had ever seen. Becky had to hold back her tears; she stood in awe and wonder as she watched the magnificent ocean rolling before her eyes. The waves were almost hypnotic as they rushed back and forth from the shoreline. Looking out beyond the waves was like looking at a piece of perfect, blue glass that never ended. As she stood there, taking in all the glorious beauty before her, Doug put his arm around her and said, "Don't you think it's time you touched it, and it touched you?"

With that said, Becky took off running towards the beautiful blue waters, and Doug was left running and laughing, trying to catch her. She stopped about three feet from the water, and turned to look at him.

"If it wasn't for you, I would never have experienced this beauty," she said. "Will you hold my hand, as I step into the ocean for the first time in my life?"

It was a magical moment. Doug looked at her with tears in his eyes.

"I would be honored to share this first with you," he replied.

There began the moment of love for them. They didn't know what lay ahead for them, but the friendship had definitely blossomed into love and they were about to become inseparable, despite Doug's marriage.

The week went by too quickly, and soon it was time for the drive back to Tennessee. What seemed like a short drive down to Florida, was becoming a very painful, tedious drive back. Becky and Doug hardly knew what to say to each other. It was fine when it was just the two of them, away from the world of nosey neighbors and gossipy friends. Now, they were headed back to a life of hiding and meeting in secret, just to be together. Doug broke the silence and said,

"I have given this a lot of thought, and I know what I'm going to do. I just need you to tell me what you think, when I am finished speaking. Will you tell me, from your heart, what you think about my decision?"

"Yes," Becky answered. "I will be honest with you about my feelings, no matter what you're fixing to tell me."

"This has been one of the happiest weeks of my life," Doug continued, "and I want you to know that I have fallen in love with you. I'm going to tell Dorothy about the two of us, although I think she already knows. I will not divorce her until my children are grown, because I don't think that would be fair to them. However, I do hope to marry you one day. For now, I am asking you to be my mistress, and allow me to stay married, in paper form only; I no longer have romantic feelings for my wife, and I haven't for over a year. Will you keep seeing me, under these circumstances, knowing that we will be the town gossip?"

"I have been thinking about you a lot," Becky answered. "I couldn't see our relationship going any other way, and my answer is yes! I definitely want to keep seeing you, because I'm in love with you. I can't give you up, at least not yet. I know you could fall back in love with your wife, and I would suddenly be out of the picture, but I am willing to take that chance because this one week has changed my life forever."

Doug was true to his word and told his wife, Dorothy, the entire story. He told her that she and the children would be taken care of, but his heart belonged to Becky. Dorothy had been a stay-at-home mother and wife, so she really had no options, but to thank him for making it as easy on her as he possibly could, and for thinking about the children.

Becky and Doug were together daily. They didn't even try to hide their relationship, which seemed okay for them, but they didn't think about the rumors and whispers their children would be left to deal with.

Everything seemed to be great for the happy couple, until Becky realized she might be pregnant. Like all women, she asked herself, *how could this have possibly happened?* What was she going to tell Doug? How was this going to affect their relationship? She certainly didn't want any more children, and he had already commented he would be glad when his two were grown. What was she going to do? It seemed her only option was to head towards Nashville and see if she could find a clinic that would "take care of the problem" for her.

Becky and Doug had spent two beautiful, fun-filled years together, and he had taken her on several trips to Florida, but had also neglected his business since he met her. Becky overheard rumors that Doug's lumber business was going bankrupt. There was no way he would want her to keep the baby if he was losing his business. Becky decided that maybe she should keep it to herself and "take care of it" without Doug ever finding out.

Becky called a woman in town, who was rumored to have "taken care of a problem" such as hers; perhaps she would give Becky the name of the doctor or clinic she had gone to. After several attempts of trying to reach her by phone, she was finally able to speak to her. The woman gave Becky the information she wanted but said,

"I have to tell you something about that experience."

"What's that?" Becky asked.

The woman began to tell her about constant nightmares of hearing a baby cry. She said that sometimes she would wake up in a cold sweat because she could hear screams of pain. She went on to say that she regretted what she had done, and wished she could go back in time and do things differently. Becky wasn't sure what to think... Maybe the woman was a little crazy. It didn't matter; this was her life. This baby was going to ruin everything she had with Doug, and she wasn't about to let that happen. She rationalized, telling herself it was best for her, Doug, and even her other kids, if the baby was never born.

Doug was supposed to be at her apartment for dinner that night. The doorbell rang right on time. Becky opened the door to find him standing there with two roses – one red, and one white.

"What are the roses for?" Becky asked.

Doug explained that someone had left him a message on his office phone, that said, "*If you really love her, you will take care of her and your new baby.*"

"Is it true? Are you pregnant?" he asked.

Becky didn't want to answer, but her hesitation was an answer in itself. Oddly, Doug didn't respond the way she had imagined in her head. He grabbed her, kissed her, and said,

"I will leave Dorothy and we will get married and raise this baby together, as a family."

Becky quickly responded with an abrupt, "No... No, I don't want things to change, and this kid will change everything!"

Doug was shocked to hear the anger in her voice, and it was quite obvious she felt no love for the child she was carrying. Becky quickly told Doug she wasn't feeling well, and dinner was off for the night. Doug gave her a kiss on the cheek and said, "One for each of you," as he handed her the two roses, and closed the door behind him.

Becky didn't know Doug left out part of the message about the baby. The anonymous caller had also given Doug the name of the doctor and clinic she would probably be going to for the abortion. The lady's voice on his answering machine also stated that some women don't make it out of the clinic; things can go very wrong, and if he loved Becky at all, he needed to stop her.

Becky made her arrangements with the doctor, and even borrowed some money from Doug; not knowing Doug had made arrangements of his own. Doug still had enough money to get things done the way he wanted them; the doctor was about to make a whole lot more money by faking the abortion, than he was going to make by going through with it. It was strictly business for the doctor, and Doug found it quite easy to convince him that it was best, for all parties concerned, if Becky was just told *things* had been taken care of.

Becky arrived at the clinic, not knowing what to expect, but she knew her life would soon be back to normal. The clinic was in a questionable part of town, and their sign couldn't be seen from the street. The doorway was on a side-street alleyway, on the lower level of a building that looked like it was at least a hundred years old. The building was in much need of repairs and lighting. The entrance was dark and dreary, but at least she had found it.

Becky signed in and filled out some papers the nurse handed her. There wasn't anyone else in the waiting room, but she heard voices in the back. Finally, the nurse led Becky back to a small room with little more than a stretcher, and a table with some instruments laying on it. The doctor came in and introduced himself. He briefly explained what he was going to do, and said for her not to worry if she didn't get her cycle for a few months. He gave her a shot of something that made her really sleepy; after that, she couldn't tell what the doctor was doing. The procedure didn't take long. Becky left the clinic after a couple hours, and was surprised at how good she felt; it was as if nothing had even happened.

A couple months passed, and life seemed grand, but for some reason Becky was putting on weight. Doug had been taking her out to eat a lot, but she didn't think she was eating enough to gain ten pounds. Becky had never had a weight problem, and she was going to tell him they needed to cut back on the fancy foods for a while. Becky still didn't have her monthly cycle, but the doctor had said it could take a few months for it to start again. Maybe her hormones were causing the weight gain.

One evening while she and Doug were watching TV, she felt a terrible pain in her stomach. The pain became so severe Doug rushed her to the hospital. Doug knew what was about to happen, but his main concern was for Becky to be all right. He wasn't allowed to go into the exam room with Becky, but he knew what the doctor was going to tell her. Becky was about to find out that she was almost five months pregnant, and it was too late to "fix it."

When Doug was finally allowed to see Becky, she was in tears.

"I tried to get rid of our *problem*," she said, "but it looks like I didn't go to the right place or something, because I'm still pregnant… I am so sorry."

Doug couldn't let her feel that way.

"Do you remember me telling you that I loved you, and I was willing to raise this baby with you?" he asked.

"Yes, I remember that," Becky replied, "but I didn't think you really meant it."

Doug went on to tell her how he'd been given the name of the doctor and the clinic, and he had gone behind her back and paid the doctor to fake the procedure. He explained that he just couldn't let his child be killed, and he wanted them to be a family. Becky was furious. After listening to her scream for what seemed like an hour, Doug finally asked, "Is our baby okay?"

Becky sighed, "Yes. I had been exercising too much because of the weight I was gaining, and it caused some cramping, but everything is fine."

Becky and Doug continued to see each other, and everyone in town knew who her baby belonged to. Becky had never admitted to her mother or anyone who the father of her second child (Dana) was. Friends and neighbors were used to seeing Becky with several different "boyfriends" who came and went from her apartment. At least the town wouldn't question who the father of her third child was.

It was Friday the thirteenth, on a cold December night, when the labor pains started. Becky was barely in her seventh month of pregnancy, so she thought maybe it was false labor. As the pain grew more intense, it became obvious that it was the real thing. Becky called Doug, and he rushed right over to drive her to the hospital.

The baby arrived that December night; it was a little girl. She was two months premature, weighed slightly over three pounds, and her lungs were under-developed. The doctor told Doug and Becky the baby was being placed in an incubator, and *if* she could survive the first night, she would still have to be in an incubator for several weeks. The doctor went on to say, "This little girl is going to have to be a fighter, to survive."

Becky felt fine and left the hospital the next morning; she told the nurses that she would be back in a few days. Without a single glance at her newborn, or a visit to the nursery, Becky left the hospital and went home to rest. She wanted to 'get over' the whole experience and get back to her life with Doug. After a few days at home, Doug took Becky out to the Black Cat for a night of drinking and fun. A week passed, then another week, and Becky still had not returned to the hospital to see her newborn daughter. Doug called and checked on the baby, but he was busy trying to get his business back on track during the day and enjoying Becky at night.

They had their first serious fight when Becky told Doug his baby had been given the last name of Johnson. Doug had noticed that Becky sometimes signed her last name as Johnson and at other times, used her maiden name, McBride. Terry Johnson and Becky had been on-and-off again sweethearts throughout high school. Terry wanted a career in the Army, but Becky thought she could do better than base housing and military pay, so she refused his offer of marriage when he proposed during his senior year. Terry went on to serve in the Army the summer after high school graduation.

Though she refused his marriage proposal, anytime Terry was in town, he and Becky were together. They became like a comfortable pair of shoes to one another. Terry was the man Becky ran to whenever her marriages failed, and he was always there to comfort her. This went on for years, until Terry finally proposed again. Becky accepted, on the grounds that she didn't have to follow him and live in a little base house. They were happy for a while, until Terry was called away on duty and Becky told him she didn't want to be tied down if he was going to be gone; Becky filed divorce papers and mailed them to his Army address.

Becky hadn't even thought about Terry since she met Doug. Doug had become the man of her dreams, even though he was married to someone else.

Becky told Doug she honestly did not realize Terry never returned the divorce papers, and she had not even thought about her marriage to Terry, since she and Doug had met that first day, in the Piggly Wiggly. Becky explained that she was truly shocked when the hospital administrator said Johnson would have to be the baby's last name, because she was still legally married to Terry Johnson. Doug was furious; he had done all he could to prove his love to Becky and assure her that he was happy about their baby, and now the baby didn't even have his last name. Doug walked away from Becky for about a week, but couldn't get her off his mind. Becky convinced him she would contact Terry, and she was sure he would want the baby's name changed as badly as Doug did.

While Doug and Becky were out dancing, drinking, and living it up, their little baby was fighting for her life. She was tiny and helpless, left alone in an incubator with no Mom or Dad to love and encourage her. A few of the nurses grew very attached to her; one of them even considered asking about adopting her, since it appeared the parents didn't care if the baby lived or died.

A month had passed; the baby now weighed a whole five pounds, and she was holding her own. The hospital had to make the call to Becky and let her know it was time for her to take the baby home. When she arrived at the hospital, a few of the nurses cried at the thought of releasing the still-delicate baby to such a woman, but they had no choice. Legally, she was the baby's mother, and legally, she was not obligated to visit the baby in the hospital. But morally, it was wrong. The nurses looked at Becky in such a way that it told her *exactly* what they thought about her.

A line was formed through the nursery as, one by one, the nurses kissed the tiny baby goodbye, and wished her health and happiness. A few nurses even took the time to hold her little hand and say a prayer that God would keep her safe, "now and always."

CHAPTER THREE

A NEW BEGINNING

Becky tried to take care of the new baby, but just like before, she found herself leaving the baby with her mother, Lois, more and more often. Robert loved seeing his newborn baby sister; he even gave her the nickname Tiny because she was so small. Lois knew Robert loved having Tiny around, she loved her too, but there was just no way she could take care of three grandchildren. Becky needed to give up some of her late night partying, and act like a mother to her children.

Tiny was about four months old when Lois received a concerned call late one evening. The caller said, "I am not going to tell you who I am, but I know for a fact that Becky and Doug have been drinking for several hours now; and they have that baby in the pick-up truck with them." The caller also said several people had seen Becky and Doug take the baby into the Black Cat; they came out with the baby, and a fifth of whiskey. Lois had to make a decision, and it was not an easy decision to make, but it had to be done. Becky needed a wake-up call; she needed to face the fact that she was putting her baby in danger.

The local police station soon received an *anonymous* phone call about two people who were drunk and had a baby in the vehicle with them. The police were told where they could find the pick-up truck. Sure enough, when the officer approached the truck, Doug and Becky were so drunk they could hardly speak. Down in the floorboard with old beer cans and trash of all kind, lay the baby girl. The police officer thought of how his son was safe at home, in a nice crib, snuggled in soft clothes and a warm blanket; tears filled the officer's eyes. As he looked down at the helpless little girl, he could hardly contain his emotions. The tiny baby was wearing a dirty t-shirt and diaper, with nothing to keep her warm except the trash that surrounded her. Once he had composed himself, the officer said, "First of all, I am taking that baby. If there is any justice in this world, she will never have to be with either of you again. You are both being taken to county lock-up."

The baby girl was taken away from Becky on that chilly April night. She eventually became part of the state welfare system, which meant being placed in a boarding home until she could be adopted.

Becky eventually found out it was her mother who had called the police that April night. What was already a strained mother/daughter relationship became even worse. Her mother's constant cut downs and the whispers around town, pushed Becky to drink even more. The 'loss' of Tiny slowly took its toll on Becky's relationship with Doug. Their happy and carefree love affair was now tense, filled with anger and resentment. Neither Doug nor Becky could explain what they felt, but everything was different. It was as if a cloud of darkness was hanging over their heads.

Doug's lumber business went bankrupt shortly after the baby was taken. The town millionaire, who once was talked about because he was so rich and handsome, was now talked about because he had let Becky use up all his money and had allowed his child to be taken away by the court system. The town had seemed to overlook Becky and Doug's blatant affair, but tossing their baby into the trashy floorboard of a pick-up truck while they got drunk was too awful to be ignored. Their small town shunned them; wherever they went, people were harsh and disapproving. When Doug and Becky went to eat at the diner, people would actually get up and leave the second they saw them.

The once inseparable couple now found themselves seeing each other less and less, until it became apparent that the love, excitement, and dreams of their future had vanished. Perhaps they would always have a love for each other, but the love they used to share had died; what used to be sparks between them, were now just a memory of what might have been.

Becky tried to regain custody of Tiny, but realized it was best if she let the court system take her. After all, Becky hardly saw her other two children, and Lois had made it clear she wasn't going to take care of another grandchild. Maybe one day Becky could see Tiny again. Although the choice had been forced on her, she knew that she wouldn't be a good mother to the baby. If Becky signed the papers to put Tiny up for adoption, maybe she would end up with a good family and a better life than Becky would ever be able to provide. There were so many *if*'s and *maybe*'s, but with all of the uncertainties, Tiny was guaranteed a better life if she was adopted by a stable family. A stable family could provide nice things, a nice home, and the one thing Becky had always longed for – love.

Doug had returned to his wife and was living in his house with his kids again, while Becky found herself alone, once more. It seemed like she would remain on a never-ending quest to find 'Mr. Right.' Over the few years she spent with Doug, Becky had changed a little on the inside. The time she spent with him had been different than with other men. It was as if she had caught a glimpse of something that was almost attainable, if she could just hold onto it. For some reason, relationships were the most difficult thing in her life. It was never difficult for Becky to get a man, or even get him to propose and buy her things; it was just seemingly impossible for her to stay connected with any one man.

Becky found it easy to get jobs and didn't have a problem with long hours of work, whether it meant standing on her feet all day at the checkout counter, or scrubbing floors as a maid at the motel.

Work came easy, but relationships seemed to be more work than she could emotionally handle. Perhaps she was destined to run from man to man for the rest of her life. Men come and go, but maybe that was a good thing for her; scars from so many failed relationships were building a barrier that might never be broken, and the most tragic scar of all was starting to form. Becky would always have to wonder where her third child, Tiny, ended up. Did she get adopted? Was she being taken care of or being abused? Becky wondered if she would ever see her again. What would happen if she did?

No one could possibly understand the feelings Becky must have wrestled with, unless they've given up a child under such circumstances. The only other person qualified to speak about how it may have felt, would be Becky's daughter, Tiny.

I am the little girl who was born that cold December night; found and taken, four months later, from a floorboard full of trash. **I am Tiny**. An attempted abortion, a premature birth, hunger, and neglect are a lot for an infant to endure and survive. My early struggles in life formed a great strength within me, a strength that has carried me through my adulthood and prepared me for the *ultimate* fight for survival.

The years began to pass, with no home to call my own. My first birthday came and went, with no family to celebrate it. The second year was the same as the first. Once again, on birthday number three, I spent my birthday alone. Three years had passed and I still had no one to call Mommy or Daddy. I spent most of my time just thinking and dreaming of being part of a family. By the time I was three years old, I had learned to read and write. My social worker, Ms. Turner, began to spend more time talking to me. One day she told me she was going to take me somewhere for a test; she called it an IQ test. Ms. Turner said that if I did really well on it, it might help me get a Mommy and Daddy because parents love to have smart children.

I took the test and Ms. Turner said I did excellent. She told me I had a score of 138, and that I should be very proud. They couldn't believe my score, so I had to take the test twice. I was so excited that I made a good grade both times. Ms. Turner made sure my scores and information were saved so they could be given to my new Mommy and Daddy, one day.

The day finally came when Ms. Turner told me there was a couple wanting to meet me. *Maybe the couple will like me and want to keep me*, I thought.

Ms. Turner made all the arrangements for the Bartlett's to meet me. She and I were going to get up early one morning and drive to a meeting place, a little ways from the boarding house.

"Why can't they come see my room and play with me?" I asked.

"Because instead, you're going to go to their house and you'll get to meet their son, Lucas," she replied.

I was so excited that I started jumping up and down.

"Ms. Turner, are they my new Mommy and Daddy?" I asked.

"Well," she said, "we need to make sure that's what you *all* want, but you can call them Daddy K and Mommy L for now."

A couple of days later, she told me it was all arranged; we were leaving early Saturday morning to meet them.

Ms. Turner and I left the boarding house that morning, before daylight. We drove for a long time, and then stopped at a park where she said they would meet us. We had only been waiting a few minutes, when a pretty white car pulled up beside us. I stayed in the car while Ms. Turner talked to the Bartlett's, then I saw her give them some papers. She came to my side of the car, picked me up, and carried me towards them. As she carried me closer, I could see they both had big smiles on their faces. Ms. Turner asked me if I was okay, and I nodded my head yes.

Ms. Turner introduced me, "This is Karen Lee."

They both smiled and said hello. As I continued to smile at them, Daddy K reached his arms out to me.

"Can I hold you, baby doll?" he asked.

I leaned forward and he took me from Ms. Turner's arms. He

smelled really good; and Mommy L was beautiful. They put me in the front seat of their car, between the two of them. Daddy K stood outside the car and talked to Ms. Turner for a long time. I heard him say they would see her later that night. I was afraid that meant they had already decided they didn't want to keep me.

We had been driving for a long time, when they stopped to get me ice cream and we took a potty break. They were really nice and asked me a lot of questions about what I did everyday. As we got closer to their house, Daddy K started telling me about Lucas and how excited he was to meet me. He pointed down the road to a long row of trees.

"You see that house, up the road from those trees, sitting on that little knoll?" he asked.

"Yes," I answered.

"Well, that's where we're headed," he said. "That's our house."

It was the most beautiful house I had ever seen. I watched all the trees as we drove up the long driveway, and then I saw Lucas.

"There he is," Daddy K said, "waiting to see you."

Daddy K got out of the car first. He hugged Lucas and whispered something to him before they both walked to Mommy L's side of the car and opened the door for her. Mommy L picked me up in her arms, gave me a big hug, and said, "This is Lucas. He's going to show you all around our home while I get dinner started."

Lucas gave me a big hug and kiss.

"Come on, let's go inside!" he said.

I heard Daddy K and Mommy L laugh as Lucas grabbed my hand and we took off running. He led me through the house and showed me every room, even the closets. Then we went down to the barn where I met his dog, his ponies, and all his cows. It was the most fun-filled day I'd ever had. After playing with Lucas, Daddy K and Mommy L told me we were going to have dinner, and after that they had to drive me back to meet with Ms. Turner.

Mommy L called for Lucas and me to wash up for dinner. I wanted to impress them so much that I came out of the bathroom with a wet head.

"Look! I washed my hair too!" I said happily.

I hoped the smile on Mommy L's face meant that she was proud of me. I delayed dinner a little bit because they had to dry my hair before we could eat.

Finally, I sat down at a table filled with more food than I had ever seen in my life. I said yes to everything they offered me. I grabbed a fork and started to eat, but Lucas quickly took my hand and stopped me.

"We don't eat until we pray," he said.

I had no idea what he was talking about; so I sat and watched them bow their heads while Daddy K thanked somebody named Jesus for the food. When he was finished, Lucas let go of my hand and told me I could eat. It was the best food I had ever tasted. Most of my meals at the boarding house were just juice and cereal. I thought it was kind of strange that Mommy L left the table crying, but I was too busy eating to think about anything else. All I knew was that I didn't want to go back to the boarding house. I asked Mommy L and Daddy K why I couldn't just stay there with them; I told them I would be really good, and I wouldn't eat too much, or be any trouble. They smiled and said I was no trouble. They promised they would come get me again one day soon.

Before I left, Lucas gave me a big hug and kiss and whispered that he would see me again. I didn't talk a lot on the drive back; I was pretty tired from my big day. I must have fallen asleep on the way back to the boarding house because when I woke up the next morning, I was in my bed. Ms. Turner was there to see me; she told me that the family really liked me and she wanted to know what I thought about them. She asked me a lot of questions, but my favorite question was when she asked me if I wanted to see them again. I couldn't get 'yes' out quick enough. I tried to find out when it would be, but I didn't understand a lot of what she was telling me, so I just waited.

After a few days, I started going a lot of places, like to the doctor and the dentist. Ms. Turner took me to get my hair cut and she took some pictures of me. I got a big surprise one night when Ms.

Turner came to visit me.

"What do you think about going to stay with Daddy K, Mommy L, and Lucas for a while?" she asked. "They decided they didn't need another visit. They want you to come live with them and be part of their family, if *you* want to."

I told her that I would love it! I couldn't believe I was finally getting a real Mommy and Daddy.

That night, Ms. Turner helped me pack all my belongings into a little red suitcase. She said she would pick me up early in the morning to go meet my new Mommy and Daddy. I could hardly sleep that night because I was so excited.

When morning arrived, I grabbed my little red suitcase and ran down the stairs to see if Ms. Turner was there to pick me up yet. It was May 1st, 1967, and Ms. Turner showed up right on schedule. We got into her car and drove for a long time. We finally stopped at a place she called a road stop; there was a big tree with a picnic table beside it. Ms. Turner carried a basket to the table and we sat down to eat sandwiches together. Ms. Turner asked me a lot of questions and kept telling me that if I wasn't happy in any way, she would come pick me up, day or night; all I had to do was call her.

"I pinned my phone number into your suitcase," she said, "and I also wrote it inside your shoe. All you need to do, if you need me, is go to a phone and put your finger in the O circle, and turn the dial, like we practiced." She explained that a lady called an operator, would ask me for Ms. Turner's phone number and that she would take care of everything else. I just had to dial the zero number on the phone.

She told me she would come see me at the Bartlett's house the following week to see how I was doing, and find out if I liked my new home.

I was starting to get a little scared, but I kept thinking about how much fun I'd had with Lucas, and I knew I had to be brave. There were a few doubts in my mind though. What if they didn't come get me? Then I started to wonder what it would be like to sleep in a different bed. I didn't have much in life, but at least I had a bed to call my own and I knew where things were. I didn't know if I would like my new bedroom. Ms. Turner had told me not to talk to strangers or trust them, and yet I was about to go away with Daddy K and Mommy L all by myself. What if they changed their minds and just stopped the car and sat me on the side of the road? What would I do? All sorts of thoughts were racing through my mind. Ms. Turner must have known what I was thinking, because she put her arms around me.

"I'm not trying to scare you," she said. "The Bartlett's are really nice people and they are so excited that you want to be part of their family. They have even prepared a pretty, pink bedroom for you, with a closet full of new clothes and toys."

"Really?" I asked.

Ms. Turner made all my fears go away, as she told me more and more about how happy Daddy K and Mommy L were that I was coming to live with them.

We were finishing our sandwiches when I saw the pretty white car pulling into the parking lot. Daddy K and Mommy L got out and walked over to our picnic table. They both gave me big hugs. Mommy L and I went for a walk while Daddy K talked to Ms. Turner. Finally, I had to hug Ms. Turner good-bye. She had tears in her eyes, as I waved good-bye.

"Remember, I'll see you next week," she said.

When Mommy L sat me in the car, Lucas was there waiting to see me. I didn't know he was trying to surprise me. He had brought me a cute, brown teddy bear that had a tear coming down its cheek.

"It has a tear, like you did when you left our house last time… but you don't have to be sad anymore," he said.

I gave Lucas a big hug and kiss, and hugged my teddy bear tightly; it was my first teddy bear, and I loved it.

We drove a long time and then I finally saw the familiar row of trees. Daddy K slowed the car down.

"Do you know where you are?" he asked.

"I remember the trees," I replied with a smile.

Lucas walked me into the house and Mommy L told him he

could show me my room. She said she was going to start fixing dinner and we could go play. Lucas kept leaning over to hug me; I thought he was the greatest big brother anyone could have. When Mommy L called us for supper, we ran to wash our hands and went to the table. Daddy K thanked God for bringing me into their family, and I saw Lucas smile when he said it. Dinner was delicious and Mommy L started crying again while I was eating. I whispered and asked Lucas why she was crying, but Mommy L heard me.

"I'm okay. I'm just so happy to see you eating everything," she said.

I didn't know how tiny I was for a three-and-a-half year old; because I only weighed twenty-two pounds, Mommy L was afraid I had gone to bed hungry most nights at the boarding home.

Daddy K and Mommy L gave me lots of hugs and kisses as they tucked me into bed. They told me they loved me very much and that I was completely safe in my new home. When they turned my lights off, my room was *really* dark; I'd never been in a room that dark before. I tried to squeeze my eyes shut and hide under my covers, but I was really scared. I peeked out from under my covers and saw wolves pacing around my bed; they were snarling and bearing their teeth at me. I could even feel them bumping into my bed as they walked around the room. I tried to be strong for as long as I could, but I eventually had to scream for help.

My scream brought results, as Daddy K and Mommy L immediately came running into my room. They both hugged me and asked what was wrong.

"There are wolves in my room!" I told them. "The wolves are really mean. They must be hiding under the bed."

Daddy K checked under the bed and in the closet and assured me that there were no wolves in my room, or anywhere in the house; it was just a bad dream. They kissed me good night again, and turned off my lights as they closed my door. The wolves returned as soon as the lights went off.

This continued to happen, night after night. My big brother began to sneak into my room, or I would go into his room, and he would protect me from the wolves. My old room at the boarding house was never as dark as my new room, and my old room didn't have wolves in it. Mommy and Daddy told me I could trust them and they would always keep me safe. Sometimes when Lucas was at a friend's house, I saw shadows when I peeked out from under my covers at night. It looked like a man was standing in the corner of my room, but he never scared me, and when I saw him, I didn't see the wolves.

Over time, the nightmares went away. I settled into my new home and adjusted to my new family, and even a new name. My brother was in 2nd grade when I came into the Bartlett family, and I remember him taking me to school one day for "Show and Tell" time. I thought it was pretty cool to get to ride on a school bus and sit by my brother in his classroom. The teacher, and several others, hugged me and welcomed me; I saw Mommy and Lucas get a lot of hugs too. I felt so happy and proud when he introduced me to everyone as his little sister. He told everyone that I was really neat and that we had a lot of fun playing together. Although I was very young, I still remember that day, and my first experience of sitting in a classroom.

Not only did I get to be "Show and Tell" for my big brother, but the church we attended also gave me a baby shower that week. I remember standing in the middle of a floor full of presents, and I was allowed to open all of them. There were a lot of people watching me, but they were all smiling and it was a lot of fun. Many people hugged my Mom and Dad that day and some of them were crying. Mom and Dad explained that although I wasn't born into their family, they loved me as if I was their own. They said I was even more special because they wanted me, and were thrilled to have my brother and me. I think they really meant it, but a 40-year age difference would prove to become a test of patience and endurance. They both turned 44 the year they adopted me, and they were also trying to grow their already-successful heavy equipment contracting business.

Dad's business became more and more important as the money rolled in and the number of employees and responsibilities grew. Spending time with my brother and me became less and less important. Mom and Dad both became unhappy. There were more raised voices and more reasons to spank us. Lucas and I became scared of Dad's belt and it was as if Mom would make up things just to see us get whipped. As things got worse, we talked about running away, but we didn't have anywhere to go so we learned to deal with it. Within just a few years, the once happy home became filled with yelling and screaming almost daily. Mom and Dad told us they were working hard so they could 'leave us something one day' and that we would thank them when we were older; but I didn't believe I would ever thank them for being so mean to us. All we wanted was a home we could feel safe in, and parents that loved us. We wanted to wake up to parents that were happy to see us, not listen to their fussing during breakfast about how many things had to get done that day. *Our day* was non-existent in their mind, and there was no care or concern about how their yelling and all the tension affected us. Most days after school, I just wanted to go hide in my room, sit beside my bed, and dream of a future when I could be free and make a home for myself that would always be happy.

Children don't understand the goals of adults to work long hours and save money for "future happiness." The only thing children understand is the day they wake up to, and how they feel they are being treated. Every child needs to feel unconditional love from their parents. Your child did not agree to the extra hours you put into work, or the debt you may have accumulated, and the stress those things often bring to the family. A child should not be the "victim" of their parent's bad choices. Your child is a blessing from God Almighty. *HE* knew the date your child would be born. *HE* formed that child in your womb and entrusted you to love and care for that child, for as long as you have breath. If your child is adopted, then they became the "grafted-in" child of your womb, the day you took them into your home. Love your children and rear them to feel safe and secure. Help them blossom with their God-given talents, and they will definitely thank you one day. You are the sculptor of their future…make a masterpiece!

Jamie

CHAPTER FOUR

FAMILY LIFE

Mom and Dad worked hard all their lives, and the hard work paid off as Dad's business grew into a very successful company. When a new Paper Mill was being built in the county, Dad had been in the right place at the right time. He approached management about being the general contractor for the Mills. A great relationship formed between the businesses because the Paper Mills could rely on Dad's labor and equipment to show up, day or night, to keep the Mills operating. The terrible odor from the Mills, that most people complained about, began to "smell like money" for our family.

Born in 1923, both Mom and Dad lived through the harsh realities of our nation's Great Depression years, and they knew how to save and conserve all they acquired. They both came from poor families and were reared on farms. Mom always said, "We were poor, but we were clean. There is no shame in being poor if you are working hard and trying your best, but there is no excuse for being dirty."

Before Lucas and I entered their lives, they had taken time to enjoy life and enjoy each other. They entertained us with stories of other towns and homes they had lived in when they followed work through Kentucky and Ohio with the natural gas pipeline. Dad was an excellent crane and bulldozer operator; natural gas lines were in great demand and operators were needed to get the work done. Mom commented that they "lived like gypsies" as they pulled the trailer they called home, and followed the gas line for work.

Dad once told us a story about a job he was called to do, which involved digging along the side of a mountain to get a gas line through; he was the dozer operator on that particular job. A crane lowered the bulldozer down the side of the mountain each morning. The dozer was held there, suspended by cables, as Dad dug into the mountainside.

"Weren't you scared that the cables would break?" I asked.

"I always made sure I dug a little ledge that I could jump towards," he replied, "and I fully intended to let the dozer go if I felt a cable snap."

His stories made me think about all the work that people like him had to do, and the risks they had to take, to make our nation great.

Mom and Dad followed work with the pipeline for several years. When that ended, Dad became a contractor at an atomic energy plant near Kentucky Lake. Lucas and I saw pictures of the little house they had purchased, and listened to stories of them taking their boat out on the lake on weekends. They had a lot of pictures of themselves with family and friends; they always looked so happy. Lucas and I didn't see them the way they looked in the photos. We didn't get to know them during the happy times in their lives. We saw them turn into people who were more concerned with building a huge business and bank account, than taking time to enjoy their life with children. It would have been nice if we had brought them smiles, and if our coming into their lives could have been their happiest times. Unfortunately, we were brought into the Bartlett family at the wrong time; we became their stress, instead of their joy.

Each day became more and more stressful, and tension grew as Mom began to tire of raising us by herself. Most mornings, Mom was awake by 4:30am in order to get breakfast on the table by 6:00am. She cooked bacon, eggs, and homemade biscuits on a daily basis. She also put together a huge lunchbox of food and a cooler of drinks to get Dad through his day at the Paper Mills. This may sound unusual to women these days, but to their generation, cooking a large meal was as natural as combing your hair; it was a necessary part of their daily routine.

Mom told us stories of going to the hen house, when she was a child, to get the eggs she ate for breakfast. I could not imagine having to gather the eggs and get wood to heat the stove, before breakfast could be prepared. Mom thought she had it easy with her electric stove, refrigerator, and coffee maker. I never heard my Mom complain about having to get up early to cook. I think cooking a great meal and seeing your family enjoy your cooking, gave a sense of pride and accomplishment to women at one time. The women who were stay-at-home wives and mothers had days filled with long hours and hard work.

After cleaning the breakfast dishes and seeing that Dad had all he needed before leaving for work, Mom began packing our lunch boxes. Mom saw us onto the school bus every morning, and was waiting at the end of the driveway to pick us up at the end of each school day. She always had our supper ready as soon as we got home from school. Her daily home-cooked meals consisted of meat, at least two vegetables, dinner rolls, and dessert. She always had a plate of dinner prepared for Dad whenever he came home from work. Mom was the one who helped us with homework and got us ready for bed every night. Most days, Dad arrived home late. It was considered "early" if we heard the sound of Dad's diesel engine coming up the driveway by six o'clock in the evening; he usually came home between 7pm and 9pm.

We weren't really around Dad much at home, except on Sundays. We were up early every Sunday morning for Sunday school and church. Lying in bed and taking Sunday as a "day off" was unthinkable. Saturday was the "day off," and Sunday was the Lord's Day.

I often heard my Dad say, "A little hard work won't kill you." However, I learned that a lot of hard work can sure make people mean. My brother and I didn't get to go on family vacations, like many of our friends. Asking to go on vacation resulted in standing at attention and saying "yes sir" and "no sir" while being lectured on the importance of saving money. We were told that it was "pure non-sense" to go sit at a beach, on hot sand, and get sweaty while the sun baked down on your skin.

When we tried to bring up the beautiful ocean, we were stopped by Dad's stories of how he and Mom had seen the ocean while he was stationed in New Jersey, during World War II. He told us that he decided to swim way out in the ocean one day. In fact, he swam so far that he couldn't see the shore; then it occurred to him that he might not be able to get back. He said he'd had his fill of the ocean after that experience. He also lectured us about the dangers of the under current and that many innocent people lost their lives because of that pretty ocean.

Needless to say, we never went on a family vacation to the ocean. However, Dad did let us stop and see it one time. Mom had complained enough that he eventually took a long weekend (Thursday through Sunday) and drove us down to Daytona Beach, Florida, and we went to see the NASA Space Center. He stopped along the beach for a few minutes; Lucas and I walked to the shore and felt the ocean with our feet. Then, it was time to get in the car and drive back home to Tennessee. We didn't get to put on swimsuits or play on the beach; we literally just stopped to see the ocean.

There is no question as to how hard Mom and Dad both worked, he with his business and Mom with her cooking and gardening. Each year, Mom planted a huge garden that was about half an acre in size. Mom grew just about any vegetable you could think of: corn, green beans, kale, lima beans, peas, carrots, broccoli, cauliflower, cabbage, leaf lettuce, radishes, and so much more. Her garden was a grocery store in itself, and nothing grown in her garden was left unused. We had fresh vegetables to eat daily. She froze and canned vegetables to ensure that she had enough food to see our family through the winter months.

There were apple, peach, and pear trees near Mom's garden. What we didn't eat as fresh fruit was used to make cobblers, jams, and jellies. She also had a beautiful grape arbor, filled with large, dark purple grapes. Mom made delicious grape juice that Dad swore kept him from ever getting colds or the flu. Of course, the grapes that weren't used for juice were used for homemade grape jelly. I don't think there was a single fruit or vegetable that my Mom didn't know how to cook, can, or freeze, and somehow use as food for our family.

It's hard to keep a kitchen clean when it is put to use from 5am to 9pm. My job was to clean the house, vacuum the pool, and use the trimmer around the yard after Lucas mowed. We had a large riding mower called a Yazoo; even with a big mower, it still took Lucas a couple of hours to get our yard mowed. We were taught hard work at an early age. Television was a luxury and it wasn't turned on until our homework and chores were finished. There were very few shows fit for us to watch, according to Dad. Whenever he was home at night, he closely monitored what we watched. Mom had strict instructions from him concerning certain shows, like Bewitched; any show with witchcraft, wizards, or magic of any sort, was strictly forbidden in our home.

The chores and strict upbringing wouldn't have been so bad, if there hadn't been so much yelling and fighting all the time. Dad was very stern, but he also tried to talk to Lucas and I in a nice tone most of the time. Mom, on the other hand, didn't care to tell us how bad her day was, how bad she felt, and how much we were grinding on her very last nerve.

One particular morning, I heard Mom and Dad fighting; it was loud, and I couldn't tell what they were saying. Dad left the house before breakfast, and it was obvious that Mom was in a bad mood. Lucas and I went on to school, hoping she would be in a better mood when we got home. When we came home after school, we put our books down and Lucas went to the refrigerator to get something to drink. Suddenly, I heard a loud thud. About the same time I saw the panic in Lucas's face, I heard Mom scream. A container of grape juice had fallen out of the refrigerator and was pouring out on the floor, all over Mom's new kitchen carpet. I will never forget that day. I stood in horror, at the end of the family room, watching her scream in Lucas's face. She yelled that he was an "idiot for not being able to see the juice was about to fall," and said she was sick and tired of having to deal with us. She screamed that everything was our fault, even the fact that Dad was working all the time. Then came the worst part.

"...and I didn't even want you two!" she continued. "It was all *his* idea to get you! Get out of my sight and go to your rooms!"

Both Lucas and I felt empty and alone as we quietly said, "Sorry," and shut our bedroom doors behind us.

Later that night, Dad called us out of our rooms. He said that Mom was sorry for what she had said and that he needed to get her some help. Dad called it *nerve problems*, but Lucas and I just thought she was mean and crazy. We knew she meant every word she said; we could see the hatred in her eyes. She could never take back telling us she didn't want us. Nothing was ever the same after that day. Mom took pills she called nerve medicine, but the pills didn't keep her from yelling and screaming and, at times, looking at us like she couldn't stand the sight of us.

Most afternoons, my routine was to eat supper, do my chores, and close myself in my room before Mom's screaming started. After school, Lucas usually needed her help with homework. Doing homework shouldn't start a fight, but most days it turned into a major ordeal. Day after day, I watched Lucas sit at the kitchen table struggling to do his homework, trying to tell Mom he didn't understand what she had told him to do. She would start yelling at him, telling him that he was being stupid. Some days, she got so mad she would pick up a butcher knife or long pronged fork and throw it at him from across the kitchen. There was no patience and no understanding, it seemed like anything and everything could set her off. The incidents were her way of getting Lucas to call her crazy or something, which was exactly what she wanted, because then she would say those dreaded words, "Just wait until I tell your Daddy what you said to me!"

I think it became an attention-getter for Mom. She would instigate a fight in order to trap you into "sassing" her. Then she would call Dad home early from work and tell him some over-exaggerated story of how awful she had been talked to. Lucas and I would try to tell Dad she was making things up, but we quickly found out that meant we were calling Mom a liar, which was even worse than being sassy to her. It became hopeless to try to defend ourselves, and I eventually saw Lucas give up. He became quiet, shy, and nervous; he would just sit and pick at his arm or face. He got to where he rarely raised his head to look at Dad when he was spoken to; he just looked down at the floor, and said the appropriate "yes sir" or "no sir" per our training. We weren't allowed to merely say "yes" or "no" to our parents; that would mean a swift slap across the face for being disrespectful.

When Mom first started calling Dad home from work to discipline us, he would use his hand to spank our behinds. His spankings became harder and harder, and eventually he began to use his belt. Most of the time, Lucas and I were both spanked because Mom thought we were equally guilty for *getting on her nerves*. Dad began to get meaner, and would often ask Mom if she could at least let him get in the door and set his lunchbox down, before she started in on something. Dad showed more aggression towards Lucas, and the whippings with the belt became harder. I would run to my room and hide beside my bed, as I listened to Lucas scream in pain, begging for Dad to quit hitting him.

What came after the whipping was almost worse. Dad would take rubbing alcohol and wipe it across the whelps on Lucas's back and legs, because he said it would keep Lucas from getting an infection. Once again, I would hear Lucas crying for Dad to stop, but it never did any good to cry. Over time, Lucas's crying transformed into anger and resentment. I couldn't stand to see what was being done to my big brother, but we were helpless, and there wasn't a thing we could do. We were sternly informed that if we told anyone about what went on in our house, they would give us something to cry about.

By the time I was 12 years old, I began to wish the Bartlett's had not picked me to be their daughter. No amount of money they promised in our future could be worth the nightmare they were putting us through. The house was filled with fighting and yelling every day, and if Lucas and I said anything that was out of line, or in any way disrespectful, it meant being spanked. We were constantly lectured about why they worked so hard. They said it was all for us, and that we should be glad they got us because we would have *money* one day. Mom would even tell me that I owed my looks to them, because if it weren't for them taking me to places like the dentist, orthodontist, and the eye doctor for contacts, I wouldn't get called pretty. It became more and more clear that I would never be out from under "owing them" for everything I was, and everything I had.

The reality of my life became more than I could stand. I worked hard in school and brought home straight A's. Mom and Dad always received comments on report cards about what a good student I was and what a pleasure it was to have me in class. However, no matter how well I did in school or how active I was in church, nothing was enough; they never acted like I was good enough to be their daughter. It was all about "owing" them for what they had done for Lucas and me, and how hard they were working for us. I didn't want to face another day in that house. There was no joy, no love, only the constant struggle of trying to do something worthy of just a little praise from my parents.

One afternoon, I fell to my knees and cried out to God that I didn't know why he made me; I wasn't wanted by my biological family and I certainly wasn't wanted by the Bartlett's. The only good I was to the Bartlett's was the work I could do for them, or to be a showpiece when they wanted to tell someone about my grades or musical ability. I begged repeatedly, for almost half an hour, for God to stop my heart. I felt suicide was wrong, but God created me, and he could take me; I didn't see anything wrong with asking him to get me out of there. I cried until my stomach hurt. As tears continued to hit the floor, I opened my mouth to beg and plead with God once more. Suddenly, a strange language came out of my mouth that I didn't understand; I had no idea what I had just said. Immediately after that happened I felt peaceful and felt like I was supposed to be quiet. I didn't say another word for several minutes; I just sat there in silence, wondering what I said and why things seemed so different. Something changed that evening. I knew God wasn't going to take me out of the situation I was in, but I believed he was going to walk with me through it all; I would know his purpose for my life, *one day.*

Lucas was a wonderful brother to me and he would get me out of the house whenever he could. He had gotten his drivers license, and with that came freedom. Dad bought him a 1957 Chevy, but reminded Lucas that he could take the keys away, anytime he felt he needed to.

Our small town had a pizza place, with a back room that had some pool tables and a few pinball machines. Lucas would take me with him to the Pizza Garden, and we would play pool and laugh. When we could get away from the house, he and I always had fun. Lucas and I talked about everything, and we never got tired of spending time together. He would even take me with him when he went on dates, just to get me away from *them*.

I tried to pay him back when I could, by washing and vacuuming his car, and cleaning his room so Mom wouldn't fuss at him. We had a very close relationship, and we often talked about how great life would be when we could get away from Mom and Dad. My brother was four-and-a-half years older than me, and I dreaded the day he might go off to college and leave me alone with them.

The years passed, and the reality hit me that my big brother was a senior in high school; he had almost made it out from under their control. I was happy for him, but was scared that Mom and Dad would turn all their anger towards me. Things at home had been getting better since Lucas's sixteenth birthday. I think they were beginning to realize we were growing up. Not only would we be leaving home, but we would also be free to tell people what life was really like at the Bartlett home.

Money was available for college; Lucas and I could go to any school of our choosing. However, when the time came for Lucas to choose where he wanted to go, he wasn't encouraged to go to a University. Instead, Lucas was encouraged to attend the local Vocational/Technical College and get a degree in Small Engine Repair, so that he could begin full-time work in the family business.

Lucas first sat in the seat of a crane when he was only nine years old. Because of it, he was capable of operating a crane, or any piece of machinery, better than operators that were twice his age. Everyone in the community knew that Lucas and I had been groomed to work in the family business. Lucas had been taught to operate every piece of equipment, and I had been taught about accounting and bookwork, including how to type, since elementary school. Dad employed approximately forty men on the job, and had a full-time bookkeeper that worked in his office at the house.

Lucas did what was expected of him; he received his degree in Small Engine Repair and went to work full-time for Dad. I was in high school at the time, and began earning credits in the business program. Upon graduating high school, the credits would be equivalent to one year of Business College. Somewhere within me, I knew that dreaming of doing anything else with my life was useless; I "owed" them for all their hard work, and for taking care of me. I'd probably stay in my small hometown forever and become an office manager for my Dad's company, with the hopes that he would turn it over to my brother and I one day. The constant threats of being dis-inherited, and being told that Lucas and I would never see a penny of their money if we didn't do as we were instructed, took its toll on both of us.

How were we supposed to pay back being fed, clothed, sheltered, and educated? Lucas and I were stuck in a never-ending cycle of love, hate, indebtedness, and a lack of self-worth. Our futures belonged to them.

CHAPTER FIVE

THE MEETING

By age 19, I had graduated from a local business college with an Associate's Degree in general business and office management. I began working full-time as office manager for my Dad's heavy equipment contracting company.

My first year of work passed quickly. Before I knew it, I was 20 years old. It was time for my annual checkup, so I took off early from work one Thursday afternoon to see the doctor. During my exam, the doctor found a lump in my right breast.

"I don't like the size or shape of the lump," he said. "Do you know if there is any history of breast cancer in your family?"

"I don't have any medical information of any kind because I was adopted when I was three-and-a-half," I replied. "All my records were sealed by the state."

"Do your parents have any information on your biological family?" he asked.

"I don't think so," I said, "but Dad has always told my brother and I that he'd do anything he could to find our biological families if there was ever a need, or a want, to find them."

Before I left, he went ahead and scheduled an appointment with a surgeon to get a biopsy.

"I don't want you to be cut on if it isn't necessary," he explained. "However, considering the size and shape, whether or not there's a history of cancer in your biological family will determine if we can wait and watch the mass, or if a biopsy will need to be done immediately."

I left the doctor's office and returned to my apartment in somewhat of a daze. I couldn't believe what had just happened. In the matter of an hour-long visit to my doctor, I now faced the possibility of having breast cancer. Not only that, but I also had to deal with an issue I'd always tried to forget – biological parents. The people who tossed me aside and didn't find me worth keeping, were out there somewhere, and now I needed medical information from them.

Mom was expecting me to call her after my appointment, so I picked up the phone to dial her number. I wasn't sure how to tell her what I had been told by the doctor. I heard her say "Hello" on the other end of the line and, suddenly, I couldn't speak. Emotions overwhelmed me as I tried to say, "Mom…." The tears began to flow and I could hear the fear in her voice as she said,

"What's wrong? Tell me! What is wrong?"

I could tell she was beginning to cry before even hearing anything I had to say. I was not the emotional type, and it took a lot to get me to cry, so she immediately knew there was a problem. I managed to tell her the doctor found a lump he did not like the size or shape of, and it could be breast cancer.

"Stay on the phone," she said. "I'm going to get your Dad on the radio."

Dad's corporation had a Motorola radio system, similar to a C.B., but with a private signal. This was before people had cell phones, and the radio was a wonderful way to make contact with Dad when he was at the job site.

I could hear Mom call for Dad on the radio, and he was quick to respond. I'm sure he heard the panic in her voice, as she told him he needed to get home as fast as possible. Mom kept me on the phone until I heard Dad enter their house. Mom told him I was on the phone and needed to tell him everything about my doctor's appointment. Dad took the phone from Mom and I repeated everything the doctor told me, including needing information about my biological family. Dad and I talked a few minutes, and then he handed the phone back to Mom. She wanted me to spend the night with them so I wouldn't be alone, but I told her I would be okay; I just wanted to get to bed early and I would be there for work in the morning.

I had only been off the phone for about fifteen minutes, when I heard a knock at my door. I opened the door to find Dad standing there. He said he had come to pick me up because I didn't need to be alone and Mom needed to see me. I questioned how he could have possibly gotten to my apartment so quickly since their house was over twenty miles away. His only response was a slight smile as he said, "I think the tires touched the road a few times."

I packed an overnight bag and Dad and I headed home. Mom was waiting with open arms when I walked through the door; it was as if all the bad memories instantly faded away, as the possibility of a tragedy stood at our family's doorstep. It was a turning point in my relationship with them and I knew that whatever lay ahead, we were going to face it together, as a family.

Dad called the doctor that evening. The doctor was adamant and said it would definitely help if there was medical history about my biological mother, or any other family members, that may have had cancer. Dad told the doctor he wasn't given any history on my birth family when they adopted me.

"I don't even have a family name," Dad said, "but I will do whatever I have to do to get the information for her."

That night, Dad sat me down and told me he had to be at work the next morning because, in over twenty years of business, he had never failed to pass out paychecks to his employees every Friday morning.

"Those men and their families count on having that money to put in the bank each Friday," Dad said. "If you ever have your own business Kimi, remember the great responsibility that comes with having employees. If your employees do their work, they are due their paycheck."

He instructed me to always write their checks first and write my check last. I paid attention when Dad tried to teach me about business;

despite his downfalls, he had become a very successful business own-er and had learned it all on his own. With a lot of hard work and be-ing disciplined in saving money, he and Mom had built a contracting business that grossed over one million dollars *annually*.

Dad said he would be back home around noon, after passing out payroll; he would head out Friday afternoon, in search of my biologi-cal family and the much needed medical history.

True to his word, Dad arrived home around noon, and ate the lunch Mom had waiting for him. I followed Mom into her and Dad's bedroom where she had a suitcase laid out across the bed, and she continued packing Dad's clothes in it.

"How long will you be gone, so I know how much to pack?" Mom asked when Dad entered the room.

"For as long as it takes," Dad replied.

Mom didn't miss a beat; she didn't question his answer, she mere-ly nodded and continued to pack. It was as if they knew each other's thoughts. Seeing them communicate without having to say a word was like watching a well-oiled machine at work. They had been mar-ried for almost forty years at the time; after being in someone's life for that many years, I suppose you grow into each other mentally.

As Dad headed for the door to put his suitcase in the car, he told me he had stopped at the county court house before work that morn-ing. He wanted to see if there were any records with the name of a biological family member that might give him an idea of where to start searching. The county clerk was an old friend of my parents, and she told him how sorry she was; although she remembered when they adopted me, the county court house didn't have records about any of my biological family members. She was sure that the information was sealed in the court records at the state capital. She went on to say that he would need to get a lawyer, and it could take some time to get the records "unsealed." Dad thanked her for her advice, but said he didn't have time to wait on lawyers and the court system. He explained that I was facing a biopsy, and possibly breast cancer, and he needed infor-mation within the next few days.

"Dad, how are you going to know which way to turn when you

get to the end of the driveway?" I asked.

He hugged me, and said, "You know who will guide me, Kimi. I'm taking my Bible and a gun. What one doesn't get me, the other one will."

Then, with a very intense look, he continued,

"I won't be back until I have all the information you need now, and may need in the future. I intend to get medical history on any and all family members I can find. You stay here with your mother, and take care of her."

Mom told Dad good-bye, and I heard him say he would phone her when he could find a place to lodge for the night. As he left the kitchen and walked out the back door, I ran to the living room to look out the window, curious to see which way he would turn when he reached the end of the driveway. He was just heading down the hill when I heard Mom call for me. I left the window and went to see what she needed. By the time I returned to the window, it was too late; I couldn't see the car going down the road in either direction. It was as if I wasn't supposed to know which way he went. I merely had to have faith, and believe he would get the information I needed.

With no idea where Dad was headed or when we would hear from him, Mom and I just waited. We tried to kill time by cooking and watching TV, but we were both wondering where he was and if he was okay. Around 8:30 that Friday night, the phone rang, and we figured it was Dad calling to say he had found a motel for the night. Mom answered the phone; she kept saying "okay" and she had a strange look on her face. She didn't ask anything except, "When?" Then she turned to me.

"It's your Dad and he wants to talk to you," she said.

I couldn't read the look on her face; it was neither happy nor sad.

"Is he okay? What's wrong?" I asked.

"Just take the phone," she said. "He will explain."

As I took the phone, a fear came over me that I didn't understand; I knew this phone call was important, and whatever Dad was about to tell me had made Mom very uncomfortable. Dad's voice was calm but serious.

"Kimi Leah," he said, "I have someone here beside me that wants to talk to you."

"Who is it?" I asked nervously.

"You have a half-brother. His name is Robert and I'm at his house," Dad said. "He and his wife have been very nice to me and very helpful. He made a phone call to your biological mother, and she will be coming over here to meet with me when she gets off work at 10 or 11 tonight. You and Robert have the same mother, but different dads."

There were so many questions going through my mind, it seemed like time stood still for a moment. Then Dad continued.

"He doesn't want to bother you, but he wants you to know that he has looked for you and wondered what happened to you; he is 11 years older than you, and has never forgotten you. He just wants to say hello to you, but he understands if you don't want to talk to him."

All I could say was, "*I have a half-brother?*"

It had never crossed my mind that I could have a brother or sister. I always figured if my biological parents gave me away then they must not have wanted children.

"You're a tough girl… You can do this," Dad said. "I'm going to hand him the phone now."

I felt myself stand a little taller and little straighter as the voice on the other end said hello. I said, "Hi," and then listened as he told me how happy he was that Dad had found them.

"I am so glad that you're okay and that you've been taken care of all these years," he said. "I will see to it that Becky, your biological mother, gives your Dad all her medical history, and any other information he needs. She will not leave this house until she cooperates. I will force the information out of her if I have to. I'm not going to let an illness take you away, now that I have found you. I promise to never call you or force myself into your life, but I'm going to give your Dad my phone number, in case you ever want to call me."

He was very nice, but I wasn't sure what to say.

"Can I speak to my Dad again, please?" I asked.

"Sure… I love you," he said, and then he handed the phone back to Dad.

As Dad got back on the phone, I asked him how he found my half-brother in a matter of hours. He started to get choked-up.

"You just won't believe the story I have to tell you when I get back," he said. "I will be meeting with your half-sister tomorrow, as well as your biological Dad. I should be home late Saturday night or early Sunday, at the latest."

When I hung-up the phone, Mom and I just looked at each other and shook our heads.

"How on earth did he do this? He only left here a matter of hours ago, and he didn't even know where to go!" I said.

"If anybody can get things done, it's your Dad," Mom replied.

The very next day, Saturday afternoon, Mom received another call from Dad. He told her that he would be heading home in a couple of hours, and that he was in a small town close to the Kentucky/Tennessee border.

Mom and I played Monopoly and watched television while we waited for Dad's return. When we finally heard the garage door start to open, we both jumped up and ran to the door to greet Dad. I stepped back to let Mom hug him first, and then I got a big hug and a kiss on the cheek. He said he needed to wash-up and then he would tell us about his trip.

Mom put some dinner on the table for him while he cleaned-up, and then we all sat at the table so he could tell us how he managed to find my biological family in less than a day. After prayer, Dad took a couple bites of his food, and then looked me straight in the eyes. With a quivering voice, he said, "Didn't I tell you *He* would help me?"

"Yes sir," I said, "but what happened? How did you even know where to go?"

Dad put his fork down, bowed his head, and began to weep. Mom stood up and wrapped her arms around his shoulders.

"What's wrong?" she asked. "Don't tell us about it if it's going to upset you like this, just wait."

I could see the tears stream down Mom's face, as she watched her strong husband weep and tremble. She wasn't used to seeing Dad cry; he could handle anything. He woke up early, day after day, and worked twelve to fourteen hour days; he never complained and was rarely ever sick.

Dad shook his head 'no' and with a tearful voice, he began a story that I will never forget.

"Kimi Leah," he began, "make sure you always remember the story I'm about to tell you. You should write it down, word for word, as soon as possible, because I have witnessed a miracle."

"I prayed before I headed down the driveway. I asked the Lord for guidance in finding your biological family and told him I needed answers quickly. When I reached the end of the driveway, I felt led to turn left. As I drove, I remembered something the social worker had told me the day Mother and I picked you up from her. She said, *'I would keep her away from the Kentucky/Tennessee border until she is older.'* I hadn't thought of that in years. Even though I remembered her saying that, Tennessee has a long border, and I wasn't sure which area to head towards. I kept praying as I drove, and I felt led to drive towards Nashville, Tennessee. Once I entered Nashville, I prayed, *'Now what, Lord? Where do I go from here?'* My mind was filled with the desire to find the nearest Nashville hospital. I entered the parking lot of the hospital, still not knowing what I was doing there, or where to go once inside."

"As I walked into the hospital, I felt led to find the maternity floor. When I found it, I proceeded to the counter and approached a nurse who was dealing with some paperwork. I said, *'Hello, my name is Kent Bartlett, and I have an adopted daughter, and I need…'* She immediately stopped what she was doing and put her finger to her mouth, as if to tell me to be quiet. She looked at the clock on the wall behind her, and said, *'Mister, would you care to have a seat and come back up here in about five minutes?'* I told her I would be glad to."

"As the minutes passed, I realized that she wanted to wait for the shift change, and as soon as there was a lot of movement, nurses coming and going, she called me to come back up to the counter. She said, *'Now would you mind to finish telling me what you were saying earlier?'* I told her the entire story of how Mother and I adopted you in 1967, that you were three-and-a-half when we got you, and that we had a son we adopted in 1959, but he was a baby when we got him. I told her about your recent visit to the doctor, and how I was trying to locate a biological family member, so I could get some medical history to see if there was any cancer in your family. The nurse listened intently as I talked, and asked me a few questions about your birth date, hair color, and size. I showed the nurse pictures of you as a small child, and pictures of you now. Kimi Leah, she looked at me with something in her eyes that I cannot explain; it was as if she expected something from the photos and was resolved with what she had seen. Then the nurse said, *'Give me a few minutes and I will be right back.'* "

"I waited for quite a while and began to worry that I was wasting time, when I saw her coming back with a paper. She handed the paper to a younger nurse and said, *'Go copy this for me.'* The younger nurse refused to copy whatever it was; I heard the younger nurse say, *'No way! That could cost me my job. Go copy it yourself, I don't want any part of it.'* "

"I wondered what the nurse was doing. She finally came back over to me and said, *'This is for you and your daughter.'* I looked at the paper she handed me and couldn't believe what I was holding; it was a hospital Birth Certificate for a little girl born on December 13th, 1963, weighing only three pounds, fifteen ounces. It also had a birth mother's name and listed the county where she lived when the child was born. The child's name on the certificate was Karen Lee Johnson, which told me it was real, because I knew your name was Karen Lee when we adopted you. We changed your name to Kimi. We thought the change from calling you Karen, to calling you Kimi, wouldn't be confusing for you."

(A Live Certificate of Birth was issued by the state after my adoption, which showed the Bartlett's as my parents and the county they lived in as my place of birth. This was the birth certificate commonly issued for adopted children. To have an original hospital birth certificate, with biological family names, was unbelievable.)

Dad continued, "My mouth must have dropped open in disbelief as I looked at the nurse in front of me. She told me that she was there when you were born Kimi. *'That tiny baby stole my heart and stole the hearts of several of the nurses,'* she said. *'One of the nurses spent a lot of time checking on her, and even wondered if she could adopt the baby.'* She didn't say who the nurse was, but the more she talked, it was obvious she was talking about herself. Kimi, she told me that you were placed in an incubator for the first month of your life, and said your birth mother left the hospital as soon as she could, and never returned to check on you. The nurses heard that she even took a trip to Florida with her boyfriend, rumored to be your biological Dad. Becky, your biological mother, told one of the nurses that the man listed on your birth certificate wasn't the real Dad. The nurse gave me all the information she remembered about your birth. Your lungs were under-developed, and you were born two months premature. She said that you were so tiny, they didn't know if you would make it through the first night."

"The nurse asked about your health, so I told her you suffered from bad allergies as a child. I mentioned the year you missed 101 days of school and how you were in bed sick most of the year. I informed her, *'We took her to doctor after doctor, until one day we found an allergist who administered allergy shots. She began allergy shots in her early childhood years, and is doing much better now.'* The more she and I talked, it became apparent this was a miracle in the making. Kimi, can you believe that I walked up to a hospital counter and just so happened to speak to the nurse that cared for you when you were born?"

"The nurse and I talked for quite a while, and then she told me she needed to get home. I reached for my wallet to give her some money for her time, and somehow thank her for all she had done, but she stopped me. When she saw me reaching in my back pocket, she said, *'No Mr. Bartlett, you don't understand. I have an adopted daughter, and if she needed help, I would hope there would be someone there for her.'* With that said, we parted ways. As I walked back to my car, I realized that God had truly held you in wait for our family, because I had just spoken to the woman who wanted you just as badly as Mother and I did."

In God's infinite wisdom he had another daughter planned for that nurse and her family. I was to become part of a family that wouldn't find me until three-and-a-half years after my birth.

"As I headed toward the county listed on your birth certificate," Dad said, "I didn't know if I would be able to find any family members, since almost 20 years had passed. Still, I could hardly believe I was holding an original copy of your birth certificate. Kimi, I knew with certainty that if the good Lord had guided me this far, then I would be guided to the right places and the right people to get all the information I needed for you. I continued to pray while I drove."

"As I entered into a small town called Gentry, I pulled off the road into the parking lot of a little, closed-down, gas station. I saw some youth hanging out, so I pulled over and contemplated where to go next. I figured if I could find a preacher, he might know if there were any people still living in the area, with the last name of McBride – the mothers name listed on the birth certificate."

"I was sitting in my car, pondering the situation, when a woman approached and knocked on the car window. When I lowered the window, she said, *'Sir, I can tell you're looking for someone. Why don't you tell me who you're looking for, and maybe I can help you?'* I replied, *'Well, I was wondering where I might find the Baptist minister in this town.'* She looked at me, and said, *'We don't have a Baptist minister right now. Why don't you tell me who you are looking for, and maybe I can help you?'* So I asked, *'Do you know where I can find the Methodist minister?'* She smiled and said, *'The Methodist minister and his wife are out of town this weekend. Why don't you tell me who you are looking for, and maybe I can help you?'* I couldn't figure out why she was so persistent with me. Reluctantly, I told her I was trying to find a woman by the name of Becky McBride, or find someone who might know of her."

"Without hesitation, the woman looked me straight in the eyes, and said, *'I don't know her, but I want you to take the next road down here on the right. When you turn on that road, take a left on the first street and go to the third house on the left. The man that comes to the door will be able to help you.'* "

"I wrote down the directions while she spoke, and went to roll up my window and thought, *I forgot to thank her for her help.* Within seconds, I looked up and she was gone. I looked both directions and couldn't see the lady I had just spoken with. I got out of the car and asked some of the youth that were standing around. One by one they each told me, *'There hasn't been any woman walking around here any-where… and we didn't see any woman near your car.'* By the looks on their faces, I could tell they were serious about not seeing anyone, and they were beginning to think that I was crazy. At that moment, I knew I had entertained an angel unaware. I was being guided once again, so I did as I was told. I got in my car, made a right down the next road, turned left on the first street I came to, and stopped in front of the third house on the left."

"I walked to the door and knocked, unsure of where I was and why I had been led to that house. A young man, in his thirties, greeted me. I said, *'Hello, my name is Kent Bartlett.'* Immediately, the young man held the door open and said, *'Please come in and have a seat.'*"

"I entered the house and sat down, still unsure of my surround-ings. The young man asked, *'What can I do for you?'* I answered him and said, *'I am looking for a Becky McBride because I have reason to believe that she's the birth mother of my adopted daughter.'* The young man and I talked for quite a while, and I explained the entire situation about why I needed family medical history for you. I assured him that I wasn't looking for the woman to cause her any trouble. I told him I was a business owner and you, Kimi Leah, had always been well taken care of financially. I said, *'I am merely on a search for any medical history that my daughter might need now, and in the future. I will be on my way, as soon as I have the information I've come for.'*"

"Now, I can usually read a person's face and get an idea of what they're thinking, but this young man had a poker face that I couldn't read at all. He just looked at me and listened, and then asked, *'Do you have any pictures of your daughter?'* So I showed him all the pictures I'd brought with me. The young man studied each one for quite some time, and then suddenly yelled for his wife, and said, *'Cindy get in here! He's got Tiny!'*"

"I felt very uncomfortable at that moment and started to get up, when he must have sensed my apprehension. He said, *'No, please don't leave Mr. Bartlett, you don't understand. You have my sister. We called her*

Tiny because she was so little when she was born.' "

"The young man, Robert, and his wife were extremely kind to me, and gave me all the family history they could think of: uncles, aunts, grandparents, etc. Robert told me you have a half-sister, about three years older than you, and that Becky had another daughter several years after you were taken from the family. He said Becky was your mother, but each of you have a different Dad. Robert said, *'Becky actually tried to straighten-up her life and raise her youngest daughter, but me and my sister, Dana, were raised by our grandmother, Lois.' "*

"Robert said he and Becky didn't get along very well because of her attitude and the way she had never been a "mother" to he and Dana. He also said they never forgot the sister they lost because of Becky; they never forgot about you, Kimi. The youngest daughter, Rhonda, is the only one who calls Becky 'Mom.' As children, Robert and Dana referred to Becky as 'little Mom' because they called the grandmother who raised them 'Mom.' Robert assured me that he would get Becky to tell me everything she knew about her health, her mother's health, and any other family members she could think of."

"When Robert called Becky, I heard part of the conversation. He told her what was going on, and that she needed to come to his house when she finished her shift at work. Robert had to raise his voice several times, and I heard him say, *'You will show up after work, or I will be there to get you, and drag you to my house!'* He yelled at her and said it was the least she could do; it was her fault that he and Dana lost their baby sister."

As Dad continued to tell me about his short, miraculous journey, he couldn't speak highly enough about how well he was treated. "Robert and his wife were more than generous and kind to me," Dad explained. "They treated me to coffee and food, and talked with me for hours until Becky arrived around 11pm that night. Needless to say, that woman wasn't happy about being told to show up after work. She entered the house mad and out of control. She even accused me of stealing you. She said she didn't want to meet you and didn't want to be bothered. The woman said, *'I worked hard to raise my youngest daughter. I don't want Rhonda knowing about Kimi, and Kimi is never to contact her!' "*

"I tried to remain calm at first, when Becky was carrying on with her yelling and accusations, but I had to stop her when she accused me of stealing you. Kimi, I never wanted to hit a woman so bad in all of my life. I got right in her face and let her know that you were legally adopted at three-and-a-half; we didn't get you when you were a baby. *'So you can just stop with your drama,'* I told her. *'Settle down and act like a human being.'* I asked Robert if there was a room where she and I could go to talk, so he led us to a back room where we could have some privacy. I imagine anyone walking down the street could have heard us yelling at each other. Finally, she calmed down when I assured her that you had no need of her, except for medical history about her and other family members."

As Dad told me all of this, I was overwhelmed with different feelings. I was hurt Becky didn't care I was alive and that I'd been taken care of. She didn't care I was having health issues and she didn't even want to meet me. I immediately put up a wall within myself and thought, *Fine then. She can have it her way. She will never have to lay eyes on me and I won't bother her precious younger daughter.* This was certainly not the sort of happy reunion I had seen on television, when adopted kids were reunited with their birth families.

Dad could see the pain in my eyes.

"I will never bother her or her kids," I said.

He put down his fork and said, "Now you need to understand that I wouldn't have met Becky at all, if it hadn't been for Robert. He led me to your older sister's house, where I met Dana and her husband, Jim. Dana couldn't stop crying and thanking me for taking care of you, Kimi. It's completely up to you, but I think you should consider meeting Robert and his family, as well as Dana and Jim."

Dad was always good at getting to the core of a situation; he made you think about the entire issue, not just the surface.

"You need to think about the situation from their stand point," he continued, "because they aren't to blame for what Becky did. Robert and Dana both sent their love and said they hope you will want to meet them."

"Robert even led me to the home of your biological Dad. He

wasn't the man listed on your birth certificate, but Robert said there were no doubts about Doug Glenwright being your biological Dad. Apparently everyone in the town had known about he and Becky's affair, but they didn't seem to care what anyone thought. Their affair lasted for several years, but ended soon after you were born."

Dad then told the story of how he met Mr. Glenwright. When he arrived at his house, there were a lot of cars in the driveway.

"When I pulled into the driveway," Dad began, "a large built man walked towards my car and said, *'Can I help you?'* So I said, *'My name is Kent Bartlett, and I have an adopted daughter. I was wondering if you would mind getting in my car, and us taking a little drive down the road, to talk.'* Much to my amazement, the man didn't question anything, he just said, *'I'd be glad to. Just let me tell my wife I'm leaving. She's having a Sunday school party with her lady friends. Give me just a minute.'* And I mean, that man wasn't gone but a minute."

"When he sat down in the car, he looked at me and said, *'I felt like I knew why you were here the minute I saw you pull in my driveway. I knew this day would come.'* I asked if Robert had called and told him about the situation, but Mr. Glenwright's response was an immediate, *'No.'* He said that he and Robert didn't get along because of Becky and the affair. I asked him how he knew who I was, and Mr. Glenwright answered, *'Have you ever felt like you were about to face something you dreaded? That deep down, gut feeling that says **it's here**? Call it whatever you want, but I knew my sins would catch up to me one day.'* "

"I drove and the two of us talked. I intentionally crossed over the state line, and pulled off to the side of the road. I asked Mr. Glenwright to start naming names of family members, as far back as he could remember, and told him to begin with any and all medical history he knew of."

Dad continued, "Mr. Glenwright was totally cooperative. He even started to tear-up a few times. He said that he'd been willing to leave his family and marry Becky to raise you, but she refused his offer over and over again. Doug went on to tell me that his wife, as well as his son and daughter, knew you existed. Once they were grown, he asked them several times if they would ever want to meet you, but both of them said no."

"I thanked Mr. Glenwright for his cooperation and the medical information. I told him, '*I was prepared to get information by cooperation or by force, if need be, and I'm glad things have gone this well.*' Mr. Glenwright replied, '*I noticed the gun in the car seat, and I knew I could be in trouble when we crossed the state line.*'"

Both of them understood they shared something in common, and they had to work together in order to help me. Mr. Glenwright told Dad that he understood he didn't deserve to meet me, but he would sure like to some day. Dad told him that he would pass along the information, and it would be entirely up to me.

Dad left that little county on Saturday, with a complete family history on both sides. As I sat and listened to his story, I knew things would never be the same.

"Kimi Leah," Dad said, "I will never forget how the Lord guided me, step by step, and I want you to remember this story just the way I have told it to you."

I knew my Dad was a man of faith, but I could tell from the tears and uncontrollable weeping, that the experience had changed his life, and he would never forget that amazing journey.

I will never forget how Dad dropped everything and took off, not knowing where to go or who he would find, but he did it all for me. Somehow, all of the harsh memories of my strict upbringing were pushed to the back of my mind. I looked at my parents with a deep thankfulness for truly being there when I needed them the most. Perhaps the fact they were in their 40's when I came into their lives became more stressful than they realized it would be. Despite all the unhappiness I experienced while growing up, I somehow felt forgiveness towards them and I knew life could have been a lot worse if they hadn't adopted me.

I arrived at the doctor's office the next week with all my medical history. There was, in fact, a lot of cancer and diabetes in the family history, on both sides. As the doctor began his exam, I saw a strange look on his face. He left the room for a while and when he came back, he told me that the lump had disappeared.

"I can't explain it," he said, "but whatever I felt before, has totally disappeared. I checked the mammogram more than once, and the mass is gone."

Mom, Dad, and I left the doctor's office that day, knowing that it was all part of a plan, a plan bigger than any of us could understand. We knew the reason for Dad finding my biological family would be revealed, when the time was right. This was just another miracle in my life's journey.

CHAPTER SIX

PATH TO FORGIVENESS

Time had not healed the wounds of my birth mother's second rejection of me. I was at work one morning when the phone rang, and I answered it in the usual way, "Hello, Bartlett's." I was surprised to find Robert, my half-brother, on the other end of the line. We had an agreement that I was not to be contacted by any of my biological family until I was ready, if I was *ever* ready, to make the first step towards a relationship with them.

Robert must have sensed the lack of oxygen I felt at that moment.

"I'm sorry," he said. "I know we told your Dad we wouldn't bother you. I just felt I needed to call and tell you that Becky is in the hospital. She has stage four ovarian cancer, and she is not expected to make it out of the hospital. I wanted to let you know because of the cancer issue… And also, I thought you should have the opportunity to meet her while she is still alive, if you want to."

He went on to give me the name of the hospital she was in, and her room number. He said he wasn't going to tell her that we spoke, in case I chose not to see her.

Emotions overwhelmed me, as I was left unsure what to say to him, and how I should feel about the looming death of a mother I never knew. She had tossed me aside as if I was a piece of trash that was of no use to her, and now I was supposed to care about her having cancer?

I thanked Robert for calling, and that was all I could muster up from within me. It felt so strange to think I was related to this person, who I knew nothing about and had no emotional feelings for. Yet he was my brother, an actual blood relative of mine, and I couldn't get my heart to feel anything. My head told me to ignore it all and just carry on with the only family I had ever known.

Robert had the advantage of remembering me and knowing that I had once been part of their family. I, on the other hand, found myself wondering if Dad had truly found my blood relatives, or if there was a mistake. If it weren't for the miraculous story Dad revealed to me, and how he was guided each step of the way, I wouldn't believe they were the right people.

Nothing was wrong with the man and woman who said they were my half-brother and half-sister; I just never expected to have siblings. I had only wondered about *her*. The *mother* was the only one I ever thought about. I wondered what she looked like. Was she short or tall? Did she have dark hair, like mine? Were her eyes aqua, and her stature petite? Most of all, I wondered, did she miss me and was she looking for me? I would have to leave the room if a TV show came on about a mother reconciling with a long lost child. My heart would ache with questions no one could answer but *her*.

I had resolved myself to believe that my biological mother would remain a mystery to me, and we would probably never meet. It was scary to think of Dad actually finding her. Once in a while, I would daydream that she was a successful business lady, or maybe a movie star, who had turned her life around and spent years looking for me. I hoped that she regretted the day she let the court system take me away from her.

My reality wasn't so picture-perfect. My story was not a happy, joyous one, like the writers portray reunited families on TV. It became clear that she was still a cold-hearted, self-centered woman. She was ugly to my Dad, and plainly told him she didn't want anything to do with me. The tides had now turned, and the woman who didn't care about my cancer scare was now lying in a hospital, fighting for her life, with stage four ovarian cancer.

As I hung up the phone, I felt sick to my stomach and my mind was racing with questions. How was I supposed to decide if I wanted to lay eyes on this woman? After all, she did make it clear that she didn't want to see me and didn't want my presence to "mess up" her relationship with her youngest daughter. What if Rhonda was at the hospital? I wasn't sure that I wanted to see either one of them. My mind told me it wasn't Rhonda's fault that Becky didn't want us to meet. My heart was hurt, and it caused a wall to come up that made me not want to see Becky's beloved child. I felt no bond with any of them. The way Becky talked to my Dad, and the way she told him she didn't have to answer to him for her lifestyle, caused me to want to suppress what I knew, and otherwise forget any of them existed.

It had been easy to think that I could ignore they existed, until now. I thought the ball was in my court, and I would decide if I ever wanted to see any of them. Now, I was confronted with the reality that the clock was ticking, and a last chance is just that – it is the last and final chance to get to do or say something. This was not a decision I could make quickly or lightly. If I chose not to go see her, would I regret never meeting my biological mother and seeing what she looked like? On the other hand, if I did go to see her, would she scream at me for showing up? Would the experience be so terrible that it would haunt me for life? Perhaps she would say things to me I would never be able to forget. I was already more hurt than anyone realized, because she didn't want to meet the child she gave away. I still didn't understand how a mother could have absolutely no love for her child.

I purposely stayed at work a little longer that night, in hopes of talking to Dad and getting his thoughts on what I should do. Mom noticed I was working late, so she told me to stay and have dinner with them. I eagerly accepted, and began helping Mom set the table. Finally, I heard the noise of that old diesel engine, and I knew Dad had just pulled into the driveway.

The three of us sat around the kitchen table, drinking coffee and having a nice dinner. In the back of my mind, I just wanted to blurt out that Robert had called me. I hadn't mentioned it to Mom, because I wanted to talk to Dad about it first. Dad was rational and full of wisdom. I knew Mom, being a Mom, would be mad that Robert had called and upset me. I knew what her reaction would be, but what I really needed was advice on what to do about meeting Becky. As we sat around talking, Mom noticed it was almost 8pm, and suggested I spend the night instead of driving back to my apartment. I kept my make-up case in my car, and Mom had everything else I needed; I always had a change of clothes at Mom and Dad's, so I agreed to stay. Mom and I washed the dinner plates and cleaned the kitchen, and Dad went downstairs to his office.

After about an hour, I excused myself and told Mom I was going to go see if Dad needed help with anything. His desk faced the door; as I approached, I could see him working on some paperwork. I lightly tapped on the door, to get his attention. I hated to bother him, but I really needed words of wisdom.

Dad looked up from his paperwork and smiled.

"What can I do for you baby doll?" he asked.

As I stepped into the office I said, "Do you have a few minutes? I need to talk to you about something."

Without hesitation, he replied, "You know I always have time for you. Come in here and tell me what's bothering you. I could tell something was troubling you at dinner tonight."

I told Dad about Robert's phone call. He listened while I explained that Becky was dying, and if I ever wanted to see her, I had to decide quickly. I wasn't sure what it would feel like to actually look into her eyes, and I didn't know if I could do it.

Dad listened patiently without saying a word, and when he felt like I was finished, he asked if I needed to say anything else. I told him no; that was all I knew about the situation and wasn't sure what to do. Dad always chose his words wisely and took long pauses before speaking, and this was no exception. He leaned back in his big, brown, leather chair, clasped his hands together, and just looked at me silently for a few minutes. I knew to remain at attention, and wait for him to speak. My brother and I were *well* trained to not interrupt an adult when they are speaking, even during moments of hesitation.

When it seemed like he was unsure of what to say to me, he finally spoke. I will never forget his words.

"Kimi," he began, "I have listened to how you feel about her and I can't tell you that I would feel any differently if I were in your shoes. However, I think you need to *think* of this differently."

He stopped and tucked his head for a moment. When he raised it again, there were tears in his eyes. I almost felt guilty for getting him involved, but he was the only Dad I knew, and upstairs was the only Mom I knew. How was I supposed to call other people family, when the Bartlett's were my family?

A couple minutes passed before he spoke again. Then, with a sincere and loving voice, he said,

"Maybe instead of thinking about yourself and how you feel, turn it around for a moment and think about the fact that, just maybe, she may need to see you and say something to you before she dies. Try to think about her and her situation right now. I know you are a Christian lady, and you can understand what I am saying to you. Your Mother and I will drive you and go with you every step of the way, if you want us with you."

The tears began to stream down my face; I knew he was right. I couldn't speak for a moment, but then, I nodded.

"Yes," I said, "Yes, you're right. I hadn't looked at it that way. I was only thinking about how I felt. I need to give her a chance to see me, if she wants to. Is there any way you and Mom could drive me to the hospital tomorrow? I would like to have you both with me when I meet her."

We got an early start the next morning and headed on a two-hour trip to the hospital. Mom and Dad cancelled all of their plans, and never complained about the short notice. We didn't talk a lot; we were all captured in our own thoughts. I knew Dad must have been wondering how his second meeting with *her* would go; he certainly didn't enjoy meeting her the first time. I could only imagine what my Mom was thinking. Mom didn't say a lot about the trip, but she let me know they would be with me as much or as little as I needed.

I couldn't read Mom's thoughts on Becky. I couldn't tell if she thought Becky was trashy, or if she felt sorry for her, or what. Mom didn't say enough for me to know how she felt about the situation. All I knew was that she was there for me. She was willing to look at a woman who gave up her daughter, when she herself cried for years because she couldn't have children. What a clash of personalities and character. I would never waiver on the fact that Leah Bartlett was the only lady who would ever be called my Mother. We may have had our bad times, but I still knew who fed me, clothed me, and took care of me when I was sick.

No one would ever be Mom and Dad to me except Kent and Leah Bartlett. I had not yet figured out how I could stay loyal to my big brother, Lucas, and yet build a relationship with Robert. Could I ever give any of them a piece of my heart, and call them my brother and sisters? Time would have to be my ally in forging a relationship with them. With Becky, time was now my enemy, forcing my hand to turn at its pace.

When we arrived at the hospital, my heart was racing. I began to question the entire meeting. I was about to ask Dad if we could just turn around and go home, when he must have read my mind. His eyes fixed on mine, as he stared at me from the rear view mirror.

"You are tough, Kimi Leah," he said. "You can do this. Mother and I are here. You just tell us when to leave and when to stay."

By that time, he was parking the car. I knew this meeting would change us all a little, and add another dimension to our family.

We all hugged and Dad led us in a prayer before walking through the hospital doors. Their love for me felt stronger than ever before. I knew they were there to protect me physically and emotionally. We stepped onto the elevator and headed to the fourth floor. As the elevator doors opened, I knew what I had to do. I now understood what Dad was talking about when he told me how he felt *led* to do certain things. It is a feeling that you can't explain, just a sense of knowing what you need to do. I stepped off the elevator and turned to Mom and Dad.

"I'm sorry," I said. "I don't know why, but Jesus and I have to face her together. I need to walk this hallway with Him. Do you care to wait here? I'll come back to get you."

It was time to take my heavenly Fathers hand and trust Him to see me through. I could see the tears in their eyes, as they both nodded their heads yes in agreement. They told me to let them know when I was ready. I let go of Mom and Dad's hands, gave them each a kiss, and looked up.

"Okay Jesus, it's me and you. Take my hand, and don't let go."

I nervously walked down the long, empty hallway toward Becky's hospital room. Then, it was there before me; the doorway I had to walk through. I took a deep breath.

"Jesus, help me," I said, as I opened the door to a pitiful site.

Lying there was a tiny, dark-haired woman, with tubes and machines hooked to her. She was all alone. There were no family members there, no husband to hold her hand and give her comfort. I instantly wondered if she regretted living for herself, being self-centered, and running from man to man.

Becky hadn't asked to see a picture of me when Dad first met her, yet as soon as I pushed the door open and our eyes met, she began to weep. Tears began to roll down her face, as her hand covered her mouth. We both froze with our eyes fixated on one another. I stood in silence, as I laid eyes on the woman who bore me. The years had not been kind to her. I saw a hardness to her face, and I struggled to see a resemblance between the two of us. All I could think of was how much I looked like Mom; I couldn't see any of myself in this woman.

As I stood there, holding the door open, not knowing whether to step in or turn around and leave, she spoke to me. She didn't say *hello* or *I'm glad you're here*. Her first words to me were, "Can you ever forgive me?"

I looked at her frail, sickly body and immediately replied, "Yes."

Yes was all I could say to that question, as I looked at her lying there helpless and hurting. All the questions I thought I wanted to ask her, and all the things I thought I would say to her, escaped my mind. I was ready to have my parents with me.

"Mom and Dad are here with me," I said. "Would you mind if they came in and had prayer with you?"

"That would be wonderful, yes. Please have them come in," she said.

I saw the pride that must have gotten her through so many difficult years, as she tried to straighten herself up in her bed, with all the machines and tubes attached to her. She reached her hand up to touch her hair, too weak to fix or fluff it, trying to make herself look the best she could. I wanted to tell her not to worry about moving or adjusting anything, but sometimes you have to let a person do what they need to do, and this was one of those moments. I watched her try to gain composure and sit up straight, as little moans of pain came from her with each move she made.

As I leaned out of the doorway, I saw Mom and Dad standing where I left them. The very minute they saw me open the door and motion to them, Dad nodded his head and they started walking. Dad had his arm around Mom's waist, and I knew he was prepared to catch her if seeing Becky was more than she could handle.

I watched all their faces, as I stood by the doorway, unsure of what the next few moments would bring. Becky's eyes fixated on Dad's as he entered the room. She saw the stern look on Dad's face that said, *I'm here with my family and you're not going to upset any of them, cancer or no cancer.* Her eyes fell momentarily, as if in shame, and then she watched as my Mom approached her.

I wasn't prepared for what I was about to witness. I stood there, speechless, as Mom walked to Becky's bedside, leaned down, and hugged her. Mom then said,

"I just want to thank you. If you hadn't given birth to her, we never would have gotten her."

At that very moment, my Mom taught me more than she realized. She exemplified the love that Christ spoke about. She showed me that you can look beyond someone's faults and find the good in them, if you choose to.

The tears fell from Becky's eyes, as Mom hugged and thanked her. I'm not sure anyone had ever thanked Becky for anything. Dad was noticeably proud of his wife, but my own pride made me think Becky didn't deserve a hug, much less a *thank you.* I wanted to protect Mom from her own kindness, and tell her that she was too much of a lady to lean down and hug this woman. It was too late; Mom had put the love out there, for all of us to see and feel. I knew right then and there, that although I had told Becky I forgave her, it just wasn't in my heart yet. God was going to have to work on my heart to mold me into the tenderhearted lady my Mom had just shown herself to be.

All I could say after that was, "Do you mind if Dad has prayer for you?"

"Yes, please," Becky said.

Dad said a beautiful prayer for her healing and comfort. After the prayer, I was ready to leave. My heart was pounding and I just needed time to ponder, and process all of my thoughts. Even though I knew it might be my only chance to speak to her, or ever see her again, all I could say was, "We have to go now. Take care." I didn't hug her or tell her I was sorry she was sick; I wasn't sure I cared.

Mom and Dad didn't question me or say anything about the quick visit to her room. They merely followed me out the door, and were right behind me as I bolted for the elevator. I'm not sure I took a breath until we were going down the elevator. My feelings didn't make any sense to me. I didn't hate her, and yet, I couldn't talk to her or hug her. Three sentences were all I could muster and each of them was uncomfortable. Mom made it look so easy to be forgiving and kind.

Dad had talked to me for years about not being bitter towards my biological parents. I thought my heart was clear, until I saw the beautiful act of my Mother hugging the woman who tossed me away as if I had no worth. I knew I couldn't have hugged Becky, and that told me I wasn't where I needed to be, in terms of forgiveness. How was I going to change the thoughts in my head about what I felt for her and the lifestyle she had chosen? Would I ever have some kind of *love* for her? Somewhere within me, I felt forgiving her meant I was justifying her actions and saying I deserved what she did to me.

Mom and Dad never complained about four hours of driving, for the five-minute visit. They did exactly as they told me, proving they were there to support me as I faced Becky for the first time. When I questioned Mom about how she could hug Becky, she said she meant every word. If Becky hadn't given birth to me and allowed me to be adopted, they never would have gotten me. I never questioned Mom again about her actions that day. I just wished I could have felt tenderness or *something* other than numbness for Becky. Perhaps there were twenty years of callouses built up on my heart. I didn't want to face the feelings of being unwanted and unloved; I wanted all those feelings to stay covered up, and pretend there wasn't any pain. Little did I know that the pain Becky caused me would pale in comparison to what lay ahead for me.

CHAPTER SEVEN

THE CONNECTION

A few months passed and I found myself wondering if Becky had died. Feeling uneasy and somewhat afraid of the door I was about to open, I decided it was time for me to call Robert.

Making a simple phone call could turn into a very complex situation. Once a connection was made, there would be no turning back. If I began talking to them, I would have to meet them.

There were so many feelings of uncertainty looming within me. What would I talk about with them? How would Robert feel when I talked about my brother, Lucas? I didn't know what it was like to have a sister. Would Dana and Rhonda understand my confusion and my feelings, or would I be damaging our relationship before it began? I started second guessing myself about contacting any of them. I thought, *maybe I should wait a few years, let the thoughts settle in my mind, and then decide if it's even wise to get to know them.*

As I pondered the "pro's and con's" of making a connection to the family I didn't know, Dad's words came back into my mind. I realized I was doing it again – thinking of my situation and not considering they knew I was "out there" somewhere all these years. They spent years wondering what had happened to me. Robert told Dad he would even look at girls about my age, when he was in a mall or traveling somewhere, and wonder, "Is that Tiny?" He told Dad that he was constantly looking, in hopes he would find me one day.

Dana had been completely overwhelmed with emotion when she met Dad and saw pictures of me. She asked Dad if he would tell me she loved me, and was so happy to know I had been taken care of. Dana said she hoped to meet me one day, when I was ready. She even told Dad that Rhonda knew I existed; she had told Rhonda about me, and said Rhonda would also be thrilled to meet me.

Dad had made sure to get all the needed medical history for me and, in his wisdom, he made sure to get phone numbers and addresses, just in case. I gathered the papers Dad had brought back to me and searched for Robert's phone number. All of Dad's notes were well organized with near-perfect penmanship. He must have taken his time when gathering and writing the information so I would be able to see it all clearly, in the event that he never made it back to audibly tell me about his miraculous trip.

He wrote all of his notes in a spiral bound tablet and kept precise information on each person he met. He couldn't have done a better job; it was truly a mission of love. I turned the pages one by one, as tears streamed down my face. Emotionally, I was unsure how to process the fact that contact had been made. Where I came from was no longer a mystery. I now had actual names, places, and even knew the city I was born in. The greatest surprise of Dad's journey was the unexpected addition of siblings.

All of this flooded my mind, along with past memories of feeling unwanted and unloved by the Bartlett's. But then, I also remembered being so sick as a child, and how Mom took care of me, night and day. I thought of how hard she worked in her garden, and how early she got up each morning to make sure that my brother and I had a good breakfast before school. She and Dad both worked hard to provide for us. At least they gave us a home, and made sure we were in church every Sunday. I couldn't imagine what I would have been like, if Becky **hadn't** given me away.

My heart filled with loyalty to the Bartlett's for giving me a home and taking care of me, and for making church a priority for our family.

I thumbed through the little notepad, and there it was: Robert's name, phone number, and his address. Dad had even made a little note to take the first street on the left and go to the third house on the left. My heart began to pound as I sat down at my desk and reached for the phone. I wasn't sure I would even be able to speak if someone answered the phone. I used a technique that had always gotten me through difficult times. For most of my childhood, even into my young adulthood, when I was upset or down about something, Dad's answer to me was, "You're a tough girl. You can do it." I repeated the words over and over again in my mind… *I'm tough. I can do this. I'm tough. I can do this.* Suddenly, the dial tone stopped as a woman's voice said, "Hello?" I sat up a little straighter in my chair.

"This is Kimi Bartlett," I said. "May I speak to Robert please?"

The woman told me to "hold on just a minute" and she would get him. I heard her lay the phone down and yell for Robert. I could hear the excitement in her voice as she said, "It's Kimi! It's Kimi!"

I was unsure what my first words would be, and my heart felt like it was coming up through my throat. Someone picked up the phone.

"This is Robert," he said.

I nervously said hello and said I was sorry it had taken me a while to contact him.

"I fully understand," he said, "I don't want to interfere with your life in any way."

I began to tell him about my visit to the hospital, and he said Becky told him I had made the trip to see her.

"Well, did she die?" I asked.

Much to my surprise, he said no. I had played out the scenario in my mind that she probably died shortly after my visit and they just decided not to tell me about it. Robert went on to explain that they were all surprised she survived. The doctors thought she would be fine; her ovaries had been removed, and her treatments were finished. They had run several tests and could no longer find any sign of cancer; her surgery and treatments had been successful and she was out of danger.

A part of me was happy for Becky and her family (which I did not consider myself to be a part of), but if she was alive, then that possibly meant another meeting with her. A lot of thoughts were going through my mind; I tried to focus on talking to Robert, but all I could think of was my mixed emotions for her and how dreadful it would be to face her again. I managed to ask Robert if it would be okay if Dad and Mom came with me to visit them around Christmas time. He was so excited; he said he couldn't wait to meet me. He seemed so nice, it actually made my nerves calm down a little, and I thought that it just might be okay to get to know him. Robert said Dana and her husband didn't have a working phone, so he would drive to her house and let her know I would be coming for a visit. I thanked him and told him I would call and give him an exact date, as soon as Dad could tell me when it would be best for he and Mom to make the trip with me.

With Christmas right around the corner, the time for the visit had arrived all too quickly. Once again, I was unsure about whether or not my visit was the right thing to do. I had managed to talk to Lucas about the situation, and plainly told him that he would always be my brother. I told him how much I loved him and that Robert could never take his place in my heart. Lucas responded in a way that only a sweet, loving brother could. "I will like him," Lucas said, "as long as he's nice to you." I could tell that Lucas was there to take care of me and protect me from getting hurt.

The "meeting" was going to be very difficult and stressful for me. Dad had engrained certain characteristics into me that would always be part of my being. One of those characteristics was loyalty. I still could not wrap my head around the idea of calling Robert my brother, or even calling Dana and Rhonda my sisters. I felt like I was being a traitor to the parents who took me in when no one from my biological family tried to keep me. I had already rationalized in my mind that if the grandmother couldn't have taken me, there were surely aunts and uncles who could have. I knew God had pulled me out of that family and given me a new start, with a different name and a different family. Now I felt like I was messing with an ordained life and trying to go backwards in time to a place I wasn't supposed to be. To make things a little easier, I decided to only see Robert and his wife, for my first visit. I asked Robert to tell Dana and Rhonda that I would try to meet them on my next visit.

I had loved Lucas since the first time I met him, when he practically pulled me through his house, showing me every room and closet and telling me that the pink room could be mine. He and I had always been close. There was no way I could let someone I barely knew damage the bond I felt with my brother. No one ever suggested to either one of us that we weren't brother and sister. I think the people who knew we were adopted, thought we were "really" brother and sister. Mom always told people we were so close we would fight anyone for one another.

There are a lot of books written about adoption, however, I don't think many of them consider the viewpoint of the child. The books are usually about the parents and how wonderful they are for taking an "unwanted" child, and how they can adjust to the new addition in the family, and so forth.

It can be very confusing to a child who is old enough to know they were "taken in" by a strange family. I always felt like I couldn't be sure I was wanted or truly had relatives, beyond Lucas and my parents. Kent and Leah Bartlett had relatives, but were my brother and I truly accepted by them? Would they consider us "family" when our parents were deceased? Was there any point in trying to get close to cousins? Did they consider us their cousin, when we weren't around? When you hear people make comments like, "Well you're not really related... You're not blood," it makes you unsure if you fit in anywhere. If your biological family cast you aside and doesn't want you, and people constantly remind you that you aren't really "blood" related to the parents who adopted you, then where does an adopted child fit in?

I had a built-in defense reaction, which Mom referred to as "being sassy." I was a strong-willed child. I had to teach myself, as a little girl, that I would be okay, if I was scared or needed something and no one was around. In fact, it was my strong will and determination that made me try so hard to impress the Bartlett's, by washing my hair on my first visit. I wanted to show them I could take care of myself and that I wouldn't be any trouble. It apparently worked; I know they smiled a lot when I came out of the bathroom and said, "Look, I washed my hair too!" If they had decided not to adopt me, I think they would've always remembered that moment and how happy I was to show them what I could do.

Although I remember wanting a Mom and Dad, I also remember how scared I was the first night I spent at their house. I was a three-and-a-half year old girl in a strange house, with people I had only met once, and I had to be strong. My personality had been set at an early age. My caseworker had informed the Bartlett's that I was a "very independent, determined child."

I believe an all-knowing and wise God gives us the attributes we will need in order to survive the situations He knows we will face in our lifetime. Perhaps that's why it is said, "He won't give you more than you can handle." We are born with certain strengths within us, which may not come out of us until the time is needed.

Once again, I was headed into a situation that was going to push my emotional strengths to the limit. I asked Dad if he and Mom would drive me to Gentry, sometime before Christmas so I could meet Robert and his family. Without hesitation, Dad said, "Just name the day, and we will make time to take you," and I knew he meant it. Saturdays were the best days for Dad to go out of town or take a day off, and I knew it would be a short trip. I remembered how quick the trip to the hospital had been when I met Becky for the first time, and I wasn't sure how I would feel when I saw my half-brother, Robert, for the first time. It wasn't something that could be pre-planned. I was still processing all the information about no one in the family stepping up to the plate, to keep me from being taken away. How did the grandmother, aunts, uncles, and the rest of the family look at themselves in the mirror each day? They all knew they had allowed a blood relative of theirs to be taken away. How could they not care what happened to the child? These are things I found myself pondering on. I felt betrayed and wasn't sure I would ever want to meet very many of my so-called "family" members.

These thoughts had consumed my mind almost daily ever since Dad called from Robert's home that Friday night, to tell me he found my biological family. My mind told me that the only way to get rid of some of the confusion was to meet them. I wanted to look into their eyes and see how they looked at me. The eyes are truly the "window to the soul," and Dad had taught me to look people in the eye when speaking to them, and read them by their eyes. If they really loved me, there would be an immediate spark in their eyes as soon as they met me. Only then would I be able to rationalize trying to build a relationship with them. They had grown up without me, and I didn't think any of them had put forth much effort in finding their long-lost relative. Even if it was a one-time meeting, I had to force myself to make the trip. If I could only handle meeting one of them at a time, then that is what I would do.

A part of me wanted to be a softy and play out the scene in the movies, where the long-lost siblings run towards each other, arms open wide, filled with joy and tears and a lifetime of plans to never be separated again. However, I couldn't pretend to have feelings I didn't have. My personality wasn't a soft, emotional one. I had to be strong-willed to be in a boarding home without parents and be told how to act in order to make someone want me. It's easy for people to want to adopt a baby, but a three-and-a-half year old has to help in the process. I was well aware that it was up to me and how I acted that would influence whether or not someone wanted to adopt me.

I wondered if any of my so-called relatives in Gentry, ever thought about what they put me through. Were they taken in by strangers and forced to live their life trying to pay back the parents who fed and clothed them? Did any of them face life alone? Did they understand they had taken away my sense of belonging? I had lived a life of humility, being told how lucky I was to be taken in. I would spend my life trying to repay the Bartlett's, but it would never be enough. I certainly didn't want to get involved in a situation where any of *these people* would make me feel guilty for not staying in touch or not visiting enough. One thing was for sure, if anyone ever complained about me not "doing my part," that would be it; I would walk out of their lives as quickly as I walked in. I was already being told what I owed to people, and I didn't need another family putting me through the same thing.

The day arrived for Mom, Dad, and I to make the trip to meet Robert. It was a pretty December day. Dad drove us in his black, '98 Oldsmobile. It was a beautiful car that was only driven on Sundays and special occasions; Mom had an Oldsmobile station wagon she drove on a daily basis. The '98 Olds was a long car that seemed to just glide over the road; the interior was a soft, deep-burgundy color with plush seats that seemed to envelope and hug you. When we arrived at Robert's, I would be proud to step out of Dad's black beauty.

We were almost to Gentry, when Dad pulled off to the side of the road. Dad turned in his seat and looked at me.

"You need to understand that Robert wasn't raised like you were," he said. "His house is not what you're used to being in. Don't misunderstand me, it was clean and they were more than kind to me, I just don't want you to be shocked when we pull up."

I told him that I understood; I knew my brother and I had been raised on one of the nicest properties in our county. Perhaps the fact we were adopted, or the fact the Bartlett's constantly made us feel indebted to them, caused us to never let their money "go to our heads." Lucas and I always had a heart for the kids that no one else wanted to be friends with; we stayed away from the cliques and the "popular" kids.

Dad pointed out the street we were headed to and when it became visible, I could tell he wasn't exaggerating. We pulled up to a small house that had a trailer attached to the right side of it. The front porch looked like it would cave in if a heavy snow fell on it. Robert's house wasn't the worst one on the street though.

The appearance of the house didn't matter to me. I reminded myself how Robert had welcomed Dad into his home, and how helpful he had been in getting medical history on family members. It was his character that my Dad had described to me, and it was Robert's kind character that made me want to meet him. We hardly finished parking when the front door opened; I saw a slender, dark-haired, well-groomed man waiting to greet us. Dad helped Mom from the car, and we walked toward the house. Robert and Dad shook hands as Robert opened the door for us to enter the house. I kept my eyes on Robert, trying to see how he looked at Mom and Dad. His eyes were kind and I saw a sparkle in them when he said hello to me. He gave me a big hug and told me how glad he was to finally "meet" me.

Robert and his wife had prepared a wonderful supper for us. We talked for several hours over food and coffee. I listened to sad stories of Robert's childhood and how his grandmother, Becky's mom, had raised he and Dana. Becky had gone from man to man, never settling down for long. He and Dana even called their grandmother "mom," and called Becky "little mom."

It was a very nice visit, and I knew he was trying to fill-in pieces for me so I could understand the life I had been taken from. I found myself watching his actions, studying his features, and looking for signs of myself in him. I thought it was cool that we both had liked coffee since we were small children. As I listened to him tell stories, I knew I'd made the right decision in choosing to meet him. I liked him and knew I would have to see him again. Dad was right, Robert hadn't been blessed with a happy childhood or money, but he had risen above it all. He was a hard-working man, trying to make a good living for his wife and family.

The hours passed quickly and Mom and Dad were very patient; it was getting late and we still had a two-and-a-half hour drive ahead of us. Robert and I hugged good-bye and I told him I would be back for another visit in the spring or summer.

As we pulled away from Robert's house, I could see him standing in his front yard. He watched us drive away until we were out of sight. As we drove, Dad said, "I knew you would like him if you just gave him a chance."

I thanked Mom and Dad for driving me to meet him, and told them I would like to go back again to meet Dana. They both encouraged me to keep my heart open to having a relationship with my siblings. Dad reminded me that it wasn't their fault, and there was nothing Robert or Dana could have done to keep me from being taken away; he knew there was anger and bitterness in me towards Becky and the fact I was given away.

Even before my medical scare, Dad had talked to me about not having any bitterness towards my biological parents. I felt like I was always being told to forgive. When Mom's "nerves" made her unbearable, when she was mean and nasty to Lucas and I, Dad would tell me to forgive her because she couldn't help her nerves. When Dad got home late and didn't have time for us, or when he was in a bad mood and "whipped" us, Mom would tell me to forgive him because he didn't mean to be so rough on us. Dad was constantly telling me to forgive the people that gave me away. I wondered if the forgiven people ever had to pay for hurting others. At twenty-one years old, I had no idea that I would learn to forgive the worst offenses. My lessons of forgiveness were only beginning; this was a mere test of my heart's capacity to forgive.

Winter passed quickly, and I did make another trip back to Gentry. I not only met with Robert and Dana, but I also met Rhonda. I was unsure about meeting Rhonda at first, because of what Becky had told my Dad, but Dana let me know that she already knew about me. Dana had told Rhonda about me years before, and she was eager to meet me. They were all very nice, and so far, I was glad I had taken Dad's advice to give them a chance.

On my third visit, a large dinner was arranged where I met an aunt and uncle, and some cousins. Becky was at the dinner as well, but she barely glanced at me. I was okay with her attitude; she thought she was tough, but she was about to meet tougher.

I had learned to put feelings into certain "compartments" and walk away or ignore things that I didn't want to deal with. My upbringing caused me to have a business-like and somewhat reserved demeanor. I didn't like drama and I didn't "carry on" about things. I never understood why some people acted "overwhelmed" with a situation. The motto that carried me through my lonely toddler years into my adulthood was, "Just deal with it." After I became a Christian and started studying my bible, I came across a verse, Philippians 4:13, that says, "I can do all things through Christ which strengtheneth me." That's when I learned where my strength came from; I knew it was God who kept me safe that first month in an incubator, and through my infant years. HE was the one that comforted me through my childhood and told me everything was going to work out for my good. Whether it was the Bartlett's making me feel indebted to them, or Becky continuing to show that she didn't care about me, I knew I could always pray for strength and the bad feelings would disappear.

An aunt made arrangements for me to meet my biological Dad at her house. I was nervous about meeting him, and knew I would never call him Dad, but I did wonder if I could see myself in him. I certainly did not see myself in Becky, when I first met her.

Mr. Glenwright arrived on time, and we shook hands when we met. I didn't think it was going to be a productive visit; however, he turned out to be quite a surprise. He began talking and didn't stop until he had told me about his *entire* relationship with Becky. He told me about how they met and that he was married at the time. He was honest about it being an adulterous affair and said he was one hundred percent sure that I was his daughter. He had offered to leave his wife and marry Becky, but she didn't want to get married. Tears streamed down his face when he told me she asked for money to get an abortion, but he couldn't let her go through with it. Doug admitted he went behind Becky's back and paid the doctor double the cost to fake the procedure. She was mad when she found out, but it didn't matter because it was too late for her to try again. "You're alive because of me," he told me. He and Becky drank a lot, and alcohol was the reason I was taken from them. He recalled the night they were drunk in his pick-up truck when an officer took me from the trash in the floorboard; the night child welfare services took control of the situation and I was placed in the "system."

Little by little, I learned about Becky and how my life could have been, if I had not been adopted. Also, the more I learned from the stories that were told to me by various "family" members, I realized that Becky had a difficult childhood. A part of me began to feel sorry for her, and the life she had lived. I felt like Becky and I needed the chance to talk, just the two of us. Somehow, I needed to make arrangements for us to meet privately. I wasn't in a hurry for a one-on-one conversation with her, so I felt it could wait until the following summer.

The city I lived in had a very nice hotel, called The Executive. It was filled with gift shops; lounge areas; restaurants; and had a nice outside pool, as well as an indoor pool and hot tub. I decided the hotel would be a safe meeting spot for us. There would be plenty for her to do, when I wasn't there with her.

Summer arrived and I was ready to make my call to Becky. I told Becky I would pay for her to stay in a deluxe suite for two nights, *if* she would come visit, so we could talk; she agreed to make the trip.

I made sure to have the room paid for in advance, and I let the hotel know I would be covering the cost of any room service charges for food, as well. The day of our meeting came sooner than my nerves were prepared for. I suppose I could have put the meeting off for years, and I still would have dreaded it. It was never going to be an easy task to ask her why she gave me up. Nevertheless, the day was here. I positioned my car in the hotel parking lot so I would be able to see her arrive; I wanted to see her without her knowing I was watching. Vehicles came and went, until I finally saw a petite, dark-haired woman getting out of a white car. It was Becky. She was wearing a nice blouse, a slim skirt, and high heels. I waited for her to go in the hotel, and then I exited my car and went inside to find her. She was wandering around the lobby when I approached her. She said hello but offered no gesture of a hug, and barely gave me a smile. I handed her the room key and let her know I had reserved the nicest suite the hotel offered.

Becky was silent as we rode in the elevator and walked towards her room. I opened the door and let her enter the room first. It was obvious that the room exceeded her expectations. She excused herself to go to the ladies room while I proceeded to turn on various lamps for her. When she came back into the sitting area, I told her that I was going to let her get settled in, and I needed to know when she wanted to meet with me so we could talk. I didn't expect what was coming. Becky put her hands on her hips, looked at me with pursed lips and a hateful glare, and said, "If you think I came here to confess my sins to you, it's not going to happen. My sins are my business and none of yours."

I stood speechless for a moment, realizing she was never going to change. I had just wasted a few hundred dollars in hopes of building some kind of relationship with her, but she was too full of pride to even think of anyone but herself. Remaining calm, I told her that the room, as well as the food, was already paid for.

"But I'm not paying for alcohol," I continued. "You can call me if you change your attitude." With that said, I exited her room and walked away without looking back.

Becky had been given many opportunities to try to get to know me and develop a relationship with me, but she had a chip on her shoulder that was as cold as ice. I was done; the ball was in her court and I wasn't going to try again.

CHAPTER EIGHT

ENGAGED

A few years had passed since Dad found my biological family, and although some positive connections had been made, it was still an awkward situation. It was going to take many more visits, and possibly several years, for me to feel more comfortable. I enjoyed my visits to see Robert and Dana; however, I was beginning to feel like someone should make the trip to see me and get to know about the life I had lived. All of our conversations revolved around memories of their childhood, which I had not been part of. They never seemed to want to know about my life. It would not be possible for us to be close as siblings if we always talked about their lives, and relatives I couldn't remember the names of, and didn't really care to ever meet. I appreciated them opening their hearts by sharing childhood stories of neglect, emotional abuse, and even physical abuse, by certain relatives. Most of what they told me about Becky only validated my feelings of disgust towards her. She caused her children to fall victim to the life she had chosen for herself. But then, to be somewhat *fair*, many of Becky's choices were the result of the way her mother constantly insulted and demeaned her. The more I listened to stories about her, the more I came to believe that all she ever really wanted in life was to be loved. It was her search for true love that led her from man to man, and feelings of failure that led to drink after drink. I wasn't sure if she and I would ever reconcile enough to form a relationship, but my heart was losing its hardness towards her.

I was still the office manager for my Dad's contracting company. I spent most of my time working, writing poetry, and spending the evenings visiting with Mom and Dad. We had become much closer over the past few years, and I wanted to learn more about their lives and what it was like to live during America's depression years. I stayed late after work once or twice each week, often times staying the night instead of driving back to my apartment. Mom and I would put on a pot of coffee and play games, like Yahtzee or Monopoly, and just laugh as we enjoyed being mother and daughter. It was a wonderful time in my life of drawing closer to my parents. I will never regret putting my social life on hold to make those memories.

Many of my girlfriends had gotten married shortly after high school, others had moved away after college. I was the odd, unmarried one, still living close to home. I enjoyed my job, and overall, life was going well, but I was beginning to feel lonely. I was 22 years old and I rarely went on dates. I had several guy friends, but I never went anywhere to meet new people or try finding "Mr. Right." Most of my weekends were spent with Mom and Dad. If I wasn't visiting with them, I used most of my alone time to read my Bible or write. I also spent many hours practicing the organ. I was the assistant organist at church and I played at least once a month. Life was better, and definitely more peaceful, but I needed a social life. I felt like life was passing me by; I didn't want to find myself 30 and single one day.

Being an adult certainly did not keep my Dad from telling me that if he ever caught my car somewhere it shouldn't be, he would take my keys from me. Dad had purchased the car and put it in the company name, so I knew he could and would follow through with his threat. He lived up to a high moral standard that was difficult for most people to understand. As his children, Lucas and I were not to embarrass him or tarnish the name he had built for us in the community. Naturally, as most teenagers and young adults do, we learned to be sneaky and get away with some things. Being perfect is not an option for any human, and I certainly wasn't perfect, but I did my best to make the Bartlett's proud.

Some friends were throwing a 21st birthday party for a girl I knew, at an upper-scale nightclub across from The Executive hotel. Gene, a dear guy friend of mine, told me that I should go to the party. He mentioned several people that would be there, and also told me he wanted me to meet someone. Gene thought he knew someone who might be the guy for me. I reminded Gene that I would be in trouble if Dad found out my car was at *that club*. He totally understood; in fact, most friends that Lucas and I had grown up with knew how strict our Dad was, so they would help cover for us at parties and get-togethers.

Gene had been one of my best friends since 6th grade, and we did a lot of things together. He agreed to drive me to the party. I was fairly curious about this 'great guy' he kept telling me about. Gene insisted that he seemed perfect for me.

"Yeah," I replied, "like I'm going to turn around and the guy of my dreams is going to say, 'May I have this dance?' "

It was the 80's, a decade filled with some of the greatest musical artists the world has ever heard. The club we were going to was the type of place you dress-up for. It was almost a contest to see who had the most awesome outfit. The men had a GQ look and the ladies were in their fanciest evening attire with perfect hair, make-up to the max, and fabulous costume jewelry. Many of the ladies even bought new clothes if they were going to the club on a Saturday night. I chose to wear a sundress I already owned, for the birthday get-together. It had a bright floral design, with short sleeves and a cut out back. It was a knee length dress and I wore white, three-inch, high-heeled pumps with it. The neckline was high, so I chose not to wear a necklace, but I found a big, gaudy pair of earrings that would sparkle and be noticed through my long, thick dark hair.

Gene picked me up that evening for the party. He looked great in his black pants and blue silk shirt. He had his shirt unbuttoned enough to show off his wide, gold necklace. We arrived at the club, and the parking lot was at full capacity. He offered to drop me off at the door, then go park the car down the street, but I told him I wasn't about to walk in by myself. I chose to go with him to park the car. The two-block walk to the club wouldn't have been so bad if I hadn't been wearing three-inch heels, but it was still better than walking in alone.

Heads turned as we walked in, which often happened when Gene and I went places. He and I both loved to dress-up, whether we were just going to dinner or out to a movie; we never wore jeans. We made a cute couple, even though we were just friends. I had known him so many years that I overlooked all the gossipers who told me that Gene was gay. I knew some of the girls he had dated, and I couldn't understand why people would whisper and tell me such things about him. Whatever he *was* didn't matter to me; he was my friend and we always had fun together.

Gene found us a small table with chairs. The place was packed, with only enough room to stand, so I don't know how he managed to get us a table *and* chairs, but he did. Gene knew the guy that managed the club, so our table was 'reserved' for the evening.

It was so crowded we couldn't find Vicky, whose birthday we came to celebrate. Finally, Gene spotted some of our friends who were there for her birthday party. Since all of us were not able to sit together, the conversations became sporadic throughout the evening. Gene was a great dancer and we made a great team on the dance floor. A couple of hours had passed and my feet were starting to throb. Gene was back on the dance floor and I was seated at our table, when I felt a tap on my shoulder. I turned to see a handsome guy with dark glasses standing behind me. He asked me if I wanted to dance, but I told him my feet were hurting and he should have asked me sooner. There was something about him that made my heart skip a beat. He gently placed his hand on my shoulder and said, "I will ask sooner, next time." Gene was walking back towards the table, as the mystery man was leaving. I noticed them stop to speak to each other and I wondered if that was the guy Gene so desperately wanted me to meet.

Gene was bright-eyed as he returned to the table.

"Well, what did you think?" he said with a smile.

"About what?" I asked.

He informed me that Kevin was the guy he wanted me to meet. I told him Kevin had asked me to dance, but I said no because my feet were hurting. I could tell Gene thought I'd made a big mistake, but I didn't think so. If this Kevin guy wanted to get to know me, he would find a way.

We were all getting tired of the dance scene, so our little 'birthday group' decided to go down the street and have breakfast at a diner that stayed open late on the weekends. Some people in our group were running around saying good-byes and inviting others to join us for breakfast, when I felt another tap on my shoulder. It was Kevin. A slow song had begun to play, and he held out his hand.

"May I have this dance?" he asked.

As I took his hand and we turned towards each other on the dance floor, it was as if there were clouds all around us; it was almost magical. People moved out of our way and gave us the floor, as he twirled and dipped me. Kevin had removed his glasses, and our eyes were fixated on each other. It seemed like we were the only ones in the room and the music was just for us. Most people do not believe in love at first sight, but for Kevin and I, that is exactly what happened.

We had danced through two slow songs, when Gene approached and said it was time to leave for breakfast with our group. I asked Kevin if he was going. He said that if I was going, he would definitely be there. I gave him a smile of assurance, and let go of his hand. As I was letting go, he squeezed my hand, brought it to his lips, and placed a very gentle kiss in the middle of my hand. Our eyes remained fixed on one another, as he kissed my hand. He made me feel like a princess.

Gene and I walked down the street to the restaurant and I couldn't wait to tell him that he had made a good call; Kevin was the one. It seemed crazy to think that someone I just met was the man I suddenly knew I would marry. Gene was thrilled for me and with a big smile, said, "I told you so."

There were about ten of us who went to the restaurant and I wasn't able to sit by Kevin, but we glanced at each other several times. Gene and I had a 20-30 minute drive ahead of us, and it was getting late. As we started to leave, I was afraid Kevin wasn't going to ask me on a date or talk to me again before I had to head back home. Gene and

I were out of the restaurant, walking down the street towards his car, when Kevin came running after us. He said he had been searching for a pen or pencil to write his phone number down, when he realized we had left the restaurant. He asked for my number and with a wink, I gave him a sly smile and told him it was in the phone book, if he was interested. He smiled, with a twinkle in his eye and said, "Oh, I am more than interested." We gave each other a smile and headed in opposite directions toward our vehicles.

That night, a fairytale romance began. On August 6th, 1986, Kevin and I went on our first date. From that day forward, we became inseparable. We saw each other almost daily and if we couldn't see each other in person, we would spend hours talking on the phone.

Every move Kevin made was as romantic as anything you could see in a movie. On September 10th, 1986, he invited me to dinner at his parents home. He had hidden an engagement ring in my shrimp cocktail dish. When I finally noticed the ring, lying in the ice under my shrimp, Kevin immediately dropped to one knee.

"Will you make me the happiest man on earth and marry me?" he asked.

It took me approximately two seconds to wrap my arms around him with a joyous, "Yes!" Kevin's mom had helped him plan the hiding of the ring, and had prepared a wonderful dinner for just the two of us. She had her dining table set with her finest china and beautiful crystal. The room sparkled with candlelight. The entire setting was perfect. Everything Kevin did was thoughtful and beautiful. I felt like a princess who had just found her prince charming. Kevin rarely showed up to see me without a red rose in his hand, and something sweet to say, like "A beautiful rose, for a beautiful lady." He loved to write poems for me, and would often draw a rose at the bottom each poem. He seemed too good to be true.

Everything was perfect, except for the fact my parents didn't think I should marry *him*. Dad had always worried about someone trying to marry Lucas or me for *our* family money. Dad was not ashamed to research the people we dated, get a background check, or find out what type of family they came from. The wonderful relationship I had built with Mom and Dad over the last few years was in jeopardy, as they cautioned me and repeatedly said Kevin wasn't right for me.

"I've driven by his house Kimi, and it's not much to look at, and I know where he works. He's never going to amount to much," Dad informed me.

Dad's snobbishness infuriated me.

"Well I'm proud of him," I replied, "because he put himself through college and got that job on his own; no one handed it to him. It may not be much to you, but he did it by himself."

I was not giving up Kevin just because he didn't measure up to their standards.

Our wedding date was set for December 13th, my birthday, which was just a couple months away. Arrangements were made and invitations were printed. I suppose it was my determined attitude that made Mom and Dad realize the wedding was going to happen, whether they liked it or not. After weeks of hearing them tell me what a 'huge mistake' I was making, one day they approached me and said they would pay for the wedding and honeymoon. Finally, there could be some peace.

The engagement festivities began. Some girlfriends hosted an intimate bridal shower for me, and Kevin's family planned a huge Princess House Crystal wedding shower for us. In addition, the church I had attended since childhood began planning a huge wedding shower for Kevin and I. Some of the women that were planning our wedding shower, were the same ladies that helped plan my baby shower when Mom and Dad brought me into their family at three-and-a-half years old.

Our church was truly an extension of our family. There were so many wonderful people there who prayed when you were sick and even showed up at your house with entire meals. If you needed help, someone would show up with a kind face and willing heart. Many of them exemplified what Christianity is supposed to be about. It was the sincere love and kindness of those precious people that caused the little church to grow and expand throughout the years. I would not have changed my wedding location if the greatest of cathedrals had been offered to me. I knew the ladies of the church would make my wedding shower and wedding day absolutely perfect for me. It was that kind of assurance, and my decisiveness, that allowed me the luxury of being engaged in September and married in December.

It was mid-October and all the wedding preparations were completed. My bridesmaid dresses, as well as my dress, had been selected. Being a typical new bride-to-be, I had purchased a bridal magazine and found a stunning dress I fell in love with. I took the picture to the Bridal House and showed it to Kyle, the owner. He started shaking his head and a huge smile started forming; he was clearly just as excited about the dress as I was.

"I just received a knock-off of this designer dress," he said, "and I can alter it to fit you perfectly."

I couldn't believe it! I walked in with a picture, and he just so happened to have the dress of my dreams. Kyle quickly brought it out for me to see, and he was right; it was identical to the dress in the magazine.

The dress was a size 8 and had to be taken down a few sizes for me, but Kyle was excellent at alterations and wedding planning. I could tell when Mom saw the dress on me, she agreed with my choice. It was definitely *the one*. It had a beautiful fitted lace bodice; long sleeves; and a long ruffled train, covered in sequins, flowing behind it. Kyle thought it would be beautiful if he covered the train with even more sequins than it already had. He ended up sewing more than 30,000 sequins on the train of my already-beautiful dress. Kyle said that when I turned the corner to walk down the isle, he wanted the dress to glisten like freshly fallen snow, and simply 'wow' people as I passed by. I left the alterations and design adjustments of my dress in the hands of Kyle.

Everything was falling into place perfectly and it was a totally stress-free experience. I had heard of brides stressing over wedding details and planning for months, even years, to make their wedding perfect. I had spent a few weeks on preparations and details, and everything was already finished. It was time to enjoy all the get-togethers with girlfriends; I had brunches and bridal showers awaiting me.

Kevin and I spent hours talking and dreaming about our future. We dreamed of beautiful vacation destinations; the type of house we wanted to live in; how many children we hoped for; and, of course, what kind of dog we wanted. I had never known life without a dog, so that was a must; Kevin was a dog lover also. My dogs had always been outside dogs, chosen by my parents, but I loved each of them through the years. I did think it would be wonderful to have a little dog that could live inside the house with me. I dreamed of a little fluff ball that would run to greet me each afternoon after work. I wanted to hug it as I watched TV, and snuggle with it at nighttime. Kevin had a schnauzer that lived in his parent's house; he was so lucky to have an *inside* dog. In fact, whether it was food, music, or vacation spots, Kevin and I liked all the same things. He had even become a member of my church. Kevin said he had been looking for a church home and wanted to get back to going to church on a regular basis. Life could not have been more perfect.

It was a nice October evening, and I was taking a chicken casserole from the oven that I had prepared for dinner. Kevin called to say he would be running a little late for our dinner date. I decided to use the extra time to make the dining table look spectacular. I found a lace tablecloth and began setting the table with my best dishes and various candles. Kevin had been taking me out to dinner a lot lately, and I wanted to show him we could have fine dining at home. I didn't want him to feel obligated to always take me out to a restaurant.

As I was finishing up some of the little details around the kitchen, I heard that wonderful knock at the door. Every time I saw him was like Christmas morning, and I simply couldn't contain my excitement as I took off running for the door. I always greeted Kevin with a huge smile and a big hug. I'm not sure he understood everything that he meant to me, or what getting married meant to me. I was finally going to have something, *someone*, I knew I belonged to. Marriage meant family, love, and togetherness. I was about to be given a new name again, but this time I was sure the motive was love. I had no doubt that Kevin truly loved me.

Before I met Kevin, I had decided my husband would always be told he was loved before leaving for work in the mornings, and would be greeted with love when he returned home. I never understood the people who didn't appreciate having another human being in their life that they loved. This was the type of connection I had waited for all my life, and it was worth more than rubies, diamonds, or any material thing. Kevin was precious to me, and I could not wait to be a loyal wife to him. I would guard and protect my marriage, and be his best friend for life.

I opened the door to find Kevin standing there with flowers and an apology, for making me wait on dinner. I welcomed him in and told him I didn't even realize the time, and assured him he was always worth the wait. I placed the flowers in a vase and began putting the food on our plates. He pulled the dining chair out for me and as we sat to eat, we held hands and bowed our heads in prayer to thank God for our meal and upcoming wedding. We were about halfway through our dinner when I heard what sounded like a faint bark.

"Kevin, what was that?" I asked.

"I didn't hear anything," he immediately replied.

I took another bite of chicken, then I heard it again; it was a little bark. I wasn't sure if the bark sounded small because the dog was off in the field across from us, or if maybe the dog was hurt. Kevin said he would step on the porch and look around. He shut the door behind him.

"I don't see anything," he said, "but maybe you should take a look."

Kevin stepped to the side as I opened my front door. I looked down, and to my surprise there was the most adorable little Shih Tzu puppy I'd ever seen, looking back up at me. She had big brown eyes and a huge red bow tied around her.

Tears ran down my face as I picked up the precious little puppy; I began kissing her and telling her that I loved her. There were no words to describe what Kevin had just done for me. I kissed and hugged him and told him that she was just perfect. He proceeded to bring in a small tan kennel, a water bowl, and even a book about Shih Tzu's.

He said he researched many different dog breeds, and wanted to find one that wouldn't affect my allergies. He wanted me to have one that could stay in the house with me, especially since he knew he would have to work some night shifts. My heart overflowed with love and joy as I watched the tiny fur-ball run around and explore her new home. She was only six weeks old and was so small she fit in the palm of Kevin's hand. She was mostly white, with a little brown on her. We began to discuss name ideas, but I immediately knew what her name should be. I thought the perfect name was Charity.

Charity meant love, and that was the chapter in 1 Corinthians we were using as the theme for our wedding. The next couple hours passed quickly, as I laughed and played with my new puppy. I was so happy, and everything was wonderful. I could hardly stop smiling as I watched little Charity run around, exploring her new home.

Suddenly, without warning, Kevin snatched Charity up and threw her into the back of her kennel. The helpless little puppy hit with a loud thud, as I screamed her name. The look in Kevin's eyes was scary, and he began screaming at me. He said that he was the one who was supposed to have my attention. His voice continued to get louder as he yelled that he wished he hadn't bought the stupid dog for me! I didn't know what to do. He began grabbing Charity's things: her bowl, the Shih Tzu book, even the red bow he'd tied around her. As he headed for the door, I began to beg and plead, telling him I was sorry if I had ignored him. I even tried to reason with him.

"But, didn't you want me to love her?" I asked. "Isn't that why you gave her to me?"

It didn't matter; Kevin slammed the door and walked out.

I did not understand what had just happened, he left me confused and crying. He had been laughing and playing with Charity just like I was. I had never seen Kevin get mad or upset over anything. I fell to my knees in prayer, sobbing. My cries were so deep my stomach ached. I prayed God would send Kevin back to me and send an Angel to protect innocent little Charity. Kevin was so angry when he left, I could just picture him tossing her out of the car as he was driving down the road. All I could do was pray. There was no way for me to know what was happening to the precious little puppy I had just held in my arms and promised to always take care of.

I knew Kevin and I would eventually have a disagreement, or that dreaded first fight all couples have to work through, but this was different. I rehearsed the evening over and over in my mind. I was certain that I saw genuine happiness on Kevin's face as he watched me play with little Charity. When did things change? How could I have overlooked something upsetting him? I agonized for hours, not knowing if I was still engaged or if he had taken his love back, as quickly as he had taken the puppy back.

Around 2am, my phone rang. I was still in tears, as I hurriedly grabbed the phone. "Yes?" I answered.

There was a moment of silence, and then I heard Kevin say, "I am so very, very sorry."

He was crying as he spoke; he told me that Charity was perfectly fine and was sitting right beside him. I let out a huge sigh of relief, knowing she was still alive and unhurt. I began asking him what happened; I tried to be calm and just let him speak. Kevin said he'd been a total jerk, and I had to agree with him. He explained how, ever since we met, I had given him my undivided attention every time we were together. He said that when he saw me play with Charity and tell her I loved her, he was afraid she was going to take his place.

"She's a dog," I replied. "How could she take your place? That doesn't make sense."

"I know it sounds stupid," he said, "but that's what went through my head. I kept hearing you say you loved her, and she was making you smile the way I'm supposed to."

I continued to listen to him apologize and rationalize his actions. He told me Charity had been fed; he made sure she had water, and he would bring her back to me as soon as he got off work. I told Kevin I loved him and forgave him, as we said goodnight. I was finally at peace again. I fell off to sleep, thanking God that Kevin was coming back and was bringing my precious puppy to me.

True to his word, Kevin arrived with the puppy, her kennel, new toys, and more heart-felt apologies for putting me through a terrible evening. I didn't take it as a warning sign of a man with a terrible temper, or anything worse, and I chose to overlook it. This was the one and only instance when Kevin was anything less than a perfect gentleman. We all have bad days and sometimes say things we don't mean. I wasn't giving up my prince charming simply because he had one little outburst.

Everything returned back to normal as our wedding day drew near. A local musician, who was also a family friend, agreed to play the organ for our wedding. Mr. Quincy had performed on the Lawrence Welk show; had been a guest on the Paul Harvey Radio Show; and had played at several World Fairs. His musical talent was extraordinary. He was a large man, and when he took over the keys on a keyboard, he literally bounced on the stool as he filled the air with magic.

Mr. Quincy's wife had died from breast cancer a few years earlier. They had a sweet little girl, who was like a little sister to me. Cynthia was only nine years old when cancer took her mother. Mr. Quincy had asked me if I would stay close to her and make sure she had someone to talk to. I gladly accepted the offer to be a part of her life. Mr. Quincy had drawn up a will, naming me as Cynthia's legal guardian if anything were to happen to him before she was grown. We were eleven years apart in age, so I always felt more like a big sister than a Godmother. She and I went to movies together, and would spend hours playing in make-up; we always had fun together.

Cynthia was now almost 12 years old, and I asked her Dad for permission to have her in the wedding, as my junior bridesmaid. Mr. Quincy was thrilled I was including her, and I couldn't wait to ask her to be part of my wedding party. She was one of those children who was always happy, and always smiling. She could brighten your day by just being around you. Even when I approached her at her Mother's funeral a few years earlier, she turned to me and said, "It's okay. Mommy isn't hurting anymore." There was a sweetness and innocence in her that was captivating. She saw life as cupcakes and rainbows and she was always happy.

Another local talent was selected to sing at the wedding. Kevin's mother worked for the Glendale's. Mr. Glendale owned oil wells and was very, very wealthy. Mrs. Patsy Glendale was a sweet, southern belle type lady. She had recorded a couple of gospel albums and had a beautiful voice. Mr. Quincy and Patsy knew one another, so it was easy for them to arrange practice times. With Mr. Quincy's talent on the organ and Patsy's voice filling the air, our wedding would certainly be a treat for our guests.

Mr. Glendale offered us his beautiful, white Rolls Royce as our mode of transportation to and from the church on our wedding day. Mark, Kevin's oldest brother, was going to arrive two hours before the wedding to pick me up in the Rolls Royce. Kyle would be bringing my dress to the church and would assist in making sure my dress was buttoned and secured properly. As my wedding consultant, he would make sure all of the bridesmaids' dresses were pressed and perfect; he was also responsible for the groomsmen having their cummerbunds, bow ties, and scarves perfectly placed.

All arrangements had been made as my 23rd birthday and wedding day drew closer. Kevin was going to be my "forever birthday present." My birthday would finally have a special meaning. Each birthday would be an Anniversary celebration, as our love grew from year to year.

CHAPTER NINE

THE WEDDING

The day had finally arrived. I awoke to a phone call, Mom wishing me a Happy Birthday. Shortly after the phone call, my doorbell rang; it was a florist with a dozen red roses from Kevin and a note wishing me a very happy birthday. I walked to the kitchen to start my coffee and realized I would never have to sit at breakfast by myself anymore. I prayed that God would make the day picture-perfect and let everything go smoothly. As I sat there looking around the pretty place Dad had built for me, I was glad he had talked me into leaving my apartment and moving onto their property. It would be a longer drive to and from work for Kevin each day, but he was gaining the luxury of a mortgage-free life.

It was a relaxing morning. My bags were packed for our honeymoon to Hawaii, and Charity had already been taken to Kevin's parents. My maid-of-honor was a dear friend I had known all my life. We lived so close to each other that we could see each other's homes, which had made it very convenient for sleepovers when we were younger. She had attended cosmetology school and was becoming a successful hairdresser. I trusted her to make my hair perfect for my wedding day. Barbara was coming over at 2pm to visit and fix my hair. She was riding to the church with me in the

Rolls Royce around 4pm, and the wedding was to begin sharply at 6 o'clock that evening.

I was expecting to be a little nervous, but I was calm as a cucumber. Maybe I just knew that I could count on all the people who were involved in making my wedding day special. I had gained a sneak preview at some of the greenery and floral arrangements at the rehearsal dinner the night before. I could tell the sanctuary was going to be beautiful. A friend of my Mom's, who owned a florist shop for many years, was in charge of all decorations. My only request had been poinsettias and a lot of greenery. It was going to be a candlelit service.

The hours passed quickly as I waited for my maid of honor to arrive. My doorbell rang at almost 2 o'clock on the dot. I ran to open the door and hug Barbara. She was beaming with excitement for me, as she went over her checklist of necessary items. True to her maid-of-honor duties, she made sure I had something borrowed and something blue; she also tested me and offered to call off the wedding, if I had any doubts. I thanked her for the offer and knew she would have marched right up in front of everyone for me and given my apologizes, if I had asked her to. I assured her that Kevin and I were truly in love and I had no doubts whatsoever about becoming his wife. She told me how happy she was for me and said it was "obvious" Kevin and I were in love. I knew she meant every word. We talked and laughed about our childhood while she fixed my hair and positioned my hairpiece; it was a beautiful rhinestone-covered headpiece that extended into a V-shape onto my forehead.

It was already 4 o'clock and I could hear Kevin's brother pulling up to my front porch in Mr. Glendale's magnificent white Rolls Royce. Barbara was as excited as I was; we scrambled to gather make-up and hair spray for last minute touch-ups. Kevin's brother was already in his tuxedo; he opened the back door for us as we giggled with excitement. The church was only a mile from my home so it was a short ride, but what a fabulous ride it was! I had never ridden in a Rolls Royce and it was quite a treat.

Mom and Dad were already at the church, along with all my

bridesmaids. Kyle had arrived with my dress and was eager to show off the results of his many hours of hand-sewn sequins. He was originally just adding sequins to the train, but decided to sew extra over the entire dress. It was stunning. I couldn't wait to put it on and slip into my gorgeous, pearl-encrusted wedding shoes.

Barbara and I took off for the specially prepared bridal room. It had a full-length mirror, marble-top tables, and velvet sofas. The room had been decorated with funds from the ladies Sunday school class my Mom belonged to. These were the ladies who were active in hosting baby showers, wedding showers, and kept up with church members who were sick or hospitalized. The ladies had a vision for the church to have a room with beautiful furnishings for occasions such as weddings. It had a Victorian parlor feel, and was beautiful. I was thrilled to be one of the first to utilize their beautifully appointed room.

Barbara held my dress as I slipped into it and Mom came in to assist with all the buttons and fluffing. I truly felt like a princess. Like most brides, I thought my wedding dress was the most beautiful dress I had ever seen. The photographer then began the first of many hours of photographs. I originally thought being at the church two hours before the wedding was going to be wasted time, but that time was quickly slipping away. Before long, it was time for everyone to take his or her position of entrance into the sanctuary.

Mr. Quincy and Patsy began the beautiful musical prelude. Mom kissed me good-bye as the usher came to take her arm and lead her to the coveted mother-of-the-bride seat. I was to remain in the parlor until I heard the song begin that was directly before the Wedding March. Kyle stayed with me to fluff each ruffle and make sure my train flowed perfectly down the hallway as I began my walk to the white isle. Dad was waiting for me as I stepped out of the parlor. He gave me a gentle hug and kiss on the cheek and told me how beautiful I looked. The sanctuary doors had been closed during the last song so there could be no peaking as I approached. Kyle was about to signal the ushers to open the doors for me, when Dad looked at me and said, "It won't bother me a bit to go in there right now and tell all these people there's been a change of plans."

I knew he wasn't trying to be mean, he just wanted to give me one more chance to change my mind. The doors were beginning to open as I smiled at him and said, "Lets walk." He nodded and proudly took my arm.

The church was overflowing with people; extra chairs had been brought in and there still wasn't enough seating for everyone, so some guests had to stand.

Mr. Quincy was right on cue. The moment the doors opened, his fingers came down on the keyboard with full force, and at full volume. The Wedding March had begun, and the notes echoed large and full throughout the sanctuary. He played as if he were playing for royalty. All eyes turned toward the doorway and everyone stood as Dad and I entered. I had to make a left to begin my march toward the alter. Kyle had discreetly and quickly positioned himself to "pop" my train upward to keep it full and flowing as I walked. I heard *ooh*'s and *ahhh*'s as I glided down the isle and the 30,000 hand-sewn sequins sparkled in the candlelight. It was a walk I only wanted to do once in my lifetime; I never wanted to forget how wonderful I felt and how beautiful the church was. There were more poinsettias than I could count; the sanctuary was awash in thick, lush greenery and the candlelight was breathtaking. The entire front of the church was covered in candelabrums; there were candelabrum at the end of each church pew, and even the windows twinkled with candlelight.

There were so many people, I couldn't catch a glimpse of Kevin as I made my way toward him. As Dad walked with me, I wondered if he was thinking about that day, almost 20 years ago, when he took me from the arms of a social worker to claim me as his daughter. He had been strict, but I was grateful for the life he had provided for me and I loved him very much. I owed the entire day to him and his hard work. As I took my final steps with Dad, I took a moment to say, "I love you." Kevin had a huge smile on his face, and I could tell my dress was a hit. He quietly whispered, "You are beautiful!"

The Pastor asked, "Who gives this woman to be married to this man?"

Dad placed my hand in Kevin's and replied, "Her mother and I."

The church was so quiet you could have heard a pin drop as the Pastor read scripture and instructed us to love one another as Christ loved the church. The love chapter, 1 Corinthians 13, was read. Although I had heard it hundreds of times before, it suddenly became personal and I knew 'the love chapter' was God's instruction for a happy marriage. Love is to be long-suffering and kind, not envious or "puffed-up." Love isn't selfish and doesn't get easily angered; love avoids evil thinking. Love bears all things, hopes for all things, and endures all things. Love never fails.

The time came for the lighting of the unity candle. Kevin and I held our individual wicks and tipped them toward our large unity candle in the middle of the candelabra. The moment our individual flames touched the unity candle, an enormous flame shot straight up in front of us, almost a foot high. I heard a few people gasp as we drew our faces back from the flame. The photographer took a picture as the flame was descending. Kevin and I just looked at each other, as if to say, "Wow."

The ceremony concluded as the Pastor pronounced us husband and wife, and Kevin was told to kiss his bride. Mr. Quincy began the Recessional March at full volume, and Kevin and I took our first steps as husband and wife. I was now Kimi Leah Bartlett Burghess. I kept my maiden name; I wasn't giving up my family, I was merely adding to it.

Kevin and I chose to have a receiving line in order to thank each guest personally for taking part in our special day. The entire bridal party formed a line down the hallway toward the reception room. It took over an hour for the last guest to finally pass through the line. The photographer then rushed Kevin and I into the reception room to get the typical wedding pictures of the bride and groom cutting the cake, exchanging bites of cake, and drinking punch. It was an absolute whirlwind as we rushed through the reception and headed back to the sanctuary for photos with the bridal party and family members. The only food Kevin and I had at our reception was the one bite of cake we exchanged for the photograph. Kevin's mom had anticipated our lack of food and told us she had a large shrimp tray and other treats waiting in our hotel room for us.

We finished our photos and said goodbye's to friends and family. We were staying in the honeymoon suite at The Executive hotel for our wedding night, and making the 100-mile drive to the airport the next morning, to catch our flight to Hawaii. Much to our surprise, Kevin's brother had made arrangements to drive us to the hotel that night, in Mr. Glendale's beautiful Rolls Royce. It had been a perfect wedding and the only odd happening had been the lighting of our unity candle. Kevin and I couldn't believe how the flame shot up like a torch. We had both seen couples have trouble getting their unity candle to light during the ceremony; we had never seen a flame shoot up almost a foot in the air, like ours did.

Morning had come all too quickly as Kevin and I scrambled to get the car loaded and head to the airport. We thought we would have an hour to relax and eat breakfast before our flight; however, we forgot about the one-hour time difference between the cities. We checked-in at the airport and had to take off running because our flight was being held for us. We laughed as we ran, realizing we didn't get any supper after the wedding and we weren't getting any breakfast either. As we took our seats, we asked the flight attendant to thank the pilot for waiting on us. First, we were headed to Chicago, where we would be changing flights. We would then be riding a much larger plane for the ten-hour flight to Hawaii.

It was a hectic morning, but that was okay; Kevin and I were both fueled by the adrenaline of love and nothing could dampen our moods. We were able to find our connecting flight in Chicago without getting lost, but we still hadn't found time to get food. With great anticipation of a food cart, we eagerly boarded the flight bound for Hawaii. Luckily we weren't in the air long until the flight attendants began pushing food and drink carts down the isles. We cuddled and talked for hours, as the jet stayed on course toward the South Pacific.

A wall separated the first-class passengers from the rest of us who were crowded in the coach section. Kevin and I both took turns peeking at the mysterious first-class section, which was curtained off from us commoners. The seats in first class were large lounge seats with ample arm and legroom between them. Special flight attendants were assigned to cater to their every need. Kevin and I talked about the possibility of being part of the elite, first-class section one day, perhaps for a future Anniversary trip. We both laughed that we would be paying twice the money to be in seats that would hit the ground first if the plane took a nosedive. It was still a nice thought to get the special first class attention. We spent hours talking about future dreams, until we finally talked ourselves to sleep, as a movie played on a large screen at the front of our coach section.

We awoke to hear the pilot announce we were "beginning our descent" toward the Honolulu airport. He reminded everyone of the time difference; Hawaii is five hours behind central time. Though our watches showed it was almost midnight, on island time we would be exiting the plane at a sunny 7 o'clock in the evening.

Passengers were greeted with beautiful, floral leis as we each stepped out of the plane. The airport was small and easy to walk through, so we quickly gathered our luggage and headed outside to find a taxi.

We arrived at the hotel our travel agent recommended, only to find it half torn down and obviously under construction. Tired and disappointed, we frantically made phone calls to try and correct the mistake. The hotel manager informed us there were two hotels with the Outrigger name; however, one was called the Outrigger East and the other was Outrigger West. Our travel agent had accidentally booked us at the wrong Outrigger. We had no choice but to spend our first night in an old, outdated room that seemed somewhat clean, but nothing like we expected and certainly not worth the $2,000 we had paid.

As soon as 8am central time rolled around (3am in Honolulu), we were on the phone once again, hoping our travel agent could transfer our reservation to the correct hotel. It took several hours and several phone calls, but the problem was eventually fixed. Finally, we loaded our luggage into another taxi that drove us to the beautiful, tropical hotel we had originally anticipated.

The next hotel was indeed better than the first. Kevin and I quickly unpacked our suitcases, put on our swimsuits, and headed for the ocean. It was a sunny 88 degrees in the middle of December, and the palm trees were draped with Christmas lights. Red bows and other various decorations adorned lampposts and doorways. We hadn't thought about what it would be like to celebrate Christmas in the tropics. There were no large evergreens and, of course, none of the snowy scenery we were accustomed to back home. Regardless, it was still pretty and the Christmas spirit was the same.

We enjoyed a beautiful, sunny day at the beach. As I stood to put my flip-flops on, Kevin knelt down and said, "Let me do that for you." He wiped the sand from the bottom of each foot, and said he didn't want the sand to irritate my feet while I walked. I couldn't believe how thoughtful he was. He promised he was always going to be there to take care of me and protect me.

Kevin and I ate dinner at the hotel and went to our room to relax and watch television. We hadn't been in our room for very long when Kevin said, "I'll be right back." I didn't have a chance to ask him where he was going when he left the room. I waited patiently as the minutes turned into an hour. I was about to leave the room to go look for him, when he opened the door and said, "Sorry it took me so long."

I asked where he had been, and he said that he needed to use the bathroom and was embarrassed to use the one in our room, so he went to the lobby bathroom. I assured him that I knew he was human and he should never be embarrassed around me. He admitted that it seemed silly, but asked me not to be mad at him if he felt more comfortable going to the lobby.

I told Kevin I wouldn't be mad, but reminded him he wouldn't be able to run to the neighbor's bathroom when we went back home. He laughed and said, "I'll worry about that when the time comes."

Night after night, Kevin would leave me waiting in our hotel room while he made his trips to the lobby bathroom. I didn't want to hassle him over it, but the entire thing seemed odd to me. I knew men often took a long time in the bathroom, but Kevin was gone over an hour every night.

We were having a fantastic honeymoon filled with love and laughter. It was already our fifth night in paradise, as we came in from the beach to cleanup and get dressed for dinner. Kevin asked if I wanted to have a little fun before dinner, but I smiled and told him I needed a break. I turned my back to him to lay my clothes out on the bed. Suddenly, he shoved me backward onto the bed, ripped my suit off and forced himself on me. Tears streamed down my face while I begged him to stop. He was hurting me; it was a painful, burning, ripping sensation. He screamed at me that I was his wife and he would "have me" whenever he felt like it. I turned my head from him as he tried to kiss me, then he said, "Oh no! What have I done?"

Kevin got off of me and I pulled the covers up tight over myself and cried as I told him how bad I was hurting. He tried to apologize and caress me, but I just wanted him to leave me alone. He said that he would clean the bathtub and fill it with water so I could soak in the tub.

It hurt to walk as he led me to the bathroom. I lowered myself into the warm water, hoping it would alleviate the pain. I couldn't believe what he had done to me; I was hurting, scared, and thousands of miles from home. Kevin came into the bathroom crying, begging me not to hate him. He tried to tell me that he just got carried away and didn't realize I was serious when I told him, "No."

I listened to him apologize over and over again. No matter how he tried to rationalize his actions, I knew what he had said about "having" me whenever he felt like it. He said he didn't mean any of it and it would never happen again.

I could hardly sleep that night as I replayed the scene over in my mind. He had shown a violent side of himself for a second time. How could I know if they were individual incidents that I needed to "forgive and forget," or if a more violent side was hiding within him? I had agreed to marry Kevin "for better or worse." I decided to consider the whole incident the "worse" part, and just try to believe and accept his apology.

The next morning, I awoke to breakfast in bed. Kevin continued to apologize and promised he would never hurt me again. He literally got on his knees and said, "I'm begging you to somehow forget what happened and love me like you did on our wedding day."

I told him to get up off the floor.

"I forgive you," I said, "but if you ever force yourself on me again, I will cut your *manhood* off in your sleep!"

He laughed a little and said I would never have to do that because he would never treat me that way ever again. I tried my best to give him a genuine hug and put the incident out of my mind.

My heart had filled with love for Kevin when we met and had continued to grow each day since. Just like a balloon that gets bigger and bigger as you fill it, my heart was full of love for him and I couldn't keep from smiling when I saw him. Now I felt different, as if my heart had lost trust in his love. I was not sure if it could be repaired. My prince charming had shattered my dreams of finding a "happily ever after." I wasn't sure what my feelings were exactly. I couldn't give up on our future because he "got carried away," as he put it. The more I thought about the look I saw in his eyes, and the force he used against me, the more I knew that something wasn't right. He had no reason to treat me like that. What happened to his promise of protecting me? I wished it were all a bad dream. Experience had already taught me that some things inside of a person never really change.

We were going back home the next day, and I had to prepare my mind to forget the bad. I would put on a big smile and share with family and friends the memories of a happy honeymoon.

The flight back home was long; I tried to smile and reminisce with Kevin about our long walks on the beach and romantic dinners. As much as I tried not to think about his violent side, my mind kept running the incident like a movie projector. I could see him shoving me; the coldness in his eyes; the hateful way he spoke to me; not to mention the pain he caused me. All I could hope for was that time would heal the bad memories, and I would forget what I saw in him that night.

Kevin would be living with me in the apartment Dad had built for me a couple years before. It was a 1,000 square foot, studio-style apartment. The living room, dining room, and kitchen were all one large room; the bedroom and bathroom were separated from the living space by double French doors. The bedroom and bathroom were one large room, with a beautiful oriental screen that provided privacy around the shower and toilet area. My home was fully furnished, which worked out perfectly. Prior to our wedding, Kevin was still living with his parents and didn't have any furniture or belongings I needed to make room for. The biggest change for Kevin would be his morning drive to work, but he said he didn't mind the extra 20 miles. It was going to be an easy start for our new life together. I had no debt, no car payment, and no mortgage or rent; Kevin only had a monthly car payment and student loan payment. We were blessed to have good jobs and a bright future ahead of us.

We arrived back home to a dining room filled with un-opened wedding presents. It was a fun first week of living together, as we opened wonderful gifts of china, silver, and crystal. Friends and family members had been generous; every item on our registry list had been given to us. There were hundreds of thank you notes to write, but each gift was well deserving of a personal "Thank You."

Our first week at home passed by quickly. Kevin's parents had asked us to come by their house Friday evening, before we went to dinner. I was looking forward to the visit and taking them a few souvenirs from Hawaii.

Kevin offered to drive his car that evening and I reluctantly agreed. Dad had told me he didn't want me riding in Kevin's car. Dad referred to it as a "death trap." It was a little Toyota MR2, and I somewhat agreed with Dad; it wasn't a safe car and it offered little to no protection in the event of a crash. We were just going to visit his parents and then go out to dinner, so I left my Cutlass behind and hopped in Kevin's car.

Kevin's mom was a fabulous cook, and I knew she would have something wonderful waiting for us. She said we were invited for appetizers, but I knew she would have a table full of food and desserts. We walked to the back door and could already smell the food. His family greeted us with hugs and kisses, eager to hear about our trip to Hawaii. We filled our plates with meatballs, cubed cheeses, and raw vegetables; everything was delicious. As we laughed and visited, time passed quickly. We were about to leave their house and go to dinner, when Kevin began telling a joke he had heard at work. I thought the joke was more vulgar than funny, so I gave a brief smile when he finished, and we left for dinner.

We headed to our favorite restaurant, Ruby Tuesdays, and were both looking forward to a couple of gourmet burgers. We were seated at a table for two, and our server arrived quickly to take our orders. After the server left our table, Kevin looked at me and said, "I'll be right back." I said, "okay" as he swiftly pushed his chair in and walked out of the restaurant into the mall area. I wondered if he was looking for a rose or something sweet to bring back to me.

I waited and waited. The server brought our food, but I asked if he could keep it warm until Kevin returned. He was very kind and said he would be watching, and would bring our food back as soon as he saw Kevin. Almost twenty minutes had passed when I finally saw Kevin walking towards our table. He had a serious look on his face, and I didn't see anything in his hands. He was barely seated when he glared at me and, in a hateful tone, said, "If you loved me, you would have asked where I was going!"

I just looked at him for a moment, wondering what he was talking about. He started getting louder and more hateful as he continued to complain.

"You didn't ask where I was going and you didn't even laugh at my joke!"

When I asked what he was talking about, he loudly exclaimed, "The joke at my parents house! The joke that perfect little Kimi didn't think was funny!"

As the server approached our table, he simply turned around and headed back to the kitchen with our food. People were starting to stare; Kevin was getting louder and more furious by the moment. I couldn't stop the tears, as they streamed down my face. The man I loved was talking to me as if he hated me.

We left the restaurant without eating, and I was wishing we hadn't driven Kevin's car. He sped out of the parking lot and took off onto back roads that I was unfamiliar with. He continued to scream at me and tell me that he couldn't be perfect. I had no idea what was wrong with him. As he hit speeds of 90 miles an hour, I tried to brace myself; the car was barely making some of the curves. I begged him to stop, but he just kept yelling that he was an embarrassment and couldn't do anything right. He continued to complain that I hadn't laughed at his joke.

"Please!" I cried, "Please just tell it again and I'll laugh this time!"

He said it was too late.

He was not the man I married. I was still trying to forget what he had done to me on our honeymoon, and now *this*. Finally, he turned onto a road I recognized and I knew he was headed home. The car flew up the driveway, with brakes screeching as he stopped in front of the porch. The car had barely stopped when he raced to my side of the car, grabbed my arm, and yanked me out. I didn't know what he was going to do to me, and no one could hear me if I screamed. He released his grip on my arm long enough to unlock the front door. As he dropped his keys back into his pocket, his hand slammed into my back, knocking me through the doorway and onto the floor. I looked ahead at the doors leading to my bedroom and took off, trying to get away from him.

My faith was all I had at that point. I dropped to my knees in prayer, begging Jesus to help keep me safe. As I knelt beside the tub, Kevin entered the room, slamming the doors shut behind him, and started walking towards me. It was as if I was in the middle of a horror movie. He hovered over top of me, almost snorting as he breathed. His head looked contorted as he bent over me; slimy, stringy saliva connected his top and bottom teeth. I continued to pray as I heard a demonic-sounding voice coming out of him. His eyes were dark and cold as he screamed, "This is it! This is what you married! Do you *think* your *God* can help you *now*?"

Immediately, I rose to my feet and got right in his face; I yelled back at him, "My God can help me now or anytime he chooses!"

I barely had the words out of my mouth when the metal blinds on the bedroom doors began to shake, and both double doors flew open.

"See! He's here!" I shouted. "He's here now! So you better back down, Satan!"

A huge breeze blew through the room; Kevin suddenly covered his face with his hands and fell to the floor yelling, "No! No!" He laid on the floor sobbing uncontrollably while I just stood there, wondering what I had married.

I wasn't sure what to do next, so I prayed for wisdom and guidance. Kevin remained face down on the floor, still sobbing uncontrollably. More than thirty minutes passed before either one of us moved or spoke. Finally, Kevin began to sit up. I cautiously watched his every move. I remained quiet as he started to explain, telling me that he couldn't stop the negative thoughts that flooded his mind. He said that he had always felt like the black sheep of his family, and felt like he couldn't do anything right. He told about past episodes; he was so out of control one evening, his parents called the Sheriff for help.

"I knew I had a problem, but I was afraid you wouldn't marry me if I told you," he admitted.

"Well, I should have been told and given the opportunity to make my own decision," I replied.

Kevin and I talked until 4am, and the more he told me, the more certain I was that he needed to see a doctor.

On Monday morning, I called his doctor's office and explained the urgency of the situation; they scheduled an appointment for that week. I kept my concerns hidden from my parents, unsure of how I would even explain Kevin's actions.

Kevin and I both talked with the doctor; he told us what he thought was causing Kevin's violent episodes. The doctor referred Kevin to a psychiatric doctor who confirmed the diagnosis of extreme Bi-polar Disorder. I had never heard of Bi-polar Disorder, and asked every question I could think of. We were told that it was controllable with a combination of medications, but Kevin would have to stay on medication for the rest of his life.

Unfortunately, Kevin refused to take the medication and continued to have outbursts. Every time I spoke, I had to "walk on eggshells" because I never knew what would set him off. My fairy tale life had ended before it even began. I fought to find forgiveness within my heart and tried to separate the Kevin I loved from the Kevin with a problem.

I tried to keep the situation hidden from my parents and had managed to put on a good act of being happily married, for the first couple months. I was at work one day, when Mom came into the office and caught me crying. She was persistent in wanting to know what was wrong, so I began to tell her about Kevin's illness. Mom was furious. She told me that I had been knowingly deceived and I didn't have to live like that. I begged her not to tell Dad, but she insisted that he needed to know.

Kevin was working overtime that evening, when Dad came to my apartment to talk with me. I told Dad about Kevin's diagnosis, and briefly explained some of his outbursts; I didn't want him or Mom to know what happened on the honeymoon or how Kevin shoved me around.

Dad listened to everything, and then asked me if I thought Kevin had cheated on me. I said I was sure he wasn't doing anything like that, but there were times when his paycheck didn't reflect his overtime hours. Kevin had explained that, although he may work almost an hour over in the evening, his employer only paid the hour if you had a solid fifty minutes or more. Most of his actual overtime was less than forty-five minutes, and then he had fifteen or more minutes of putting away tools and so forth. I never questioned the missing hour here and there, and believed his explanation.

Dad then asked me if I believed Kevin had an illness. I told him I had read a little about Bi-polar Disorder, and it was a mental illness that would never go away.

"So you do believe he's sick?" He asked me again.

I wasn't sure what he was getting at, so I said, "Yes sir."

Dad looked at me for a moment and said, "I want you to repeat your marriage vows to me."

I could tell he was serious, so I began.

"I promise to love, honor, and cherish, for better or worse, in sickness and in health…"

He immediately said, "Stop there," and I knew what he was about to say. Dad leaned towards me and told me that I had agreed to marry Kevin, and stay married, in sickness and in health, and he expected me to honor my wedding vows. I had no choice but to say, "Yes sir."

To my Dad, divorce was an unacceptable option. He was very strict on the sanctity of marriage, and believed there was only one excuse for a spouse to dissolve their marriage. Adultery was the only acceptable excuse that could be biblically justified, in my Dad's mind. His daughter could not be divorced for anything less than provable adultery; any other reason would mean tarnishing the Bartlett name and bringing disgrace to the family.

My fate was set. Dishonoring my Dad would mean losing my job, car, home, and money. Divorce would not only mean giving up Kevin, but giving up my family as well. Life had already been a difficult journey I didn't understand, and now this.

I had no choice but to look beyond the bad times and continue to love, protect, and defend my ill husband. I thought back to how alone I felt when I came to live with the Bartlett's; my strong-will helped me through many scary, lonely times. I knew I could face any outburst or violent episode Kevin put me through. Though he had an illness, I wanted to believe that he truly loved me, and that's what I had to cling to,

"Till death do us part."

The Wedding

CHAPTER TEN

FIRST MONTHS OF MARRIAGE

Over the next few months, the wedding bliss had passed. The joyful, newlywed excitement had worn off as Kevin and I fell into our daily routines. Each day we woke up early and headed our separate ways to go to work. After work, I would rush home to do some cleaning, catch up on laundry, and start cooking supper before Kevin rolled through the door. Amidst the daily grind, was the ever-present "walking on eggshells" so as not to say or do anything that could throw Kevin into a violent Bi-polar episode.

It was early in March of 1987, only three months since our wedding day, when I woke up one morning feeling nauseated. I didn't give it much thought that first morning; however, by day three of waking up nauseous, I felt compelled to ask Kevin to stop at the pharmacy and pick up a pregnancy test on his way home from work.

Kevin came home on time for a change, and had actually remembered to stop at the pharmacy. As I took the small box from his hand, I shuddered at the thought of the power and suspense contained within its cardboard walls. I had so many concerning thoughts about Kevin's illness. My dream of having a precious daughter to love, play with, and nurture into a beautiful young lady, was now a dream that scared me.

The "what if's" raced through my mind, as I pondered how I could possibly raise a child with a Bi-polar husband. Kevin must have seen the concern on my face, as he interrupted my thoughts.

"Don't worry," he said, "if we are having a baby, I promise to love and protect him or her, and I would kill myself before I could hurt my child."

His words were somewhat reassuring, but this was not the kind of life I had fantasized about for myself, and my future children.

It was a long, sleepless night. I tossed and turned; thinking of all the possible outbursts Kevin could put me through during my pregnancy and after the baby's arrival. He liked being the center of all my attention and would still get frustrated from time to time if I dared to tarry too long playing with our little Shih Tzu. How would he handle all the time I would need, and want, to devote to an infant?

The sharp sound of the alarm suddenly interrupted my thoughts. I slowly rolled over to look at the time; it was 6am, and time to find out if our family of two would become a family of three. With the pregnancy test in my hand, I made my way to the bathroom and followed the directions carefully. As soon as I came out of the bathroom, I handed the test strip to Kevin and asked if he would tell me what it said. If I read the results myself, I knew I wouldn't be able to see Kevin's immediate reaction. I kept my eyes glued on him, watching his every expression as he held our future in his hands. Before he even spoke, the answer was clear. I saw his eyes widen and his lips curl into a smile as he shouted, "It's positive! We're having a baby!"

At that instant, all of my worries turned into excitement and wonder as Kevin and I just stood there staring at each other. We both had to get ready for work, so there was little time for planning. However, we agreed that I should leave work early and drive into town to see the doctor. I had been meaning to call the doctor for a few days anyway; there was a persistent pain in my side that seemed to be getting worse rather than better. Now that I knew I was pregnant, I couldn't put off the doctor visit any longer.

When I arrived at work, I couldn't help but share the news with Mom, but the news of my pregnancy didn't bring the excited response I was expecting. Instead, she was rather aloof and acted as though I just told her we were getting another dog. There was no hug, no excitement, and no talk of how happy she was for me, just a cold, blank stare.

"What about his illness?" she asked.

"He has medicine," I reminded her, "and the doctor never told us that we shouldn't have children."

I wasn't going to dwell on things that I couldn't change. Facts were facts; he was a Bi-polar and we were pregnant. I would deal with his episodes and learn to shelter our children from his illness. We had only been married three months; I was already learning how to put a smile on my face and pretend we were the Ken-and-Barbie couple everyone said we were. After I had my talk with Dad and realized I had no choice but to adjust to Kevin's illness, a new "me" had begun to form. I was no longer the happy dreamer; there was no point to think that life could be happy. My spirit of joy had been squashed by reality. I was constantly being screamed at, shoved, and thrown around; then, I had to quickly ignore my own feelings and focus on forgiving Kevin as he cried and apologized for whatever he had just said or done. After only a few months, there was little of "me" left, and I could only imagine what future years would bring. Perhaps a baby would keep me going and give me a reason to keep fighting. Maybe I would eventually begin dreaming a happier future was possible. I prayed daily for strength and for the wisdom to separate Kevin's love from his illness.

Later that afternoon, Kevin met me at the doctor's office. The nurse performed another test and confirmed our pregnancy.

"I'm sorry for showing up without an appointment," I told her, "but my side has really been hurting, and I didn't know if the pain had anything to do with the baby."

The nurse became very solemn and said, "Just a minute. Let me get a room ready, I'm sure Dr. Newberry will want to see you."

She led Kevin and I to a room and before I could hardly sit down, Dr. Newberry was in the room and immediately asked the nurse to bring in the ultrasound machine. I had never seen an ultrasound machine before and wasn't sure what to expect.

"Is this going to hurt?" I asked.

Dr. Newberry laughed.

"Not at all," he replied, "but I need to take a look at something. The worst thing about this machine is the cold goop I have to put on your belly."

He was right about that.

He began the ultrasound, and it wasn't long until he found what he was looking for.

"Yep. There it is," he said. "Just as I thought."

"Is it my baby? Can I see?" I asked excitedly.

He turned the monitor so Kevin and I could see the screen. Then he took my happiness and turned it to terror, as he explained I had to go to the hospital immediately for emergency surgery. He showed me my fallopian tube and pointed at a small image.

"Do you see that?" he asked. "That is your baby, in your tube."

I was so ignorant that I just smiled and said, "Yay! My baby!"

He quickly corrected me.

"No, you don't understand," he began. "Your baby cannot live in your tube. You have an ectopic pregnancy that is about to cause your fallopian tube to burst."

"Well, can't you just put my baby where it needs to be?" I asked.

I still didn't understand the situation.

The more Dr. Newberry explained, the more my eyes welled up with tears. He wasn't giving me any good news about my baby, and now he was telling me that my own life was in danger. He instructed Kevin to drive me straight to the hospital, and said that he would call ahead to get me admitted quickly. I couldn't believe what was happening. I had already prepared my mind and heart for my baby. I was excited about having a little person that was 100% related to me, who I could love and who could love me back. While I was daydreaming about holding my precious baby, Kevin's illness seemed to take a back seat in my thoughts. I wanted a little girl to pamper and adore, but I would welcome a precious little boy as well. I already had names picked out too; the boy would be Bradley Kent, and the girl would be Kasey Lee.

As Kevin and I walked to the car, I could not put into words the many thoughts and feelings I was experiencing. We were both stunned at what the doctor had just told us. My brother and sister-in-law, Bobbie, had gone through the terrible loss of several babies; each lost during her first trimester. The babies were all lost in her womb and I had never heard of a baby getting "stuck" somewhere else. All I knew was that if you had a positive pregnancy test, a baby was being formed inside of you. The doctor's explanation about this thing called an ectopic pregnancy was more than I wanted to know about, much less experience first hand.

We quickly arrived at the hospital, where the admitting nurse was waiting for us with the necessary paperwork, ready for a signature. She must have seen the uncertainty and confusion in our eyes.

"A nurse will be in your room to get you settled and will explain everything to you," she said. "Feel free to ask her about anything you don't understand or are unsure of in any way."

She was very kind to us, and I could tell she was trying to bring comfort to a very confused-looking young couple.

Kevin walked along side the wheelchair as I was taken to a hospital room. Once we were in the room, I was given a gown and told, "Put this on, and a nurse will be in shortly to ask you a lot of questions."

I changed into the ugly hospital gown, and crawled onto the most uncomfortable bed I had ever sat on. I'd never had an operation before, and I was trying to be brave, but my insides wanted to burst forth in tears. My surgery was scheduled for early the next morning (since I had eaten before my appointment with Dr. Newberry, he had to delay the surgery). I was going to be cut open, have my baby taken out of me, stitched up, and left wondering, *Why?*

After I answered all of the questions the nurse needed to ask me, Kevin went home to gather some items for me. He called each of our parents to let them know I was in the hospital, scheduled for surgery the following morning. Kevin's parents arrived at the hospital within an hour of my admittance. As the hours began to pass, I couldn't believe my parents still hadn't shown up to see me.

"Kevin, what did you tell my parents when you called them?" I asked.

"I spoke with your Mom. I told her you had an ectopic pregnancy, and the doctor said it was very serious and required emergency surgery," Kevin answered.

"Well, what did she say?" I inquired.

"She was quiet and said she would tell your Dad when he got home from work. Then she hung up the phone," Kevin replied.

With each hour that passed, my heart broke as I realized that my parents weren't coming to see me. They apparently didn't care if I lived or died, nor did they care anything about my baby that would never be born. My baby was being taken from me in a very scary way, and I wanted my Mom and Dad with me.

By 10pm that night, with still no visit or call from my parents, I went into my defensive mode. *That's fine*, I thought to myself, *I don't need them. God has always taken care of me and He can deal with their hatefulness.* The real truth was that I wanted to curl up into a ball, cry, and have a pity party. It was bad enough that my doctor had given me terrible news, but now my parents were rejecting me and obviously didn't care what I was going through.

While all of these thoughts were racing through my mind, I was also extremely worried that Kevin would get stressed and have a violent outburst. I was still learning about Bi-polar Disorder, but I had noticed that stress and multiple issues at one time, were often the trigger for an episode. Such stress would make Kevin beat his head into cabinets, hit himself, or start taking his anger out on me. A part of me was apprehensive about being alone in the hospital room with Kevin, and him having access to all my IV lines and medicines. What if he decided that if the baby didn't survive, neither should I? All of these things were bottled up inside of me, and I had no one to talk to. So, I resorted to the only thing I knew to do; I told Kevin I needed time alone to pray.

Morning came more quickly than I had hoped. At the crack of dawn, the doctor was in my hospital room to explain what he would be doing during the operation, and the process that would take place afterwards. I knew nothing about holding rooms, operating rooms, or recovery rooms. Knowing what to expect made the surgery seem a bit less frightening, and I had to believe that everything would be fine.

Before I was wheeled away from my hospital room, Kevin asked the doctor if we could have a quick prayer. After we prayed together, Kevin followed behind me while I was taken to the holding room. The nurse allowed him to stay and talk to me a few more minutes while she was getting some medicine ready. Kevin tried to comfort me; he could tell I was still hurt that my parents hadn't shown up to see me.

"I'm sure they will show up at some point," Kevin said, "but as soon as I'm allowed to, I will be here to see you after your surgery."

Then, the nurse told us it was time for Kevin to leave. He gave me a kiss, and we said our goodbyes. My bed was wheeled into a bright room that was full of machinery. There were several other nurses in the room, who moved me from my bed onto a hard, cold table. I remember thinking how uncomfortable the table was, when a nurse interrupted my train of thought.

"Sweetie, can you count backwards from 100?" she asked.

As funny as it may sound, I thought, *why does she want me to count?* But I began counting anyway, "100, 99, 98…"

The next thing I knew, I was waking up in the recovery room. My first surgery was already over, but I did not feel well. Despite the warm blankets that the nurses had put on top of me, I was very cold… cold and nauseated. I was awake enough to know that I needed something to throw up in, but I was so sleepy from the anesthesia I could barely get the words out, to let the nurses know. As I tried to sit up and figure out where a bucket or container was, the pain of surgery hit me like a ton of bricks, and it was terrible. There were two nurses with me, one on each side of my bed. Their voices were kind and soft, as they patted me and said, "Don't try to sit up sweetie, you just had surgery."

They tried to instruct me to lean to the side if I needed to throw-up, but I was still so medicated and sleepy that they both had to help turn me. I was later told I stayed in recovery longer than most people, because of the nausea I was experiencing.

Finally, I fell asleep and was taken back to my hospital room. I slept for a couple hours, and awoke to find Kevin holding my hand. His parents were in the room, and my parents had finally arrived. At the time, I was still groggy from the anesthesia so I let myself drift back to sleep.

Later that evening, when I was more awake, my Mom and Dad came over to my bed to talk to me. They told me Dr. Newberry explained to them how serious my condition had been, and how lucky I was that my fallopian tube hadn't already burst.

"Where were you?" I asked them.

"We didn't realize how serious it was or we would have shown up last night," Mom answered.

I just stared at my parents for what seemed like five straight minutes, before I could even figure out what to say back.

"You were told I was having emergency surgery," I replied, "and that should have been enough."

As the tears rolled down my face, I knew I would never forget them abandoning me. They knew Kevin was a Bi-polar, and yet they weren't there to support me or help me; they just left me at the mercy of my Bi-polar husband.

The real truth behind their absence was clear in my mind. Kevin and I had just gotten married in December, and it was only March. They thought I must have been pregnant when we got married; that was the real reason they didn't show up when Kevin called them. They didn't want their precious reputation tarnished; they weren't about to call anyone at their church to pray for me, or ask anyone to be there and pray with me before surgery. My Dad was a deacon in the church, but I wasn't nearly as important as the embarrassment they might face. If people thought I had been pregnant before I got married, they would have been humiliated. When the doctor told them I was only six weeks along, and that the fallopian tube can burst at 5 – 6 weeks, I'm sure they were thrilled at the news. It wasn't until after the doctor explained what an ectopic pregnancy was, and that I could have died, that they called the church and asked their friends for prayers.

How did I know the answer to why they didn't show up? Because

I had lived under their *conditional* love ever since the day they adopted me. I had been told for years, how lucky I should feel that they took me into their home, clothed me, and fed me. I could not comprehend the concept of parents loving their children, just because they loved them. How I wished my baby could have survived; it never would have doubted being loved by me. I would have made sure that no matter the problem, he or she would know that my love was unconditional and unending for them.

Memories came back to me of the time my Mom pointed her finger in my face and yelled, "You wouldn't even have your looks, if it weren't for us! We took you to the dentist, and paid to have braces put on your teeth! We put you in glasses, and then paid for you to get contacts! You just remember that we are the reason you have what you do!"

What is an adopted child supposed to say back to statements like that?

I knew I would owe my parents forever, and to top it off, my dream of having a husband who loved me unconditionally, had turned out to be a total disappointment. Perhaps true, unselfish love didn't really exist in the human realm. I was beginning to learn that God was the only true friend I had, and the only one I could trust. When I prayed and read my bible, I felt a peace that no human being had ever made me feel. It was almost as if I could hear God saying, "Everything will be all right." If I was ever blessed with another child, I wanted to teach them about the Lord, and put a love inside of them for his Word, and make sure they understood the power of prayer. Relying on *people* to make you feel loved, and believing that *people* truly care about what you're going through, was not a reality, at least not in my life. Most people in my life had been more disappointment than joy.

I thought I had found a true path to happiness on earth, when I met Kevin. Now that dream was over.

After a few days, the doctor discharged me from the hospital and told me I would have to see him in six weeks for a checkup. I returned home, hoping that Kevin wouldn't get aggressive during the course of my recovery. I asked him if he was taking his medication, but that seemed to irritate him, so I dropped the issue. I knew that prayer would get me through my recovery.

The weekend before my six-week checkup with Dr. Newberry, Kevin surprised me by taking me to dinner at Olive Garden. We lived about 40 miles from the restaurant. Regardless of the drive, which could take an hour if you fell behind traffic, it was a favorite dining destination for many people from our small town. I was excited about a wonderful Italian dinner, and trying to put the past weeks of recovery behind me. I was told that my surgery was laparoscopic, and less invasive than typical surgery. Despite it being called "less invasive," it was my first operation of *any* kind, and I was in a great deal of pain during the first month of recovery. All I knew was that I didn't want surgery ever again; it was excruciatingly painful and uncomfortable to do simple things like sleep or walk.

It seemed as though Olive Garden was always crowded, but luckily we didn't have to wait very long to be seated. The waitress took our drink orders and gave us time to look over the menu. When the waitress brought our drinks to the table we went ahead and ordered our entrée's. As salad and breadsticks were being brought to our table, I couldn't help but smile. It was so nice to be out of the house, having a nice dinner after weeks of such a painful recovery.

I took a bite of a breadstick when suddenly, a horrendous pain pierced through my side. Kevin saw the look in my eyes as I jumped slightly.

"Can you describe the pain?" Kevin asked frantically.

"It feels like I'm being stabbed," I replied weakly.

The stabbing pain in my side was becoming more excruciating. Within moments, my lower abdomen started to throb and swell. Different pains seemed to be coming from all over my body; a sharp pain hit my shoulders, radiating down my back and through to my chest. The pain was so severe, I thought I was dying.

"I don't think I'm going to make it. Write this down," I instructed.

I began telling Kevin my final wishes and what items I wanted to leave to my friends and family members. He grabbed a pen and napkin, and scribbled my words down as fast as he could. The pain had become so unbearable that it was getting difficult for me to speak. My stomach felt like it had swollen to the size of a basketball, and my shoulders were beginning to ache so intensely, I could hardly breathe. Somehow, I managed to get a few more words out.

"I think I'm passing out," I said faintly.

Kevin quickly threw some money on the table, scooped me up in his arms, and rushed me to the car.

I could feel how fast we were going, as Kevin drove me back to the hospital, over 40 miles away. It felt as though the tires weren't even touching the pavement. We flew down the road and after only 20-something minutes, we screeched to a halt in front of the emergency room doors. Kevin jumped out and quickly came to my side of the car. He lifted me from the seat and ran into the emergency room, carrying me in his arms.

"She needs a doctor immediately! She can hardly breathe!" he screamed.

Nurses came rushing over and we were quickly taken back to a room where a nurse put an oxygen mask over my nose and mouth.

"Try to relax," she said. "Tell me about your pain."

I did my best to describe the various pains in my side, abdomen, shoulders, and chest, when the nurse interrupted with another question.

"Have you ever had surgery before?"

"Yes," I replied, "I was just here six weeks ago to have an ectopic pregnancy removed."

At that point, the nurse could tell I wasn't exaggerating about the amount of pain I was in.

"I'll try to get you something for pain, honey," she said. "If I can, I will, but I need to check with Dr. Newberry first. Just give me a few minutes."

Once again, I was admitted to the hospital. While Kevin and I waited for Dr. Newberry to arrive, the nurse brought me some Tylenol to help ease my pain.

When Dr. Newberry arrived, he wanted to know what happened.

"I rushed her here from Olive Garden," Kevin began.

"Had she eaten?" Dr. Newberry asked.

"She had eaten part of a breadstick when the pain hit her, but that's all she had," Kevin answered.

"I'd just been to dinner myself," Dr. Newberry said. "It's a good thing I wasn't drunk when I got the call."

Instantly, I looked at Kevin, expecting him to go into a rage. He wasn't the best husband in the world, but he was extremely protective of me when it came to other people. After the comment Dr. Newberry had just made, I was afraid Kevin would hit him, but thankfully, he didn't.

"Was that the problem the first time?" Kevin asked angrily. "Is that why we're back here again? Were you drunk when you operated on her?"

"I need you to get out of the room so I can examine her," Dr. Newberry said, completely ignoring Kevin's question.

"I want to stay," Kevin replied quickly.

"I can't do my job if you're in here," Dr. Newberry snapped.

Reluctantly, Kevin did as he was told and left the room. The doctor began to push around on my stomach, which caused me to scream in pain. When I told him that my shoulders were killing me, he explained it was because my belly was filling up with blood. He did a quick ultrasound to confirm.

"Not all of the pregnancy was removed from your fallopian tube during the last surgery, and it is causing internal bleeding." Dr. Newberry continued, "Your appendix wasn't removed either, and that is causing the pain in your side. I will have to remove the rest of the pregnancy, remove your appendix, and examine further while I'm in there. This surgery will require a six inch, bikini-line incision."

I was prepped for emergency surgery, once again, and Kevin was told that he needed to contact family members. Meanwhile, my head was spinning; I couldn't believe that I was about to have another operation. Just when I thought my recovery was almost over, things had taken a turn for the worst. It didn't seem real; but I was in such severe pain that I barely even realized when I was taken to surgery.

Upon waking up in the recovery room, I quickly learned the difference between laparoscopic surgery and a traditional incision. I didn't like to show emotions in public, especially when I was hurting, but the pain was so awful it made me scream. Once again, the anesthesia was causing me to throw-up, and each time I tried to move or lean, the pain was excruciating. Tears were streaming down my face; it seemed like the pain extended from my shoulders to my feet. I couldn't help but wonder, *Why is this happening to me?*

Eventually, the nausea subsided and I was wheeled back to my hospital room. My Mom and Dad had actually shown up this time. Kevin said they had both been crying, because the nurse explained my condition and how severe the internal bleeding had been. His family had also arrived shortly after he called and told them the news. Though it was nice of everyone to be there for me, I was in terrible pain and didn't feel like talking to anyone. I just wanted to sleep, so I could escape from the pain.

Dr. Newberry came to my hospital room the next day and explained how the surgery went.

"We had to do a blood transfusion because you lost three pints of blood from internal bleeding," he began. "If a blood test had been done after I removed your ectopic pregnancy, we would have known that some of the pregnancy was still in your fallopian tube."

Dr. Newberry continued to explain, and I couldn't believe what I was hearing. Even though he didn't get all of the ectopic pregnancy during my first surgery, it would have shown up on a simple blood test, and in turn would have prevented my internal bleeding! Not only that, but he was also supposed to remove my appendix during the first operation! Apparently, if your appendix is exposed to air, the doctor is supposed to remove it; otherwise, it almost always leads to appendicitis. The way I saw it, he should have known better. I wasn't sure which was worse; the fact that I had to endure a second surgery, or the fact that it could have been avoided if Dr. Newberry had done his job right the first time.

Regardless of the mistakes made by the doctor, there was no way to change the past. After that operation, my hospital stay was a lot longer and I knew the recovery was going to be difficult. I would just have to rely on the Lord to heal me, and handle my recovery day by day.

Kevin had cried several times throughout my hospital stay.

"I was so scared," he said, with tears in his eyes. "When I was driving you to the hospital, I was afraid you weren't going to make it. I was so worried that I was going to lose you. Kimi, I would be totally lost if anything ever happened to you."

Maybe the fact that Kevin nearly lost me would knock some sense into him. I began to wonder if that was the reason for my sudden health issues. Kevin had a good life and a wife that loved him; keeping our marriage together should have been enough motivation to take a couple pills everyday. I hoped and prayed he would try harder to keep up with his medications and doctor visits, for the sake of our marriage and our future. Only time would tell if Kevin would be willing to make the effort.

CHAPTER ELEVEN

MORE BURDENS TO BEAR

The weeks passed slowly during my recovery, as I spent most of my time alone. Mom would bring paperwork to my apartment on occasion, but I mostly sat by myself and pondered the events that had taken place since my wedding day; the day I had hoped would change my life for the better.

How could all of the dreams that were so dear to my heart, fewer than six months ago, seem so senseless now? With each Bi-polar episode Kevin put me through, my old-self faded away and I became a fortress for survival. I wasn't interested in seeing girlfriends or going out for fun; and the bounce I had in my step when I knew Kevin was coming to see me, was long gone. Instead of a flurry of excitement and anticipation to see him, I now dreaded every passing minute as time drew near for him to walk through our door. I was never sure what might set him off.

My parents never checked to see how I was doing or asked how Kevin was treating me; and the less time I spent with my girlfriends, the less I heard from them. It was as if everyone knew something wasn't right between Kevin and I, but no one really wanted to know what was going on behind closed doors. The old saying, "out of sight, out of mind," was definitely proving true.

I just needed one good friend that I could rely on and pour my heart out to. It was during those quiet moments, when I reflected on all I was going through, that I began to find the Lord more and more each day. A person's level of faith is built stronger with each storm that passes through their life. A strong faith has learned to trust in the unseen anchor of God's love, to see them through the most violent of storms.

Within two years of my marriage, my Dad decided to retire, which left me without a job. Dad's dream was to build a business that he could one day hand down to his children, and he worked very hard to make it a success. All my life I heard him say, "Why do you think Mother and I have worked so hard? Don't you know that we want you and Lucas to have more than we had?"

When I was a child, I didn't understand my Dad's stern attitude. However, as I grew older, I realized how exhausted he must have been. Every morning, he left our house by 6 or 6:30am, and often didn't return home until 9 or 10 o'clock at night. He never took a sick day, never complained about getting up early for work, and certainly didn't complain about only having Sunday afternoon as his *free time*. In fact, when I consider how many people think they're entitled to sleep late on Sundays, rather than take themselves and their families to church in honor of the Lord's Day, I'm amazed. It is hard to comprehend a man who loved his Lord so much that he chose to never take a day off for himself. My Dad managed to work long hours all week, and was an active Deacon in our church. Our family attended church service every Sunday morning, every Sunday evening, and we rarely missed a Wednesday evening.

Many a night I can remember my Dad coming through the back door, and telling Mom to grab him some clean clothes because he needed to visit some "church folk" who were in the hospital. If he wasn't visiting someone in the hospital, then he was visiting a shut-in that he said was on his heart. He felt bad if he went too long without visiting or praying with someone. Somehow, with all of his service to others and building a successful contracting company, he also managed to adopt two unwanted children, take them to church regularly, and teach them the importance of serving others.

Though I disagreed with my Dad on some issues, including his methods of discipline, I always had high respect for him. He was quite a man to watch and learn from. Many of the strengths he taught me, became my guide when the time came that I could no longer run to him for advice. Most of that resilient generation of people who lived through the Great Depression era are no longer with us; it's sad that we've lost people of such wisdom and strength.

My Dad's heart was broken when he tried to give his company to my brother and I, and Lucas refused the generous gift. It was a business that had grown from a small operation of a backhoe and bulldozer, to a family owned corporation worth over two million dollars. Dad had worked night and day, for years, to make it successful. He always told us he worked hard so we could "have something one day." Dad assured Lucas and I that, if we chose to run the family business, he would be on the sidelines to help us with the daily operations if we needed him. I knew he had taught us well enough to keep the business running and make it profitable for our families and future generations. Lucas knew all about the equipment and was capable of operating any piece, from a small dump truck to the largest truck crane. He was not only a great equipment operator, but our employees loved him. Anyone describing him would have said, "Lucas is a good ole boy." However, that description would have been followed by something like, "But, he just won't stand up for himself," or, "He won't make a move without being told what to do."

Some situations in life are complicated to explain if you haven't walked a day in someone else's shoes, as the saying goes. Lucas had a love/hate relationship with Dad because of the many whippings he had endured, as a child; many of which were done in anger and were way too harsh.

Our family didn't speak of the trials that took place within our home; those things were to be kept private. Even if Lucas and I had wanted to tell someone that we weren't happy, we had nowhere to turn. Dad was one of the most successful and influential men in our county, and no one was about to step up and confront him about how he should treat his children.

Unfortunately, Lucas turned down Dad's offer to run the company because his wife had already told him that it was too much work and she didn't want him to run it. Bobbie wasn't shy about putting her two-cents in, during our family meeting to discuss the future of Dad's company. She plainly stated, "I don't care what Lucas says. I don't want him working all hours, day and night, like Kent has. I would rather live on less money and have Lucas home more."

With that said, Lucas rejected Dad's offer, and that was the end of keeping the family business. My family didn't care how the decision affected me, which was no surprise. Lucas's rejection meant that the family business was being taken away from me, and there was nothing I could do about it. Dad said he knew I could probably run it, but it was not a job for *just* a woman.

In one voiced opinion, by an in-law, everything my brother and I had endured during our childhood was suddenly pointless. Lucas and I could have taken our rightfully deserved place and been owners, not just workers. All of the fighting and screaming that always ended with, "Don't you know we are working hard so you can have something some day!" meant nothing now.

I had given up on my own dreams, in hopes that I would one day be co-owner of the family business my Dad spent his life building. Now, it was all over. Lucas and I would never run the company together. I couldn't believe that Bobbie didn't realize my Dad had already done the hard work. We didn't have to keep Dad's hours and build the business; we just had to maintain it. She didn't grow up in the Bartlett home and endure years of lectures, humiliation, and a constant feeling of unworthiness. Lucas and I were the ones who went through it all, and we should have been able to reap the benefits of the business that kept us from vacations and happiness. This was one more disappointment in life that I had to just accept.

Through our entire childhood, Lucas loved me, and I loved him. We had always been close, until he got married. The Lucas I grew up with would have never let anyone hurt me. When I was young, I often missed school due to terrible allergies. On such days, Lucas made my room his first stop when he came home from school. He never failed to check on me back then or all through our growing-up years. Now he was different.

There was nothing I could do but watch, as my once-close brother was pulled further and further away from me. He acted as if refusing Dad's company had nothing to do with me. He left the meeting without telling me he was sorry; he barely looked at me as he headed for the door, and there was no good-bye. By that point, I guess it shouldn't have surprised me. Lucas had heard about how badly Kevin treated me, and yet he never confronted Kevin or even asked me about it. He didn't show any concern over my past surgeries, and never talked to me like he used to. I missed the brother I thought I would always have as my friend.

My Dad's company was sold off piece by piece; hundreds of thousands of dollars were lost because it wasn't sold as a single company. The farm became Dad's new workplace, and he had decided to keep a few pieces of equipment there. At the time, little did I know Lucas had taken a few pieces of equipment to his home and started Lucas Bartlett Contracting, Inc. The backhoe, dozer, and other equipment that Lucas used weren't leased from my Dad; he just took them and used them free of charge. My Dad continued to pay the insurance on the equipment, in addition to paying for all the fuel, and any repair costs.

In my opinion, an established business with guaranteed steady work, would have been much more valuable than taking a few pieces of equipment and starting a completely new business. It didn't make any sense to me. We would have had instant work and instant income if we had kept Dad's business. Why would they refuse my Dad's company, then turned around and form their own corporation? It was obvious that I was the only person losing out on income, and the benefits of my Dad's equipment.

Since I no longer had a job, I wanted to figure out something I could do for myself. I talked to Kevin about the situation, and he suggested I think about Interior Design. Kevin said I had a talent for picking colors and placing furniture in just the right spot. We discussed my options in regards to college; I didn't see how I could go back, considering I was in my late 20's.

Before I could give much thought to the idea of going back to college, my health issues struck again and I had two more laparoscopic surgeries. I regularly suffered from large cysts and had constant pain from scar tissue and adhesions, mostly the result of my first operation being handled incorrectly. Several people told me I should have filed a lawsuit against Dr. Newberry, but I just couldn't. I knew he hadn't intended to cause me such troubles, and I chose not to take the issue to court.

Despite the surgeries I had endured, which were supposed to fix things, by late 1990 I was still experiencing pain in my lower abdomen. Instead of returning to Dr. Newberry, I decided to see my medical doctor, Dr. Adams. After my visit, she told me I should probably see a specialist, and tell him about the ectopic pregnancy, all the complications and surgeries. Dr. Adams said she knew of a very reputable specialist, but he was about 150 miles from our home. I knew I could trust her recommendation and asked her to schedule the appointment for me. She was able to get an appointment for the upcoming week.

The specialist had requested my hospital records, as well as the videos of my previous operations. He concluded that my right fallopian tube and ovary needed to be totally removed; otherwise, they could cause very serious trouble for me in the future. Although I wasn't happy about the prospect of another surgery, I understood why it was necessary. The doctor put in a video from my most recent operation to show me what my insides looked like. I'm obviously not a doctor, but I could plainly see how diseased my right fallopian tube and ovary looked.

"I can't believe this was left in you like this," the doctor said. "This will cause you nothing but serious trouble in the future. It needs to come out now."

The doctor believed I would have a better chance of conceiving, once the diseased ovary was removed. Surgery was scheduled, and once again I tried to mentally prepare for not only the surgery, but also the time I would spend at home, alone, during the weeks of recovery.

My parents offered to get a room at a hotel, so they could be near us in case Kevin or I needed anything during my hospital stay. I was shocked, but very glad they offered. I didn't want to be in a strange city, alone with only Kevin, for the operation. Mom and Dad followed us in their car, and we headed out for another surgery. We arrived several hours early; I was led to my room, and given the usual hospital gown. Each nurse I encountered was friendly, helpful, and acted like they truly cared about my level of comfort. They were making the unbearable thought of another surgery, somewhat less stressful. I was about to have my sixth surgery and I knew what to expect; the sleepy shot, the operating room, the recovery room, and the inevitable pain that would be awaiting me after surgery.

The surgery went well, and for the first time I didn't experience nausea in the recovery room. My parents, as well as Kevin's parents, were at the hospital. I was glad they were there not only for me, but also for Kevin. I worried about him sitting by himself for hours, with nothing to do but think. Their presence made it easier for me to rest and recover. After a couple days, the doctor told Kevin he could make a pallet for me in the back seat of the car, and take me home. The two-hour drive seemed to take twice as long; I felt every bump in the road, which sent pain shooting through my abdomen. No one likes surgery, and after having my sixth, I was getting tired of going through the whole process. The past four years had seemed to bring nothing but bad luck for me.

Once home, our somewhat normal routine began again. I still woke Kevin up around 5:45am each morning, but I didn't go downstairs to fix breakfast. Instead, it was his job to bring something upstairs to me, before he left for work. He was faithful to bring me a thermos of coffee each morning, along with enough snacks to get me through the day, until he got home from work.

A few months after my ectopic pregnancy, I had made the decision to move off my parent's property and let Kevin provide a home for us. I thought the responsibility of a house payment might keep him focused, and somehow result in fewer Bi-polar outbursts.

Kevin and I moved into a nice 1,400 square foot home. We lived there about nine months, before we came across a beautiful two-story home that was located about a mile from Kevin's parents' home. We fell in love with it. It was 2,500 square feet, with four bedrooms and two-and-a-half bathrooms. All the bedrooms were upstairs, which seemed fine when we purchased the house; however, after an operation, steps become an enemy.

The steps were extremely difficult for me after this surgery. The lifting and pulling to get to the next step brought tears to my eyes. While Kevin was at work, I stayed in my room all day. I knew not to try going up and down the steps by myself.

Charity stayed by my side all day, everyday, during my recovery. She and I only grew closer; I talked to her about everything. She listened each time I cried in pain from surgery, and each time I cried because of Kevin. My sweet Shih Tzu was by my side through it all.

Slowly but surely, the days turned into weeks; moving around was getting easier and the pain was beginning to subside. One morning, about four weeks after my operation, I decided to go down the stairs and see what Kevin was fixing in the kitchen. It was Saturday, so he had the day off work, and I could smell something wonderful being cooked. Kevin had left our bedroom several hours earlier to go make coffee. He brought me a large cup of coffee, but I guess I fell asleep after I drank it, because it was after lunchtime when I woke up the second time. I didn't remember hearing anything from Kevin since he brought me coffee, and I was afraid he might be waiting for me to wake up so we could eat breakfast together.

After putting my robe on, I slowly made my way down the stairs to the kitchen. Kevin was frying sausage patties; he had already cooked some eggs and had another pot of coffee ready. He seemed to be in a good mood, so I headed around the kitchen island to kiss him. As I started around the island, I told Kevin how good everything smelled, and said, "I don't want my sausage edges to be crispy, please."

I barely had the words out of my mouth when I saw the rage start. His head snapped sharply in my direction, and his eyes pierced through me with pure hatred. He threw the skillet across the stove; grease and sausage went flying.

"I guess I can't do anything right! Is that it?" he screamed. "Is that it?"

He grabbed the belt from the back of my robe and twisted it tight, until it was digging into my gut. As he wrapped the belt around his hand, he began to slam me straight into the kitchen cabinets, over and over. The pain was horrific. It felt like my incision would literally bust open.

Finally, Kevin quit. He took off down the hallway and up the stairs. I could hear his footsteps; he was running to our bedroom. Choking back tears, I yelled after him,

"I hate you! You have ruined my life!"

The pain was so severe, I held on to the cabinets to keep from falling to the floor. I prayed I wasn't bleeding internally. My tears hit the floor, as I looked around at what he had done. Sausage was scattered across the stove; grease covered the counter tops and was dripping down the cabinets, onto the floor. All I did was make a simple request and–

Suddenly, I heard a gunshot ring out from upstairs. The second I heard the shot, a wave of mixed emotions washed over me. Each step I took sent pain shooting through my body, but I managed to make my way to the stairwell. I pulled myself up each step, using the banister for support. While I made my way up the stairs, I called to the only person I could.

"Jesus, help me deal with whatever I have to face up here," I prayed. "I need your help."

When I found Kevin, he was sitting on the floor in our closet, holding a gun in his hand. As I walked towards him, he looked up at me; his face was red and streaked with tears. I could tell he had been pulling his hair and had probably been hitting himself in the head. I knew the typical fits he threw and how he needed to talk for hours about what he had done; I just stared at him, waiting for him to say something. It didn't matter to me that he was holding a gun; I think being shot would have felt better than being rammed into cabinets, especially after having surgery.

Kevin sat there looking up at me, his tears hitting the floor.

"I couldn't even kill myself right! I was afraid I would go to Hell, and I couldn't do it," he said. "I don't deserve to live for what I've done to you. You deserve so much better than me... I heard what you said, when I ran up the steps."

A part of me wanted to apologize for what I'd said, but the reality was that I was miserable and tired of his abuse.

"Well, I'm sorry for using the word *hate*," I managed to say "I never should have said I *hate* you."

Once again, I found myself consoling Kevin and making sure he was okay. He never asked how my stomach felt or if I needed to go to the hospital. I stood there and listened to him talk about his feelings for so long that I finally had to interrupt. I told him I absolutely had to get off my feet, or I was going to fall down. I was always afraid that an interruption while he was talking, would cause him to go into another rage, but at that point, I was in so much pain I didn't care.

The hours passed slowly as Kevin sat down on the bed beside me and cried uncontrollably. He laid his head in my lap like a little child, and made promises to me of how he would never hurt me again. All I heard was "blah, blah, blah," because it always happened again. He would give some excuse for not taking his medicine and make promises to stay on his medication, from that point on. Then he would beg me to give him another chance to prove he could be the man I fell in love with.

That incident was a changing point in my life, a change that's hard to explain. I didn't leave Kevin, but something inside of me died that day. I took all my starry-eyed dreams of a happily ever after and buried them so far down in my soul that it would take a miracle for me to believe true love existed for me. I merely wanted to get through life and hoped that maybe one day in the future, retirement would make Kevin nicer. We talked about retiring to Florida one day, and that became my focus. I forced myself to believe retirement would restore the Kevin I fell in love with. There would be no stress from work, just a beautiful ocean shore to walk along each day. I had to believe things would get better in the future. That became my goal: make it to retirement! Make it to the ocean one day, and Kevin's Bi-polar episodes would end.

If only that could have been reality; if only anything I believed we had, had been true. How does anyone really know when to give up on love? Aren't there always questions like, *What if I had tried a little harder?* Or, *Is there something I could have done differently?*

I didn't want to ever ask myself those questions. I was determined to get Kevin and I back to what we had when we first met. I wanted to believe that the Kevin who asked me to marry him, would be able to control his illness one day and be the loving man I once adored. We just had to get to a stress-free environment for him, and things would be better and our love would be restored. I had to look beyond the present and hope for the future.

Kevin had a good job with a large aluminum company, and I had decided to take Interior Design classes in a nearby town. At times, things seemed to be getting somewhat better; then Kevin would have an episode, and I was reminded that it was never going to end. My Interior Design studies became my escape. I got involved by joining the Design Club, and was eventually nominated for Club President. It was nice to have something to focus on that made me feel like I still had worth.

My grade point average stayed a constant 4.0 through each semester. It was early April 1992, and I was looking forward to finishing my courses by December. On that particular day, I was driving back home after my classes when I suddenly became so dizzy I could hardly see. I pulled into the parking lot of a nearby McDonald's, and just sat there until my dizziness subsided. After a few minutes, I went inside and told the manager that I desperately needed a phone; I explained how dizzy I was and that I needed my husband to pick me up.

Thankfully, I was able to reach Kevin, and he said he would be on his way to get me. I informed him that I had opened a package of cheese crackers and ate one while I was driving.

"Maybe someone poisoned the crackers..." I said. "I didn't check the seal before I tore the package open."

Kevin just laughed.

"I'm sure the cheese crackers were safe," he replied.

I went back outside and sat in my car, waiting for Kevin to show up. Each time I moved my head, the dizziness returned and everything started spinning. To top it off, I was beginning to feel nauseated.

Within the next half hour, Kevin and his mom, Martha, arrived. Martha was very inquisitive about how I was feeling and was almost smiling as she asked me questions. While I was trying to explain how dizzy and sick I felt, I didn't understand why she and Kevin kept looking at each other. Martha must have seen the curious look in my eyes.

"Well, Kevin, are you going to say something or am I?" she said.

"Kimi have you considered that you might be pregnant?" Kevin asked with a grin.

As the words hit me, I think I stopped breathing for a moment. I had been so wrapped up in my studies; it never occurred to me that I might have another chance to be a Mommy. I just sat there in somewhat of a fog.

"I already called the doctor," Kevin said. "I told them what was going on and that I would be bringing you straight there."

Martha was grinning from ear to ear.

"I think the test will be positive!" she said excitedly.

What if I was pregnant, but it was another ectopic pregnancy? I had mixed feelings about everything that could still go terribly wrong. Since I wasn't sure what to think or how to feel, I just decided not to think about it until we reached the doctor's office and I had a blood test. The last time I had gotten excited about a baby, it turned out to be a terrible, painful experience. I had even hoped that a baby would make Kevin stay on his medication and fight to control his outbursts. Kevin was such a romantic and sweet man when he was being himself, but the Bi-polar side of him was almost demonic at times.

Kevin held my hand as we drove back towards home to see the doctor. I could tell he knew I was thinking about his illness, and everything it affected. There was a lot of silence between us. In the event that I was indeed pregnant, we both had things to consider. I only had three classes to finish in the Fall semester, before I would have my Associates Degree in Interior Design.

We arrived at the doctor's office, and as we walked through the door Kevin leaned towards me and said, "I love you, Kimi. No matter what."

There were about five or six people waiting in the doctor's office; however, before I could even sign in, the door opened and a nurse kindly signaled for me to go on back.

"Come right this way, Kimi," she began. "So, you need a blood test to see if you're pregnant?"

"Yes," I answered. "I suppose it could be possible, but after all the surgeries and problems I've had, I kind of doubt it."

The nurse smiled and said, "Well, we will know shortly, sweetie."

While waiting for the results of the blood test, Kevin and I were asked to take a seat in the lobby. We hadn't been waiting very long, when the nurse opened the door for us again.

"Kevin and Kimi, could you both come here for a moment?" she asked.

Together, Kevin and I went to hear what the nurse had to say. I was so afraid we would be told I had to go to the hospital because something was wrong, again.

"I'm not supposed to do this because the doctor isn't in the office right now," the nurse said, "but under the circumstances and because of all you have been through, I couldn't wait to tell you that the test is positive! You are pregnant, Kimi!"

"Really? Are you sure?" I asked in disbelief.

The nurse smiled and replied with a laugh, "It is more than 100% positive."

Kevin and I were so excited; we both started jumping up and down, yelling with excitement. When I realized I was jumping, I quickly stopped and grabbed my stomach.

"Oh, I can't be jumping! I might hurt our baby!" I said.

Kevin began to laugh, along with all the other people in the lobby who were smiling at our exciting news. Kevin and I left the doctor's office with smiles from ear to ear, and Martha was ecstatic when we told her the news.

It was the absolute greatest news I could have hoped for. A baby was a dream come true for me. I knew I would love a boy or a girl, but I felt this was my daughter. My heart told me that my son was lost in the ectopic pregnancy. I can't explain how I knew, but I felt as though it were a fact. I could already envision my daughter and I laughing, shopping, going out to eat, and being best friends.

With all the excitement and love that was overflowing in my heart, my mind interrupted, *"What about Kevin's episodes?"* Six years of living with unprovoked outbursts, and never knowing what might "set him off," left each happy moment with a sense of uncertainty. Now, I would have to protect my child, as well as myself. All I knew for certain were the promises in the Bible: that God would not give me more than I could handle, and He would never leave or forsake me.

With His great wisdom and love, God knows each baby that He creates, and I was thrilled that he had blessed me with the honor of being a mother. I would cling to my faith and knowledge of God's Word, and protect my child for the rest of my life, with or without Kevin.

CHAPTER TWELVE

THE CALM BEFORE THE STORM

The months passed quickly as my baby grew and I grew as well. By November, I had gained fifty pounds. I ate three full meals a day to make sure I was getting enough nourishment for my baby. The moment I found out I was pregnant, I gave up everything with caffeine and not a drop of medicine entered my system. When I became very sick with a cold, I asked the doctor if the medicine could hurt my baby. I was told anything that went into my system would go to the baby. I chose to pray my way through the cold and let my body heal itself. I couldn't risk anything hurting *her*.

This baby meant everything to me, and I knew it was depending on me for the best care, for food, and most importantly, for love. In order to give my child the safest way into the world, I chose natural childbirth. The mind is a powerful thing, and as my expected delivery day drew closer, I prayed daily for a quick delivery and for the safety of my unborn child. My prayers became more and more specific; I prayed for a daughter with dark hair, blue-green eyes, perfect-shaped little ears, and a nose that looked more like mine than Kevin's. I also prayed for her soul; I asked the Lord to make sure she accepted Him into her heart, and remain faithful to Him all of her life. I dedicated my daughter to the Lord, and wanted her to always stay close to Him. In my heart, I believed that was the greatest thing I could ask God to do for her. With Him, all things are possible.

On November 23rd, at approximately 6:30pm, my water broke. Kevin scurried around to load our bags in the car, and then rushed me to the hospital. By 10:45pm, I was holding my daughter in my arms. She was a beautiful baby girl, in perfect health, with a head of dark hair; she was precious. With a lot of prayer, I had a successful natural birth, with no medication of any sort. I certainly don't judge any woman who chooses pain relief, because I totally understand the need for medication. The pain is almost unbearable, but the results are so wonderful. My choice to go natural is not for everyone. It was just something between my Lord and I.

Kevin and I were so excited to have our little girl; we stayed up all night talking about her and dreaming about fun times for the three of us. My sweet little Kasey was hungry every two hours, so I began to watch the clock, and the door, happily anticipating the next time the nurse would bring her to me. I had never been a babysitter or taken care of young children, but I knew I would always find a way to take care of Kasey, no matter what. Something inside of me knew that she and I would always be close, and our bond would be strong.

We had our Thanksgiving at the hospital that year, and it was a blessing to have been given the gift of a precious baby girl. I wasn't sure how long it would be until Kevin had his next episode, but I knew no one would hurt my baby, ever.

After I studied the benefits of breast milk, as opposed to formulas, I chose to nurse Kasey for the first six months of her life. Breast milk is the natural choice and is full of much-needed antibodies. During most of my childhood, I was sick with allergies, and I wanted to do everything in my power to keep my daughter healthy.

Nursing Kasey turned out to be a great benefit for Kevin. When Kasey needed to be fed in the middle of the night, he usually slept right through it. I didn't really mind, since it gave me time alone with her and I didn't have to worry about him getting agitated because he was tired. There was very little sleep those first weeks at home, as most parents can attest to. In fact, there were many times that I would crawl out of bed to get Kasey before I even heard her on the monitor. It was as if I could feel her fixing to call out to me.

There is one particular night that I will never forget. Kevin and I were in our room watching television, when I felt like I wanted to see Kasey. Her nursery was located in the bedroom closest to ours, on the second floor of our home, and I knew it would only take a second to check on her.

"You shouldn't bother her because you might wake her up," Kevin said, as I slid out of bed.

"I can't help it. I just need to look at her. You just keep watching your show and I'll be back in a few minutes," I replied.

"You might try to go more than two hours without seeing her," he said with a smile.

"Shhh," I said, smiling back at him. "We need to be quiet when I open the door to her room. I don't want to wake her, I just want to look at her."

I quietly stepped into the hallway and turned to close the bedroom door behind me, when suddenly I heard a voice.

"Kimi…"

I wondered why Kevin was calling me, so I tried to quietly re-open our bedroom door.

"What do you want?" I asked. "I was just about to open her door when you called my name."

"I didn't call you," Kevin said with a puzzled look on his face.

I just looked at him with a "sure you didn't" expression and proceeded to close the door again. I stepped towards Kasey's nursery and as my hand touched the doorknob, it happened again; the muffled voice called out to me.

"Kimi!"

Once again, I re-opened our bedroom door, which startled Kevin. He quickly changed the television channel, which was odd, but I was more focused on why he was calling my name.

"Kevin, please stop. You're going to wake Kasey," I said. "I had my hand on her door and was just about to open it when you called me again."

"I promise you that it's not me calling your name," Kevin said with total sincerity. He had a strange, confused look on his face and I could tell he was telling the truth.

"Maybe you better answer next time," he continued. "I think God is trying to get your attention or something. It's not me saying your name."

Before the words were even out of his mouth, I began to realize how unusual the voice had sounded. It was somewhat muffled and loud, but yet it wasn't loud; it was just clear and strong. *Kevin might be right*, I thought.

"Well, I still need to check on Kasey because I keep getting stopped every time I get near her door," I said.

For the third time, I quietly closed our bedroom door and stepped toward the nursery. As I turned the doorknob, a chill washed over my entire body. When I opened the door, I was amazed at what I saw before my eyes. There was a magnificent white cloudiness all throughout Kasey's nursery, especially above and around her crib. Immediately, I knew I was in the presence of angels. My arms were covered in goose bumps; every hair stood on end; a chill covered my body, and my legs became weak. The room was aglow with their angelic presence, and I knew the Lord had sent them to watch over Kasey.

"I'm sorry to bother you, but I would like to see my baby girl. Thank you for watching over her," I whispered to the angels.

My legs would hardly move, but I was determined to look at her. The room almost felt thick, for lack of a better description. It was truly breathtaking to be in the presence of God's angels.

I whispered, "I love you," to my precious daughter and slowly backed myself out of the room, not turning my back to them, out of respect.

"Please continue to watch over her," I asked the angels.

Then I closed the nursery door, leaving Kasey in their tender care.

What caused angels to guard Kasey that night? To this day, I don't know the answer to that question or what the significance of that night was. Daily, I asked the Lord to send angels to protect Kasey, and I'll always be glad I did, because whatever bad thing could have happened to her that night – didn't.

I opened my bedroom door and Kevin jumped out of his skin; once again, he quickly changed the television channel. I didn't even ask him why he was so jumpy; I just blurted out,

"Angels are in the nursery guarding Kasey."

"That doesn't surprise me," Kevin replied calmly. "Don't you pray for her all the time?"

"Yes, I sure do," I answered.

Kevin just smiled and turned the television off.

"Well, at least you know she's safe," he said.

That was true. Kevin rolled over and fell sleep, but I sat up for a few hours, pondering the events of the evening. I realized why my name had been called out; God was telling me that Kasey and I would always be safe.

I had already experienced the Lord coming to my defense, and He had just assured me that He would be there for my daughter, as well. Often times I wondered what happened to the angel that appeared in the unity candle picture, from my wedding. After that night, I knew that I was not forgotten, and an angel would always be nearby.

Kevin began to work a lot of overtime, leaving me with all the responsibilities at home. It was getting to the point where he would just get up after eating and leave his dishes sitting on the counter, as if I were his servant. When I first met him, he was very tidy and picked up after himself; he always helped with dishes, laundry, and other household chores. Now, after six years of marriage, he was gone more than he was home, and when he was home, it just meant more work for me. Outside of our home, I truly had no life. Kevin made a comment one evening that he was glad to know his wife was home, taking care of his child.

"A lot of the men I work with have wives that are cheating on them and running around to bars, while they're at work," he said.

I didn't mind being at home with our precious baby, and I certainly had no desire to hang out at bars. However, there was something wrong with the way Kevin said it. There was a certain look in his eyes when he said, "I'm glad to know I can pick up the phone, day or night, and find you at home taking care of our daughter." A feeling of imprisonment suddenly hit me, and I realized that Kevin wasn't just telling me how grateful he was, he was telling me that I *belonged* at home.

Girlfriends never asked me out anymore, and Kevin and I rarely went to the movies or did anything social. The extent of our social life was either going to see his parents, or going to see mine. I had become isolated from the world. Day after day, it was just little Kasey and I.

As Kevin worked more overtime, I realized that I needed to do something for myself. Since the day I found out I was pregnant, my work towards an Interior Design degree had been put on hold. *Maybe I could open my own studio,* I thought to myself. *After all, there were only three classes I hadn't been able to finish.*

I called a couple of my design teachers and asked them what they thought about me opening a design studio, even though I still had a few classes to complete. All of my teachers were very excited for me; they assured me that I was very much a designer, and reminded me that I had a 4.0 GPA to prove it. When I told Kevin about my idea, he completely supported me and even helped me search for what would one day be my design studio.

A little house on a well-known street went up for sale, so Kevin and I went to look at it. It needed a lot of sprucing up, but I could tell that it would make a lovely design studio and gift shop. I had already picked the perfect name for it: World Designs. Though it took a lot of time and hard work, the studio looked absolutely beautiful once it was finished.

On July 7th, 1993, Kevin and I officially opened World Designs. It was a wonderful business and I was proud to call myself the owner. As our little business continued to grow, I was glad that Kevin seemed to enjoy it as much as I did. When he wasn't working at the factory, he was always helping at the store. In fact, he was quite the salesman. I was rather impressed with his willingness to go around the store with hand cream testers, and offer it to the ladies who were shopping. He once sold an entire display of hand-held back massagers, simply by demonstrating them on our customers. I was happy to see him take such an interest in our business. He even tried to get me into computers and something called the Internet. Since I had a degree in office management and bookkeeping, I had no interest in a computer. When I had been the office manager for my Dad's contracting company, I did payroll for almost 40 employees the old fashioned way, using withholding tax tables and a one-write check system. My ledger and journal always balanced to the penny. I didn't need any technology beyond my IBM typewriter and an adding machine.

Kevin insisted that computers would one day become a necessity, so I bought him an I-Pac, which was like a hand-held computer. I thought it was crazy to pay five hundred dollars for a hand-held device, but he assured me it would come in handy for him at work. He asked me about getting an Internet card for his I-Pac; since I didn't really understand it, I told him to just get what he needed. It wasn't until years later that I found out what a mistake that Internet card was.

World Designs took off and started to grow into a successful business. For my interior design work, I had to carry wallpaper books, fabric samples, and furniture pieces in the store. Due to requests for various gift items, we expanded with a fabulous body and bath line, Camille Beckman; which is a well-known company to this day. We even turned one of the former bedrooms into a gourmet room. The gourmet room was stocked with over 65 varieties of whole bean coffees, as well as teas, cocoas, and candies. It was such a wonderful little store, and I loved every minute of it.

From time to time, Mom and Dad would stop by World Designs, and I could see the delight in their eyes when they arrived to a store full of customers. On more than one occasion, Dad told me how proud he was of my success. He advised me to grow the business slowly, so I would have something to hand down to Kasey one day. Since opening the store, Kevin was even having fewer episodes and seemed to be truly happy with our choice to become business owners.

Before I knew it, four years had passed. World Designs had become such a success, we found ourselves calling City Hall for permission to add square footage to the back of our store. While we were waiting for an answer, the flood of 1997 hit our town. Kevin was working night shift one evening, and around 8:00am the next morning I received a call from him. As soon as I heard his voice, I knew he had bad news.

"I came by to check on the store and see if we had any water damage," Kevin began, "and I'm standing in about a foot of water."

"You mean you're standing *inside* our store, in a foot of water?" I asked.

"Yes. I'm sorry, but it's true," he replied. "Everything is ruined."

I could not believe what I was hearing. Our beautiful store was almost a total loss. All of the rugs, expensive hatboxes, and beautiful pictures that were left leaning against French inlaid tables; it was all ruined!

The ironic part was that I had just opened a letter from City Hall; they had denied our request for a building permit, because our store was "in a flood plane." In fact, most of the street we were located on was in the flood plane. Before I purchased the building for our business, I didn't know to check a flood zone map. I didn't know of anyone who checked for things like that. Not a single person I had spoken with, not even the realtor, told me the street had poor drainage or that the building was in a flood zone.

Many people suffered losses from the flood of '97, and we were no exception. Our next big surprise came from the insurance company. When we called our insurance agent, we were told, "You didn't purchase separate flood insurance, so your losses are not covered by your policy." Kevin and I were completely devastated. Our carpet, wallpaper, drapery, furniture, and thousands of dollars of merchandise were all ruined. Any and all profits we expected to enjoy from our hard work had just vanished along with the floodwaters.

After a lot of tears and long discussion, Kevin and I decided to forge ahead. We owned the building, and some of the merchandise that was on shelving and hanging on the wall, could still be salvaged. With rubber boots and rubber gloves, we began our massive cleanup project. We weren't about to give up.

At the time, my Mom and Dad still lived about twenty miles from us. Because of floodwaters, many people in the area were isolated and without power. I didn't worry about my parents too much; I knew they would be okay without power. Their generation knew how to survive on very little, and both of them grew up without electricity. I always loved to hear the stories about their childhood.

Mom and Dad both came from poor, farming families. Mom thought it was a treat to simply walk to her refrigerator and grab eggs for breakfast. She liked to tell about how it was her job to gather and clean the eggs before breakfast, when she was a little girl. For those of you who don't understand what it means to gather eggs, it isn't exactly glamorous. As my mom would put it, "I hated cleaning that sh*t off those eggs!" She and I laughed every time she talked about it. Those stories helped me appreciate all the comforts we often take for granted. Mom and Dad were both 44 years old when I came into their lives, at age three-and-a-half. I didn't always like how my parents were so much older than my friend's parents, but it gave me the privilege of learning about "olden times."

Over the past year, I had been taking Mom and Dad to a lot more doctor appointments, and I could tell they were progressively getting more and more forgetful. One evening, Dad called to ask if I could drive them to a doctor's appointment the next morning; he said the appointment was at 8am, and Mom had asked him to call. I told him I would be there around 7am to pick them up. Let me take a moment to reiterate the fact that my parents lived 20 miles away. I had to drive 20 miles to pick them up, then had to drive 20 miles back for them to see their doctor. After their appointment, I had to drive them back to their house, and finally drive myself back home. Just taking them to see their doctor, meant 80–100 miles of driving, and it was something I was frequently asked to do.

That particular incident stands out in my mind, because I arrived the following morning to find Mom and Dad in their pajamas. They both looked surprised to see me at their door so early.

"Why aren't you two ready yet?" I asked.

"What are we supposed to be ready for?" Dad asked with a puzzled look on his face.

I reminded him about the phone call the night before, and their doctor's appointment. I could tell that Dad had no idea what I was talking about, yet he tried to cover up for it.

"Oh, that's right. I was thinking the appointment was tomorrow," he said.

Mom had a blank look on her face and I could tell something wasn't right, but they hurried to get dressed, and we raced back to town for their appointment.

When we arrived at the doctor's office, Mom and Dad sat down while I went to the front desk to check them in. The nurse at the desk politely stopped me.

"Kimi, they already had their appointment," she said. "This is the third time they've tried to come back for it. Could you come back and speak to the doctor for a moment?"

I told Mom and Dad I was going to the restroom and would be right back.

Dr. Adams asked me to come into her office, and she began telling me her concerns. She said that I needed to check on Mom and Dad frequently because they were showing signs of dementia. It was too soon to know if it could be Alzheimer's, but they were both showing signs of forgetfulness. I told her that I had noticed some problems, such as the non-existent appointment I had just driven them to.

I went back out to the lobby to get Mom and Dad and they just followed me out the door, without mentioning their appointment. They suggested we all go eat breakfast, which sounded good to me because I hadn't had time to eat before picking them up that morning. We decided to eat at Grandy's, and after we finished our breakfast, we sat and talked for a couple hours. The more we talked, and the more questions I asked, it was obvious they were living in somewhat of a mental fog. Some of my questions were answered with ease, but other questions were answered with a strange, empty stare. Then, one of them would try to cover for the other, and change the subject.

Something was wrong with Mom and Dad, and I felt like I needed to discuss the matter with my brother. One day, I tried to mention the problem to Lucas, but before I could finish, Bobbie interrupted me. She told me that she thought Dr. Adams was exaggerating the issues.

"Kent and Leah are getting up in years and all old people forget things," Bobbie informed me.

Lucas barely spoke, except to agree with Bobbie that our parents were "just getting older." Lucas had no idea how many appointments I had driven Mom and Dad to, or how many times they would call me, only to turn around and call again five minutes later. Mom and Dad never remembered anything we had talked about; they usually didn't remember calling me at all. Every time I tried to explain the problems Mom and Dad were having, neither Lucas nor Bobbie would listen to me. I had to make regular trips to check on Mom and Dad. I worried about how I would get to them if we had another flood or a bad winter. I desperately needed my brother to understand that something was wrong with both Mom and Dad; it was not simple forgetfulness.

My to-do list only seemed to get longer as the weeks flew by. I was busy trying to keep my business going, taking care of little Kasey, and keeping Kevin happy; all in addition to taking Mom and Dad to their many appointments, some necessary and some non-existent. Life was getting pretty hectic.

One evening, Dad called to tell me he'd received a call from Dr. Adams about a recent x-ray. I was about to get a shower when the phone rang, so I was in a little bit of a hurry.

"Oh, that was nice of her. Everything look good?" I asked, but the answer I received was not at all what I expected.

"Well, no. It was not good news, Kimi," Dad answered.

I just stood, frozen, afraid to ask the next question. I could already feel the tears welling up in my eyes.

"What is it, Daddy? What's wrong?" I asked nervously.

"Now I don't want you crying Kimi Leah, but it's colon cancer," he said calmly.

"No!" I said, choking back tears. "No, it can't be!"

"Now you dry those tears up right now," Dad said sternly. "You have to take care of that sweet baby doll, and she doesn't need to see you upset. I was wondering if you would go with mother and I to talk with the surgeon, Dr. Sherman."

I tried my best to hold back the tears.

"I will be there for every appointment and anything you need," I said.

After I hung up the phone, I sobbed until I could barely breathe. My Dad had always been so healthy. I could literally count, on one hand, the number of times he had stayed home from work because he was sick. He was like the energizer bunny that just kept on going.

When I went with Dad to his next appointment, the surgeon explained how he would remove the cancer from Dad's colon. Dr. Sherman said he would make a zipper-cut straight down Dad's stomach, remove about a foot of his colon, and stitch him back up. Removing the cancer seemed like a breeze compared to scheduling the surgery. Dad had decided that he wanted to be "cut" by the "correct sign of the moon." He had to find an updated Farmer's Almanac, and then carefully study the charts in order to pick the correct date for his surgery. Luckily, the surgeon had also grown up on a farm and still farmed a little on the side; he completely understood Dad's logic and didn't mind waiting for Dad to figure out the correct date.

I thought it was quite an ordeal, until Dad explained why he believed in the Farmer's Almanac. He told me, "When I was a boy, I helped my Dad castrate our pigs. We studied the almanac in order to know when to cut the pig. If you cut the pig when the sign of the moon was right, there would be little to no blood. However, if you cut the pig during the wrong moon, the pig could bleed to death." He swore that he had seen the old Farmer's Almanac save the lives of many animals. Eventually, Dad figured out the date, and surgery was scheduled to remove the cancer from his colon.

My Dad must have been cut during the correct sign of the moon because his surgery was quick, and everything went smoothly during and after his surgery. I think he had a great surgeon, but I wouldn't dare argue against the value of the Farmer's Almanac.

Despite Dad's cancer surgery going so well, the memory problem was getting noticeably worse. During Dad's hospital stay, Lucas had even noticed it. When I reminded Lucas I already told him there was a problem, Bobbie quickly interrupted, "Anesthetic can cause an older person's memory to get worse, and that is all it is!"

By then, it seemed hopeless to convince Lucas we needed to discuss how we were going to take care of Mom and Dad. Once again, Bobbie thought she had all the answers. The opportunity to run my Dad's business was gone because of her; now she was preventing Lucas and I from discussing what to do when Mom and Dad could no longer live by themselves.

By 1998, Mom and Dad had declined even further. Both of their memories were so bad, Dr. Adams made an appointment for them to see a specialist at the University of Kentucky Medical Center, in Lexington. The doctor was renowned in the study of geriatrics and Alzheimer's disease. He had even written articles that were featured in Newsweek Magazine. I thanked Dr. Adams for helping me get my parents to such a renowned specialist.

In order to get Mom and Dad to their appointment, I had to make arrangements for us to be in Lexington overnight. Lexington was several hours from home, and their appointments were scheduled for 8am. We needed to drive to Lexington the day before, and find a hotel near the UK Medical Center. I wasn't sure what I was in for and I was a bit nervous about taking my parents several hours away, by myself, and staying overnight. It would have been nice if Lucas had offered to help me, but Bobbie had him convinced their only problem was old age.

When I arrived at Mom and Dad's house to pick them up, they weren't ready, and questioned why we had to stay in Lexington overnight. We had already discussed it at least 10 times before, but I tried to be patient and explain the situation, again. Once I had explained it again, they both understood my reasoning. Mom and Dad had great respect for their doctors, and thought it was rude to inconvenience a doctor by being late.

"Yes, we can't risk being late and missing our doctor appointment," Dad said.

Finally, we got on the road, but it much later than I had hoped; I knew it would be harder to find my way around Lexington once it got dark outside. This was before people used smart phones and GPS; I had a good, old-fashioned map, and that was all. We were a couple hours into the trip when their personalities began to change. Out of the corner of my eye, I noticed Dad unbuckling his seat belt. He turned around and looked at Mom in the back seat.

"Are you okay?" he asked.

"Well, I guess I am," she said with a puzzled look on her face.

Dad turned sharply in my direction, and I could tell he was upset.

"I think it's about time we went back home," he demanded.

"Dad, please put your seat belt back on," I said patiently. "We are going to a doctor's appointment, and I have a little further to drive."

At that point, I wasn't sure if I would make it to Lexington or not. I'm not sure what was going through Dad's mind, but he was very uncomfortable. It was almost amusing to watch he and Mom work in unison with their agitation. The more Dad fidgeted, the more Mom talked.

"I think this is uncalled for. We have a doctor back home," she said.

I don't think she could have named where home was, but she didn't like seeing her husband uncomfortable.

The drive was pure stress for me, hour after hour. It didn't get any better once we found a hotel room. Dad began looking under the beds and searching through their suitcases, in a panic.

"Dad, what are you looking for?" I asked curiously.

"Well, my wallet is gone. I know I just had it, but now I can't find it," he said.

I had just watched him take his wallet out of his back pocket and put it under his pillow.

"Dad, I think you put it under your pillow," I said.

"Well, if it is, I certainly didn't put it there!" he said scornfully, glaring at me.

Once Dad found his wallet under the pillow, I watched as he and Mom began to whisper to one another; they kept looking at me as if they didn't know who I was. It became a little unnerving, so I reiterated who I was, and started to talk about family times. The more I talked about home and family, the more comfortable they became. Finally, we were able to get settled down and go to bed for the night.

The morning wasn't as confusing for them as the night had been.

"Now where are we going this morning?" Mom asked.

"Well, we are going to a doctor's appointment, and then I will drive you both back home," I replied.

That answer seemed to appease them. I was able to get them ready, and then we headed towards the UK Medical Center.

Dad was a huge UK Basketball fan, so I started to talk about the University in hopes that it would keep him comfortable with his surroundings. Luckily, I found the doctor's office with little trouble, and even found a parking space close to the door. The Good Lord must have been guiding me because I truly didn't know how I managed to get us to Lexington the night before, or find the doctor's office so easily.

The doctor did a panel of blood tests on both Mom and Dad, along with three hours of questions, agility tests, memory tests, and general questions about their day-to-day routines. It was close to lunchtime when the doctor finished all of the tests, and he asked if we would come back after lunch so he could talk to us about the results. I told the doctor that was fine, and I would have them back by 1pm.

We found a place to eat and made small talk. Neither of them commented on the battery of questions they had just gone through. I wasn't sure if they even remembered where they just came from. They had an empty look, which is hard to explain to someone who has never been around a person with dementia.

By the time we headed back to the doctor's office, I was already exhausted and I wasn't looking forward to the hours of driving that lay ahead. When we arrived, the doctor called me back into his office, and had Mom and Dad wait in the lobby. I sat down and tried to brace myself for what the doctor was about to say.

"I am so sorry to tell you this, but it is my belief that both your Mom and your Dad are in the first stages of Alzheimer's disease," he said.

Tears began streaming down my face. The doctor was sympathetic and patted my shoulder while I cried.

"Kimi, do you have anyone that can help you with your Mom and Dad?" he asked. "The disease will progressively get worse. For lack of better words, the brain begins to look like Swiss cheese. You will need to make some tough decisions concerning their care."

Through my tears, I tried to explain the situation with Lucas.

"My brother doesn't believe anything is wrong with them except for old age," I said. "I can't get past his wife to talk to him about their condition."

"A lot of people can't face the reality of someone they love, having a mental problem," the doctor replied.

"Well, I'm more than used to that issue, because my husband has a severe case of Bi-polar Disorder."

As the words left my mouth, I could actually see the concern in his eyes, which I wasn't used to seeing from anyone.

The doctor gave me phone numbers for various support groups, as well as a list of behaviors to watch for as the Alzheimer's disease progressed.

"Once a person is diagnosed, the life expectancy is seven to ten years," he said. "I would advise you and your brother to contact a lawyer and discuss protecting their assets."

There was a lot of information to take in, and it had already been a very long twenty-four hours. I shook his hand as I stood up to leave.

"Thank you for taking the time to see them," I said.

"I could tell Dr. Adams thought a lot of them," he informed me.

"And if you need anything, you are welcome to call me."

As I left the doctor's office, I wondered what to do next. I waited until we got in the car to tell Mom and Dad the news.

"I have bad news about the doctor appointment you just had," I began. "You both have Alzheimer's disease. The doctor said you're in the first stages, and he suggested we talk about what the next few years will bring. We need to prepare, as a family, for some things before the disease progresses. I want you to know that I will take care of you, just like you took care of me when I needed someone."

There was total silence for at least a minute before Dad spoke.

"Now I know we forget a few things now and then," he said, "but I heard about some vitamins that are good for memory, and we will be just fine. Don't you worry about us baby doll."

I could tell they weren't going to accept their fate, which may have been a good thing. Who would want to believe their brain would become so diseased that it would look like Swiss cheese? Who would want to accept that all of their memories would be lost, along with their dignity? My heart broke for them. My parents had worked so hard and helped so many people, and now this was *their future*.

Their diagnosis of Alzheimer's disease and their future was now part of my future. My mind was racing the entire drive home. I didn't know how I would manage caring for both of them, along with my Bipolar husband and my five-year old daughter. I could feel the storms of life were headed my way.

Thankfully, I knew who could calm the storms, and I would have to trust Him to see me through.

CHAPTER THIRTEEN

DOWNWARD SPIRAL

By early 1999, it was obvious that I couldn't do everything on my own. Mom and Dad's Alzheimer's continued to progress, and so did Kevin's Bi-polar Disorder. I was beginning to feel older than my parents. After working at our store all day, I would pick Kasey up from school, drive 20 miles to take dinner to Mom and Dad, then drive 20 miles back home to get Kasey ready for bed, and take care of Kevin's needs. I knew something had to give, so I decided that my only option was to give up our store. Kevin had a good job that could support us, and I simply couldn't keep going at such a non-stop pace.

I had been in deep prayer about the store and was having a difficult time letting it go. The store was like a baby to me, and it was doing great. Finally, I made an agreement with God. I said, "Lord, if you want me to sell my store, someone will have to walk right up to my desk and ask me if I will sell it to them." I wasn't going to advertise it for sale, because I wanted to know that the Lord was in control of the situation; if He mysteriously brought someone to my doorstep, then I would know I was doing the right thing by letting go.

Well, be careful what you ask for.

It was a particularly busy day at the store, when a man walked through the front door and introduced himself as the previous sheriff of the city. I shook his hand and said it was nice to meet him.

"I know this is a strange question to just come out and ask you," he said, "but would you consider selling your store to me?"

I felt tears welling up in my eyes, as I knew the Holy Spirit was at work, and I was a participant of the Lord's mysterious works. God had heard my cries and knew that I only trusted Him to give me guidance. I braced myself on my desk, and with a shaky voice I replied,

"Well, I guess I have to. When do you need it?"

"You don't *have* to," the ex-sheriff said. "I'm sorry, I didn't mean to upset you."

"Oh, no, you didn't," I said. "The Lord had you come here today and ask for my store. These are tears of amazement; I just witnessed God answer my prayer about what to do with my store. He really does hear us and care about the small stuff."

As it turns out, the ex-sheriff was also a Christian. We were both delighted to engage in a conversation about the Lord and how He works things out for those who love him.

Kevin and I began a huge sale, and rented a storage unit to keep some of our shelving and displays. Since I was giving up my store for my parents, I believed the Lord would restore my business to me one day. Even though they didn't realize it, Mom and Dad needed more help with each passing day. I remembered the day a little three-and-a-half year old girl needed someone to take care of her; they took me in when I needed someone and I wasn't about to let them down. None of the bad memories mattered anymore. All was forgiven, and it was time for me to help the parents who gave me a home and a name to be proud of.

Trying to get Lucas to discuss how to handle Mom and Dad's personal assets was a battle to say the least. Not only did Bobbie insist that nothing was wrong with Dad, but she had also convinced her mother, Agnes, to talk to me about it. One day, Agnes decided to share her thoughts with me.

"Why Kimi, you know Kent Lee doesn't have that ole old-timer's disease. Leah may have some problems, but not Kent Lee," she said.

I couldn't believe that she and Bobbie had been discussing and "diagnosing" my parent's medical condition amongst themselves.

"No, I don't know that he *doesn't* have it, because a renowned doctor said they both have Alzheimer's," I responded.

Agnes just pursed her lips and shook her head.

"Well, you will never convince me that Kent Lee has it," she replied.

As time progressed, Mom and Dad had to start wearing adult diapers, they went through several home-health nurses, and eventually had to be put in a nursing home. Of course, neither Agnes nor Bobbie ever came to me and apologized for the way they acted. Lucas never acknowledged that he should have been more supportive, and not one of them (Lucas, Bobbie, or Agnes) ever admitted they were wrong; both Dr. Adams and the specialist were correct in their diagnosis of Alzheimer's disease.

Because Bobbie convinced my brother there was nothing really wrong with my parents, once again, hundreds of thousands of dollars were lost. Mom and Dad were both diagnosed in 1998 and they both died ten years later, in 2008. The specialist that diagnosed Mom and Dad said seven to ten years was the average life span after diagnosis, and he was correct.

Lucas and I had ample time to get assets transferred and legally protected, if only Bobbie had trusted someone other than herself. The five years that Mom and Dad were in the nursing home, cost their estate over $600,000. I could not understand Lucas and Bobbie's logic in causing our family to throw away Mom and Dad's hard-earned money. Why couldn't they have believed me when I told them the doctor thought it was Alzheimer's? I had spent much more time talking with my parents than either one of them, and I certainly didn't know why Bobbie's mother thought she knew anything about the change in my parent's memories.

Because I chose to spend quality time with Mom and Dad, I saw them changing before anyone else did. I was glad I had spent the night at their house so many times, and let them share stories about their childhood and early-married life. Those stories would be cherished and locked in my mind, to share with Kasey one day. That was a treasure from my parents that only I had.

During the course of Mom and Dad's illness, Kevin became more and more addicted to our computer. I knew he used a computer at work, so I couldn't believe the first thing on his mind when he got home was to run to our office and turn on the computer. I wasn't a techy person and I had too many responsibilities, to engross myself with useless behaviors.

A terrible tornado ripped through our town in the year 2000, and caused a great deal of devastation on the west side of our town. St Patrick's Day was approaching, and Kevin said I needed a night out of town. He made arrangements to take me to dinner, and for us to spend the night in Nashville. He had booked us a room at a quaint little bed and breakfast in the historic downtown area. I was excited about a night away; I certainly needed a break from responsibilities. Kevin said we were going to take our bypass to the west, so we could see the tornado damage. I had heard that several homes had their roofs blown off, and some homes were completely demolished.

The night seemed to be going well. We dropped Kasey off with Kevin's mom, and we headed out for a night of entertainment. I had only taken our bypass westward a couple times. The tornado-damaged area was approaching on my right, and I was looking out my window when Kevin suddenly yelled, "NO!"

I didn't have time to turn my head in his direction before I felt the impact, and it was fierce. As I jolted forward, the seat belt locked tight across my chest. My right leg took a beating against the dashboard when the front of our BMW came crashing inwards.

I didn't know if we were going under a semi or if we had hit an embankment; I had no idea what just happened, but the pain was severe. My chest felt like it was crushed, my neck was hurting, and I couldn't move my right leg.

I was hurting so bad that, at first, I couldn't speak. It felt like I had been severely beaten from the inside out, and I needed Kevin's help.

The car was making an unusual noise that sounded like a scream, and I could smell the strong stench of gasoline. I looked forward and could see some kind of liquid spewing all over the windshield, as the car continued it's high-pitched scream. Without saying a word, Kevin unbuckled his seat belt, threw his door open, and quickly got out of the car. I couldn't believe he had left me in there without even asking if I was okay.

I turned my head enough to see Kevin standing by the back bumper on the driver side; he was looking down at something.

"I can't get out! Help me, I'm stuck!" I said, trying to shout.

It was quiet for a moment before I heard Kevin respond.

"Get out of the car!" he yelled. "It could blow! Gas is everywhere!"

He still wouldn't come to my door or try to help me get out. The smell of gasoline was almost intolerable, as was the pain in my chest. I knew where to turn, and I began to pray.

While I was in prayer, I heard Kevin scream, "Turn the engine off before it blows!"

"I can't reach the key," I yelled back. "I can't move that far!"

"You have to turn it off! It's going to blow up if you don't!" he shouted.

I closed my eyes and prayed, "Lord Jesus, you know I can do this with your help. I can't leave Kasey with Kevin. Please help me Lord, I need you now."

I mustered all of my strength and reached for the keys; with only the tips of my fingers, I was able to turn the car off. Gasoline was still spewing; my right leg was throbbing; and the pain in my shoulders reminded me of the time I experienced internal bleeding. Still, there was no Kevin at my door to help me. I will never know for certain why he hesitated to help me, but my heart tells me that he saw an opportunity.

I slowly placed my hand on the car door and tried to push it open, but the crash had bent the front of the car back so far that my door was stuck. Once again, Kevin yelled, "Get out of there, Kimi!"

I grabbed the door handle, and tried one more time.

"Push it Jesus! Get me out of here!" I cried.

Immediately, the car door flew open with ease. It wasn't my power that opened the door. Knowing that the Lord had saved me once again, I pulled myself out of the car and fell straight to my knees.

"Thank you Jesus. Thank you for being there," I prayed out loud.

As I knelt by the car, thanking the Lord for His help, Kevin grabbed me by the arm and yanked me up.

"You're kneeling in gasoline! Pray over in the grass if you have to," he said angrily.

He obviously wasn't thrilled to have me safely out of the car.

I tried to take in the scene; there was a Chrysler New Yorker on the other side of the road, with the back end shoved up to the front seats.

"I think the lady said there are kids in that back seat!" Kevin said fearfully.

The way the car was bent up, the kids would most certainly be dead. I cried out for God to help them. Then, out of nowhere, a woman came up to me; she put her arms around me and asked if I was hurt.

"There are children in that back seat. Please, pray with me!" I begged, completely ignoring her question.

"Okay sweetie. I will pray with you, but let's get over here in the grass," she said as she patted my shoulders. "An ambulance is on the way for you."

I watched Kevin run over towards the other car, and I saw a tall, thin man walking towards him. Later, Kevin told me the man said, "There are no children in the car, but the lady needs help." We never knew where the man came from, or where he went after Kevin ripped off the driver-side door and pulled the lady out of her car. I knew Kevin had a lot of strength, but it was quite a sight to see him grab that door and pull it right off the car.

We were taken to the hospital and, out of the three of us involved in the wreck, I was the only one with injuries. As it turned out, the pain in my chest was caused by the impact of my seat belt. My right leg had a huge cut down the front of it; I couldn't move it very well, and I couldn't move my toes at all. Considering that both cars involved were totaled, we were all very fortunate to be alive.

After several months of therapy, and seeing various specialists about the pain in my leg, I was finally diagnosed. I had something called Reflex Sympathetic Dystrophy, or R.S.D. for short. I was told that a lot of athletes suffer from R.S.D. due to repeated injuries. It's basically permanent nerve damage to the injured area. I had to use one of my Dad's old walking sticks because my leg would go numb unexpectedly, causing me to fall down. It was like trying to teach your leg how to walk again. After a few months, it became easier to cope with my leg and I was able to bend all of my toes again, except the big one. To this day, it doesn't bend.

Kasey tried her best to help me get around; she was always so attentive to my needs. Kevin was putting in a lot of overtime, so Kasey and I were together and on our own, most of the time. When I thought back to the wreck and what could have happened, it scared me to think about leaving Kasey in Kevin's care. He wouldn't spend time with her when he was home, even if I asked him to. On many occasions, I warned him that she would never have a close relationship with him if he didn't make more time for her. He always said that he *meant* to spend time with her, but just got caught up with other things. Anytime I went to run an errand or go to the grocery store, Kevin would agree to play a game with her while I was gone. However, Kasey told me that he would just run off to the computer or bathroom as soon as I pulled out of the driveway. It was becoming a pattern, and a huge problem.

One morning after getting Kasey off to school, I was making my coffee when I smelled something strange coming from the garage. I opened the kitchen door, which led to the garage, and instantly saw the problem. At the end of the garage sat our four-foot tall propane tank, right beside our new BMW. The tank was hissing and leaking propane, which accounted for the strange smell. It was apparent what Kevin had been doing in the garage the night before.

Immediately, I dialed the number to the factory and told Kevin's supervisor that it was an emergency and I had to speak with Kevin. Within minutes Kevin was on the line.

"Why did you move the propane tank into the garage?" I asked.

"I just thought we might as well have it in, instead of it sitting on the side of the house," he answered.

"Well it's leaking propane and the smell is coming into the house. What should I do?"

"Did you get the car out of the garage?" he questioned.

"No… Should I?"

"Get the car out of the garage and then call me back," he responded.

"Okay, I'll call you back in a minute," I said, as I hung up the phone.

Quickly, I grabbed the car keys from the hook beside the door. As I placed my hand on the doorknob to open the door to the garage, a voice said, "No!"

The voice was so audible and strong that it made me feel nervous inside. That's when I realized *who* it was. Once again, the Lord had shown up to take care of me. The entire scene rushed through my mind, like I was watching a movie. I could see myself starting the car, and it exploding. I was actually about to get the car out of the garage like Kevin told me to. As all these thoughts raced through my mind, I knew I needed a friend, so I called Trisha, a girlfriend who lived nearby. I told her what was going on and she said she was calling her Dad, and would be right over. Trisha's Dad was going to call the fire department so they could safely remove the propane tank.

When Trisha arrived, her first response was,

"I told you he was trying to kill you! Do you believe me now?"

"Kevin wanted me to call him back after I moved the car," I replied. "He probably thinks I'm dead by now."

Like any "good" wife, I waited a little while and then surprised Kevin with a phone call. The shock in his voice said it all. He almost stuttered as he answered the phone.

"Ki…Kimi?" he said.

"Yes, are you surprised to hear from me?" I asked.

"Well I just figured you were busy and forgot to call back," he replied. His voice was shaking as he spoke.

"Yeah, sure," I said. "I think you're shocked because you expected that I was blown up by now."

"Oh I'm sorry, some of the guys were talking and I didn't hear what you said."

"You heard me loud and clear, and you know what you tried to do!"

I slammed the phone down and looked at Trisha.

"I told you!" she said.

For obvious reasons, Trisha and I spent several hours talking that day. Soon after I called Kevin, the fire department showed up to remove the propane tank.

"Why is there a four-foot propane tank in your garage ma'am?" one of the firemen asked.

"We purchased the tank for the year 2000, just in case there was a problem with power," I answered. I decided he should hear the entire story, so I continued, "It was outside, along the side of the house, in a safe place, until last night when my husband decided to set it beside the car I drive."

The look on his face said more than words could have.

"You be careful ma'am," he replied.

"Thank you," I said. "God has my back."

Kevin and I never mentioned the placement of the propane tank or what caused the leak. Just like the car wreck a couple years before, it was obvious that Kevin's illness was causing him to do things beyond his violent fits. I became more watchful of his actions and made sure I always had an escape route. Kevin's Bi-polar episodes happened more frequently and were becoming more intense; he was getting more violent towards himself even, and his personality began to change.

One night, I watched Kevin repeatedly beat his head into the kitchen countertop. He was slamming his head into the countertop so hard that I expected his brain to start oozing out of his ears. I screamed and begged for him to stop, but he just wouldn't listen.

"I'm no good! I don't deserve to live! You deserve better!" he yelled.

I never could get Kevin to tell me what he was talking about or what brought on that episode. As his episodes became more severe, there were many occasions where I never knew what caused him to go into a rage in the first place. He would be thinking about something, and then he'd get a strange look on his face and start hitting himself.

All I knew, was that something was really bothering him and causing him to feel worthless. He began to ask for prayer more often, and on two different occasions he approached the preacher during alter call and cried to him about something. I never questioned him about it, since it seemed like a spiritual matter between he and God.

By 2003, I was experiencing constant ovarian pain and swelling in my lower abdomen. After seeing Dr. Adams, she decided it would be best if I had a complete hysterectomy. With my mom in the nursing home and no other woman to talk to, I trusted my doctor and had a complete hysterectomy at the age of 39.

I listened carefully to all the advice about hormones, and other issues that can result from early onset menopause. Some magazine articles said one thing, but other articles would say something different, so I decided to go with my usual plan. I prayed and told the Lord, "You know I had this operation done, so I'm trusting you to take care of all my needs."

From that moment on, I decided that since God had helped me through natural childbirth and so many other things, He could handle my hormones as well. He did just that. I never took hormone medication or anything of the sort. I understand that some women may need medication and additional help through menopause, and they should follow their doctor's advice. At the time, I felt like I had too many other issues to deal with, and my health was last on the list.

CHAPTER FOURTEEN

THE BEGINNING OF THE END

Spring Break of 2004 was fast approaching for Kasey, and the thought of cold weather at the beach wasn't appealing. Kevin and I decided we would take a much-needed family vacation later that summer, when the ocean and pool waters would be warmer. While Kevin and I were sitting at the kitchen island, discussing our future trip to Florida, we heard what sounded like a meow. The meows continued and seemed to grow more panicked. There were woods behind our house, and Kevin surmised that a cat must have gotten itself stuck in one of the trees.

Kevin and I headed out towards the woods, behind our Australian Shepherd's dog pen. There was a chill in the air, and the blanket of leaves covering the ground was damp and cold. We searched frantically for the cat, but the more we walked, the more difficult it became to determine which direction the meow was coming from. After an hour of searching, we realized we were going to have to give up. We weren't any closer to helping the cat, and maybe if we left the woods, it would come down from wherever it was.

We headed back to the house and I put on a pot of coffee. Kevin said he didn't want any coffee, but decided to make himself some cocoa.

"You mean you're refusing a cup of coffee?" I asked in disbelief.

"I know it's shocking," he said with a laugh, "but I've been trying to limit myself to a cup or two at work, and that's all."

I touted about my love of coffee and what he was missing, and continued with my cup of deliciousness.

By the next morning, I felt feverish and there was pressure in my chest; it felt like an elephant was standing on it. Kevin went on to work, but said he would check on me throughout the day. I made a pot of coffee and took it back to my room. I stayed in bed, bundled up, and progressively felt worse with each passing hour. Luckily, the following week was spring break and I wouldn't have to wake up early to get Kasey ready and off to school. However, I could already tell that I wasn't going to feel like doing anything with her. Since we were staying in town for spring break, Kasey and I had planned on going shopping, going out to eat, and doing some other fun things. I didn't want to let her down. If I didn't shake my cold, or whatever it was, I wouldn't be able to take her anywhere.

When Kevin came home from work he brought me some over-the-counter remedies, which proved to be useless. I basically lived on cheese crackers and coffee, every day. I'm one of those odd people who can drink coffee any time of the day; I will actually sit on the beach, in the hot sun, with a cup of coffee in my hand. Kevin knew how much I loved my coffee, and he had become much more attentive about making sure he had it ready for me each morning.

The entire week of Kasey's spring break, I remained ill. To make things worse, Kevin worked a lot of overtime, so Kasey just sat on the bed beside me and watched television. It wasn't much of a spring break for her, but there was nothing I could do. As the days came and went, I was actually feeling worse, rather than better. I tried to tell Kevin that I needed to see the doctor, but he was too busy working and couldn't, or wouldn't, take time-off to get me there.

The following Monday morning arrived, and it was time to resume the school routine. Kevin put a baby intercom in Kasey's room so that I could give her a wake-up call in the mornings, rather than get out of bed to wake her. Kasey answered the intercom the moment I said, "Wake-up sweetie, it's Mommy." Her sweet voice came right back and said, "Hi Mommy. I love you." I told her I loved her too, and then I could hear her little footsteps begin their journey to the bathroom to get ready for school. If she hadn't been such a mature, intelligent child, we wouldn't have survived what lay ahead for the two of us.

As the week progressed, my fever grew higher and higher. By the middle of the week, my temperature had reached 103 degrees. I knew it was time to get to my doctor, somehow. With both of my parents in the nursing home and Kevin working so much overtime, I had no idea how I was going to get help. I called Dr. Adam's office and left message after message with her nurse. I finally got a call back from the nurse, only to be told that several people had the flu and that was probably what I had. I was instructed to drink plenty of fluids and just stay in bed.

For the next week, I continued to tell the nurse that I needed to talk to Dr. Adams because something was wrong; I didn't just have the flu. The nurse was almost argumentative with me; she said that I needed to be patient because it can take a couple weeks to get over the flu. I tried to explain that I was in my third week of being sick, and I knew something was terribly wrong with my lungs. To no avail, I was dismissed as an ignorant patient. I was left lying in my bed, scared and alone; I knew something was wrong, and I desperately needed a doctor.

Kevin continued to come home late from work, and little Kasey was doing her best to take care of me. She got herself up for school, then came straight to my room to give me a good morning kiss and help me to my bathroom. She would fix herself breakfast, bring me water and a snack, and then kiss me good-bye before walking down the driveway to wait for the school bus. Kasey was only 11 years old at the time, but I knew I could count on her to bring me water, food, and help me get to and from the bathroom each day. She was my only reliable source of help.

My sickness was beginning to scare me. It felt like my lungs were filling up with fluid, and I could hear a gurgling sound each time I took a breath. It was getting harder to breathe, and deep breaths were no longer possible. My body ached from my chest down through my legs, and Kevin had very little time to listen or care about how sick I was. The only way Kevin helped, was by making sure I had my morning cup of coffee.

By the fourth week, it was apparent that I had been left unattended for way too long. My voice was failing, my fever was staying at a constant 103.5 degrees, and one day, paralysis began to set in. When Kasey arrived home from school that day, I didn't want to scare her; I calmly told her that I needed something to drink, and asked if she could call her Daddy for me. Though Kevin was at work, Kasey was able to reach him on the phone.

"Go watch some TV while I talk to your Daddy, okay?" I said.

"Okay Mommy," she replied. "I'll be back to check on you in a minute."

As Kasey left the room, I quickly directed my attention to Kevin.

"I need you home, now! My legs won't move!" I said urgently.

"What do you mean?" he asked.

"My right leg will not move," I replied, "and I can barely get the left one to move. I've been trying to tell you how sick I am, but all you want to do is come home late and run straight downstairs to the bathroom! You don't even show up in our room 'til midnight or later. I would've starved by now if it weren't for our precious daughter!"

Something I said must have triggered sympathy in Kevin.

"I'm sorry," he said sincerely. "I didn't realize how bad it was. I'll leave here in a few minutes. I will call Dr. Adams and tell her that I'm bringing you in."

After being sick for weeks, I couldn't believe I was finally going to get some help. I knew Dr. Adams would prescribe some much-needed antibiotics for me, and I could begin recovering. I was tired of watching Kasey take care of me; I wanted to be able to watch movies with her, play games, and take her shopping. It wasn't her place to take care of me, but I was thankful that she was mature beyond her years and capable of taking care of herself.

Within thirty minutes, Kevin was rushing through our bedroom door, apologizing as he entered. He said he was sorry for not taking off work and getting me to the doctor when I first became ill. My body and lungs ached so bad that I couldn't even begin a fuss with him about what a lousy, uncaring husband he had been over the past few weeks. Kevin placed one of his arms underneath my head, and began to lift me from the bed. At the thought of finally getting help, I had no control over my tears as they began to flow. I was so sick, and my only source of survival for the past month had been an eleven-year-old girl bringing me baby aspirin, lunchmeat, and water each day. When Kevin noticed I was crying, he became worried.

"I'm not hurting you am I?" he asked with concern in his voice.

"No, you just don't understand how sick I am. Just get me to Dr. Adams, please," I replied.

I was sitting on the side of the bed, as Kevin continued to support me.

"Now slide down, until your feet are on the floor," Kevin instructed.

I tried to move myself down from the bed, but I could tell that my right leg still had no feeling in it at all, and I could barely move the left one.

"I can't stand up," I told him. "I cannot feel my legs. You're going to have to carry me."

I think embarrassment was setting in with Kevin, as he realized how much he had been neglecting me.

"Don't you worry about anything," he said assuredly. "I will get you there, if I have to carry you all the way."

"You may have to do just that," I replied with a faint smile.

Kevin carried me from our room, down the hallway, and placed me in our car. On our way to the doctor, we dropped Kasey off at her Grandma Martha's. I always hated to be apart from Kasey, but we didn't know how long I would be at Dr. Adams, or if she would send me to the hospital. Kasey kissed me good-bye when we got to Grandma's house, and said, "I hope the doctor gives you good medicine, Mommy. I love you." I told her that I loved her too, and thanked her for taking such good care of me.

Kevin was breaking the speed limit, as he began to realize he hadn't taken care of me at all the past four weeks.

"You don't have to drive so fast," I said. "At least you're finally doing something for me."

"I can't believe how stupid I was. I should've had you to Dr. Adams three weeks ago," he apologized.

I had no argument for him.

"Please just don't work yourself up into an episode. I can't take it right now," I said.

He assured me that he was okay, but was sorry for being a lousy husband.

As we sped into the parking lot at the doctor's office, I told Kevin, "I'm sorry, but I can't walk in. My legs are the same. I still can't feel the right one at all."

Kevin told me not to worry about it, and placed his strong arms under my legs and around my back. He lifted me from the car and proceeded with a slight run, yelling for help as we entered the lobby doors.

"Get the door open, my wife needs Dr. Adams now!" Kevin shouted.

A nurse jumped up and opened a side door, as Kevin carried me in his arms. We caused a scurry of excitement; nurses began to yell, "Get Dr. Adams, quickly!" We were rushed into a room, and Kevin had barely placed me on a table before Dr. Adams walked in.

"What has happened to you Kimi?" she asked.

"I don't know Dr. Adams, but I've been trying to talk to you for three weeks now, and I couldn't get past your nurse. My lungs are filled with fluid, my fever is a constant 103 degrees, and now my legs won't move," I replied.

Dr. Adams placed her stethoscope to my chest, and began to listen. It only took a second.

"You are going straight to the hospital, Kimi. I'm sorry you weren't able to get through to me. I will take care of that, believe me," she said sternly.

Dr. Adams then turned her attention to Kevin.

"You get her straight to the hospital, and don't stop anywhere else. I will call the hospital now. You carry her straight through the front doors, and someone will be waiting to escort her to a room," she said.

Dr. Adams knew of Kevin's Bi-polar Disorder, and would often ask how he was treating me. I don't think she was happy with Kevin for not getting me to her office sooner. Dr. Adams had been my doctor since I was 18. She was not only my parents' doctor, but was also Kevin's family's doctor. She knew all of us by name, and was loved and respected by each one of us.

Dr. Adams' office wasn't far from the hospital, so it didn't take us long to get there. The valet parking made it convenient for Kevin to get me inside quickly. He tossed the keys to the valet attendant and rushed to my side of the car, to lift me out and carry me inside. The sliding glass doors opened, leading us into the main lobby, and our eyes raced to see where to go next. True to her word, Dr. Adams had an orderly waiting at the front door with a wheel chair.

"Are you waiting for someone named Kimi?" Kevin asked the orderly.

"I am," he answered, "and I was ordered to run her immediately to x-ray."

Kevin gently placed me in the wheelchair, and the orderly began a quick sprint through various hallways, finally reaching the *X-rays Only* area. The breeze felt nice on my face as the orderly rushed me through the hospital halls, but I was beginning to feel exhausted. Even lying on a hard table while being x-rayed, sounded wonderful. I hadn't stayed awake or sat up this long in over three weeks. I could tell my fever was high and it felt like there was a huge weight sitting on my chest. The numb feeling in my legs was making me anxious, but I was doing my best to push the negative thoughts from my mind. I just kept telling myself that I needed some antibiotics and all would be fine.

Things were moving very quickly, and before I knew it, the x-rays were finished and I was wheeled to a hospital room. The nurse asked me questions concerning my allergies and things of that nature. Dr. Adams entered my room while the nurse was asking me questions, and the nurse immediately excused herself. Dr. Adams had a concerned look on her face.

"Tell me exactly when you first started feeling sick and everything you can think of from then until now," Dr. Adams said.

I began recalling, as best I could, the week before spring break when Kevin and I had gone into the woods to look for the cat we thought was stuck in a tree.

"I had been feeling tired for some time, but my lungs started to ache during spring break week," I told her.

"What were you eating and drinking during this time?" she asked.

"Kevin would bring me coffee each morning, but I haven't been getting much food. Kasey has tried her best to help me, because Kevin seems to be gone all the time."

I couldn't help but cry, while Dr. Adams patted my shoulder and explained my condition.

"You're a very sick woman, Kimi. I've already looked at your x-ray, and it has me concerned. You definitely have a severe case of pneumonia, but there are other spots that I can't figure out, so I've called in a pulmonary specialist to look at your lungs. I've also called a rheumatologist, as well a doctor that specializes in infectious disease, and an allergist. I'm not sure what all is wrong, but you have five doctors working your case and we will figure out what this is. Try to rest when you can, because each specialist will be in to see you and run whatever tests they feel necessary, and I will be conferring with each of them."

"Dr. Adams, I'm scared because my legs won't move," I told her.

"I'm more concerned with your lungs than I am your legs, at this point," she said as she patted me. "I promise I'm going to do the best I can to figure out what has caused all of this."

I knew she meant it, and I knew I could count on her. Dr. Adams knew all the concerns on my mind; the constant stress I felt over both my parents being in the nursing home, and the daily issues of trying to deal with a Bi-polar husband, not to mention having a young daughter to take care of. I could see the concern in her eyes as she patted me. While she exited my room, she told me to get some rest.

The next morning at 4:30am, the pulmonologist, Dr. Olsen, entered my room. He began listening to my lungs and asking questions about the woods behind our house.

"I've only been in the woods one time, trying to find a crying cat," I said.

"I'm going to perform a procedure on you in a couple hours. I'll give you a light sedative and place a scope, called a bronchoscope, in your mouth," he explained. "It will pass your larynx (voice box) and continue down your trachea (windpipe), so I can see what's taking place in your lungs."

"Exactly how serious is it?" I asked.

"There is definitely something causing a severe infection in your lungs. The infection may be moving into your extremities, which is why you are having trouble moving your legs," he answered. "I feel that if I can isolate what is causing the lung infection, we will know how to treat the remaining symptoms you are experiencing. If I can't see what I need to with the bronchoscope, you will need a more invasive surgical procedure. I have Dr. Sherman on standby, and he will perform the actual surgery, and I will be there as well. It will entail making a small incision in your throat, just below your neck, which will allow us to see a larger area and take any necessary biopsies."

"You're going to cut my throat?" I asked nervously.

"Dr. Sherman has performed this operation many times," he assured me. "He will make the incision as small as possible, but yes, there's always a chance something could go wrong."

Dr. Olsen continued to explain the potential dangers, such as nicking my voice box, which could cause permanent hoarseness; or damaging blood vessels around my trachea, which could cause excessive bleeding and increase complications during the surgery. Despite the dangers, we both knew that I had no choice. I could still hear gurgling in my lungs when I breathed, even though I'd been hooked up to strong IV antibiotics for twelve hours already.

Dr. Olsen said he had already consulted with Dr. Adams and she was in agreement; this was the next advisable procedure and should be done immediately. There was no problem scheduling the procedure; I had only been given a few ice cubes after the IV was inserted in my arm, and no solid foods were ordered for me. I actually didn't mind the miniscule ice cubes, I was hurting so bad that food was the last thing on my mind. Dr. Adams wasn't sure what she and the other specialist would decide was necessary treatment, so she put me on strict orders for IV only.

Kevin was at home, so I called and told him Dr. Olsen was going to do a procedure and it could lead to surgery before noon that day. Kevin said he would shower and head to the hospital. I tried to rest and not think about having my throat cut, or what could possibly go wrong during the procedure. Nurses came and went over the next couple hours, taking my vitals and bringing paperwork for me to sign.

At 11am, an orderly arrived with a wheel chair to take me to the operating room. Dr. Olsen had scheduled a room in case emergency surgery became necessary. Kevin still hadn't arrived, even though I had called him five hours earlier. There I was, alone, facing a scary procedure that I was anxious about, and I had no support and no one to talk to. I couldn't believe my husband wasn't there to support me; it didn't look like Kevin would even show up in time to have prayer with me. Someone must have known I wanted prayer, because a chaplain showed up in the operating room and offered to pray with me. I was almost embarrassed for Kevin, and tried to cover for him. I told the chaplain and nurses that Kevin must have fallen back asleep after I called him, and I was sure he would show up at some point.

I was being moved from the wheelchair to a hard bed when a nurse came over to me and said, "Your husband has just arrived. Do you want to see him? It will have to be quick because Dr. Olsen is ready for us."

"Yes, please," I answered.

I saw the "I'm sorry" in Kevin's eyes, as he bent to give me a kiss.

"Sorry I'm late," he said.

"Thanks for showing up," I replied.

The nurse interrupted and told Kevin that he had to leave because the doctor was ready for me. At that point, I didn't want to think about Kevin or how disappointed I was in him. I just needed to pray and trust my Lord.

Dr. Olsen asked me if I was ready, and I nodded my head yes. He explained that I would be sedated, but not completely "knocked out" for the bronchoscope. The nurse said, "Okay, here comes some happy medicine," and I was out. That's all I remembered, until suddenly my eyes opened and I was wide-awake with a tube down my throat. I couldn't breathe and began grabbing at Dr. Olsen's arms. I wasn't struggling for air for more than a second or two, when I must have been given more "happy medicine." The next time I woke up, I was in recovery. Dr. Olsen ended up having to call in Dr. Sherman to do surgery; he removed six enlarged lymph nodes and was sending them off for further testing.

The nurse said the doctor would be in my room to talk to me after I was more awake. When I was wheeled back to my room, Kevin was there, doing something on our laptop computer. He put the laptop down and helped the nurses get me back into bed. My throat was sore and I was instructed to not speak for the next few hours. I was very sleepy and just wanted to rest, but I noticed that Kevin immediately went back to his chair and began doing something on the laptop, as soon as I started to close my eyes.

We weren't techy people and didn't pay bills on the computer or anything of that sort, so I couldn't imagine why Kevin had even brought a computer to the hospital. We only purchased the laptop because Kevin said he could keep up with e-mails from work, and play games on it with Kasey. I was already regretting having the computer in our home. Kevin was either running off to the bathroom with his I-Pac or going downstairs to check e-mails on the laptop, for hours at a time. This new technology seemed to be taking all of his at-home time away from Kasey and I. He rarely played any games with her, like he said he was going to when we purchased the computer. Now he couldn't even sit with me in the hospital without bringing it.

I wasn't sure how long I had slept, but I awoke to find Dr. Adams, Dr. Olsen, and Dr. Roy, the rheumatologist, standing at the foot of my bed. Dr. Adams began by saying they had news about what they had found so far. I listened intently as each one of them explained what they felt was causing my problems, and what tests they each felt were still necessary.

"Your lungs are heavily infected and mold is actively growing on your lungs," Dr. Olsen announced.

I listened to terminology that I didn't understand; however, I understood my diagnosis. I had Histoplasmosis and possible Sarcoidosis, and mold was growing on my lungs. None of the doctor's had heard of mold growing on someone's lungs and they weren't sure how it happened. I was placed on very strong anti-fungal medication, which I would have to take for a minimum of six months.

The allergist had examined my records and felt he had nothing more to add to the other doctors' conclusions, so he excused himself and said he would be glad to see me, if I needed him. I never did actually see him during my hospital stay; his work was done behind the scenes. I felt that the three doctors in front of me were the best in their fields, and I was content and confident with the care I was receiving. I was told that Dr. Todd, who specialized in infectious diseases, was reviewing my case and would be in to talk to me the following day. I asked Dr. Adams if I could speak with her, as the other doctor's were leaving my room. She came close to the side of my bed, and patted my hand.

"Am I going to be okay?" I asked.

"I'm sure trying sweetie," Dr. Adams answered. "I have the best doctors looking at you, and if they can't get to the bottom of what's wrong, then no one can."

I asked her about their findings, and she explained that Histoplasmosis results from bird droppings.

"It could have laid dormant in your system until something invaded your immune system and weakened it," she explained. "I'm very perplexed about the mold growing on your lungs. Dr. Todd is very knowledgeable about infectious diseases. He's intently studying the lung images Dr. Olsen took, and he feels your case is very interesting."

Dr. Adams took her time in speaking with me, which I greatly appreciated.

More blood tests were taken and I had to take breathing treatments for my lungs. I noticed my fever was getting better, and came less frequently. I just wanted to get better and go home. I missed my sweet Kasey and I wanted a normal life again. Much to my surprise,

Bobbie and Lucas came to check on me. I was also visited by one of my cousins, and some people from my parent's church. Bobbie even surprised me with a cup of McDonald's coffee on three different mornings. I really appreciated her being there, and hoped we could become closer as sisters-in-law. Kevin spent very little time at the hospital with me. Kasey was being taken to and from school, then spending the rest of her time at her Grandma Martha's; I missed her so much. Each day consisted of waiting for the next lab tech to draw blood, or an orderly to wheel me down for another chest x-ray.

A week passed, and the panel of doctors had gained no further insight as to why mold was growing on my lungs, or why I had developed an autoimmune disorder and Histoplasmosis. Lupus was ruled out. Lymphoma was ruled out. There was still no explanation for the six enlarged lymph nodes that were removed during surgery. Apparently, it was much easier to tell me what I *didn't* have wrong with me, instead of what was causing my illness.

Finally, Dr. Adams said all my doctors felt they had ran every test they knew of. After looking at all of the results, there was nothing more to add to their findings. They were sending me home with an inhaler for my lungs, along with strong anti-fungal medication and antibiotics. I was given instructions for protecting my lungs, and arranged follow up appointments with Dr. Todd, the rheumatologist, and Dr. Olsen, the pulmonologist. Dr. Adams talked to me in length about her concern over the mold that was growing on my lungs. She wanted me to see her every three or four weeks for the next six months, possibly for the next year.

I eagerly called Kevin to tell him that I was being released from the hospital. There was no answer, so I left a message and waited for him to return my call. Within a couple hours, Kevin arrived at the hospital, and we began the long process of signing discharge documents and gathering my items from the hospital room.

After a stop at the pharmacy, we were headed home. I knew exactly what I wanted as soon as we got there; I wanted to make a pot of fresh, hot coffee. Drinking hospital coffee was like drinking grounds that were diluted through a dishtowel. The color didn't even look like coffee, but rather like a weak cup of tea. I preferred a strong cup of coffee that was definitely black in color. Kevin must have read my mind.

"Would you like some good breakfast blend coffee when you get in the house?" he asked.

"You know I do!" I replied excitedly.

We smiled at each other, yet there was a distance between us I couldn't figure out. Something just didn't feel right.

Kevin helped me into the house because my legs were still very weak, and my right leg didn't want to move when I told it to. I still had the walking stick Dad had given me after our car wreck in 2000; the walking stick and I were going to be companions once again. Kevin walked me towards the kitchen, and sat me down at the kitchen island as he turned towards our coffee maker. Kevin filled the coffee pot with water, and then stopped.

"When was the last time you checked the filter on this coffee maker?" he asked.

"What do you mean, filter? What filter?" I replied.

Kevin was already pulling something from the back of my coffee maker.

"This filter," he said. "Wow! Look at that! There is slime and mold all over this!"

I watched as he pulled a long, slender, plastic piece (which housed the filter) from the water reservoir on my coffee maker. There was long, green slime hanging from the filter sleeve. I couldn't believe what I was seeing.

"You've been bringing me coffee from that for weeks. Why didn't you notice it?" I questioned.

"I had no idea. I just thought about the filter when I started to make the coffee," Kevin replied.

An unusual feeling came over me, just like the day when the propane tank was leaking and Kevin told me to get the car out of the garage. Many thoughts flooded my mind; Kevin knew I was highly allergic to mold. In fact, he knew all of my allergies and ailments. He also knew that I never went a day without coffee. Kevin *made sure* he brought me a cup every morning while I was sick.

Recovery was long and difficult. I didn't like using an inhaler, but my lungs still wheezed, and I knew I had to keep it with me. I kept my medications close to me and was cautious about the color, shape, and size of each pill I took. My inhaler was kept under my pillow, and I became diligent about fixing my own food, unless Kasey was bringing me something. The autoimmune disease had made me weak and I spent a lot of time in bed over the next several weeks.

Kevin would take time off work to drive me to and from my various doctor appointments. I remembered to tell Dr. Adams about Kevin showing me the green slime that was all over my coffee filter sleeve. As I explained it to her, Dr. Adams raised an eyebrow and slightly turned her head.

"Oh really?" she responded. "Now that's interesting. Hmm... How has Kevin been doing with his illness?"

I talked to her briefly about how distant Kevin was acting, and that I didn't have a good feeling about the mold; I had found an article on our computer's history, about how to grow mold. I told her about the propane tank incident and other similar episodes.

"I think it would benefit you to speak with a counselor, Kimi. You've been through a lot, and now with both of your parents sick with Alzheimer's... I don't see how you do it," Dr. Adams said.

I thanked her for the advice.

"I pray a lot, and that is my counsel," I replied.

She smiled and said she would see me the following month.

It felt like my life consisted of doctor visits, medicine, and feeling bad most days. I was too young for this to be happening to me, and I didn't understand why it seemed like something was always going wrong in my life. A lot of nighttime prayers were ended with a tear soaked pillow. I found myself crying almost every day. Kevin seemed to be distant from me, even when he was home. Many nights I would cry myself to sleep, with my back turned to him.

Summer of 2004 was approaching and we decided that a trip to Destin, Florida, would be nice; perhaps the ocean air would help me heal. I was still weak, but was excited about sitting in a beach chair and watching the waves roll across the white sand. I had a love for the ocean before I ever saw it with my own eyes. Pictures in magazines made it appear to be a place where magic happened and dreams came true. I believed Kevin and I would be okay if we could just live near the beach one day.

We arrived in Florida, to sunny skies and beautiful waves rolling toward the shore. Kasey was so excited; it was contagious. Funny how the world can seem so much brighter when you view it from the smiling eyes of a child. We changed into our swimsuits and gathered our items for the beach. It was so nice to look out at the beauty of the ocean. The water was so blue, and the sunlight danced like diamonds glittering across the water's surface. We were having a wonderful vacation so far, and it felt like the sunshine and salt air were healing my lungs.

Evenings consisted of finding a nice restaurant, then playing some putt-putt golf or driving around and taking in the sites. One evening, we decided to drive to some outlet stores in a popular shopping area. Kevin was excited when he saw a Bose store, and I spotted a purse shop across the parking lot from the Bose store that I wanted to check out. Kasey chose to go into the Bose store with her Dad. I told them that I would just walk across to look at some purses, and be right back. It sounded like an easy arrangement; however, it turned out to be a terrible decision on my part.

It was getting dark, and as I headed across the parking lot, I began to feel fatigued. My legs were unsteady, and I realized I shouldn't have tried to walk across an uneven cobblestone parking lot by myself. I was about halfway across the street when my right foot hit an uneven stone and I went tumbling facedown. It all happened so fast. I didn't think I could take the pain of my chest hitting the ground, so I quickly tried to turn and catch myself. Unfortunately, my right elbow took the weight of the fall. I heard a loud pop and pain surged through my arm.

I could see headlights coming towards me, as I lay in the pathway of an oncoming car, on the dark cobblestones. A couple of ladies and their husbands came running to my aid, waving their arms for the car to stop. They tried to lift me, but my arm was hurting and my legs were extremely weak. I couldn't get up. I began to cry and tried to tell them that my husband and daughter were in the Bose store. Two of the men said they would go let Kevin know I had fallen down and was hurt. I expected Kevin to come rushing to help me, but all I saw was the two men coming back. They said they yelled for a Kevin Burghess, but no one answered. I begged the men to try again, because I knew Kevin and Kasey were both in there. The men agreed to go back into the store, and the ladies stayed by my side, trying to direct cars away from me. Finally, I saw Kevin and Kasey come running towards me.

We thanked the couples for all of their help, and for staying with me. Kevin carried me to our van and we rushed to the local hospital. After a long stay in the emergency room, my elbow was x-rayed and I was told that it was broken. I was put in a sling and given a prescription for pain medication. We eventually left the hospital and headed back to our hotel. I just wanted to crawl into bed and cry myself to sleep. Just when I thought I was feeling better, I had to have a bad fall and break my elbow. It felt like someone had put a curse on me. I just wanted a normal life, without things going wrong all the time.

As my thoughts spiraled into my own private pity party, I glanced at the sweet, caring face of my precious daughter. When I felt like crying, I just thought of her. I could never be sure what Kevin was going to act like, but I knew I could count on the relationship between Kasey and I. We were best friends and I prayed we would always stay that way.

CHAPTER FIFTEEN

NOVEMBER 13TH, 2004

This date will forever be etched into my memory. It was one month before Kevin and I were to celebrate our 18th Wedding Anniversary. In fact, the 13th of every month was always a date we recognized. Kevin's Mom would often bake us a cake or find some way to help us enjoy all of our 13th's. However, this November was a cruel turning point in our marriage, and a challenge to all that my faith stood for.

Kevin arrived home from work late Friday evening on November 12th. He said he had fallen asleep in his car in the parking lot at work. I told him it seemed like he was doing that a lot lately; it had been happening at least once a week for the past several weeks. Dinner was always cold by the time he got home, and I was never able to reach him on his cell phone, which left me wondering if he had been in a wreck or simply had to work overtime. A couple years before, a man we knew from church was killed on the same road that Kevin traveled for work; the man had fallen asleep on his way home from work, so my worries were not unwarranted.

Kevin gave me a quick kiss along with a brief apology, and said he needed to go downstairs to the bathroom before he ate dinner. It was about 7pm and I had kept his dinner warm for over an hour already.

"Okay, but please hurry. I've been waiting to eat supper with you," I said, as he headed to the basement.

The minutes slowly turned into an hour, so I finally went downstairs and knocked on the bathroom door.

"Are you awake?" I asked.

"Sorry, I fell asleep. I'll be up in a few minutes," Kevin answered.

I decided to go ahead and put the food on our plates and get the table set for dinner. Then I waited and I waited. One hour eventually turned into two; I went back down the stairs and knocked more strongly.

"You need to come eat dinner now. It's on the table and I've waited two hours," I said.

"Sorry, I fell asleep again," Kevin replied.

As I turned to head back up the stairs, something went through my mind; it was as if I heard someone say, "Liar." A feeling came over me that I couldn't explain, but it was an anxious feeling; the kind you get in your gut right before you get bad news.

Kevin finally came upstairs to eat, but dinner wasn't pleasant. I just stared at him as he explained that he was so tired, he would fall asleep any time he sat down.

"That's why I'm always telling you 1am shouldn't be bedtime, yet you go downstairs every night lately, and don't come to bed until 1am or later," I replied.

"I know. I go downstairs to the bathroom and end up falling asleep on the toilet. Believe me, I don't want to. It isn't comfortable," Kevin responded.

"That's why I'm constantly asking you to go to our master bathroom, so I can wake you if you fall asleep," I said.

That was the extent of our dinner conversation. After Kevin had finished eating, he stood up and looked at me for a moment.

"I need to go to the bathroom again. I'll be back upstairs in just a little bit. I promise I won't be long," he said.

I couldn't believe my ears. It was after 10 o'clock at night and Kevin was going back downstairs. I was beginning to notice that he always took his phone with him. He didn't help with the dishes or even offer to pick up his own plate and carry it to the sink. It was as if he expected me to have his dinner ready, put it on the table, and cleanup everything when *his majesty* was finished. He hadn't always been that way.

When we first got married, Kevin would help with dishes and would even vacuum. His actions had gotten progressively more self-centered over the past few months. He was even less attentive to me in his "husbandly duties," which wasn't like Kevin at all. Despite all of the Bi-polar episodes we dealt with throughout the years, we never lost the intimacy of our marriage and romance never became dull. So for Kevin to not be in our bed at night, but rather in a downstairs bathroom asleep on the toilet, I knew there was a problem.

The one thing I had always been assured of during our difficult times was the fact that, even though I had to endure his Bi-polar episodes, I never had to worry about his love and fidelity. Kevin would sometimes teach Sunday School, if our teacher needed to be out of town. He would always stress the importance of being faithful in your marriage; it was not okay to look at other people. He would quote Christ's own words that, "If a person even looks at another person with lust in their heart, they have committed adultery."

The security of our wedding vows helped me endure many difficult Bi-polar episodes. We married in sickness and in health, and Kevin knew I would stand by his side through anything, because the only excuse for divorce was adultery.

I had been reared to accept adultery as the only reason God would grant a divorce, and free a person to re-marry without the shame of living in sin. Kevin shared the same beliefs I did, and didn't hold back in telling other couples it wasn't okay to look, even if you didn't touch. He would say that you shouldn't look because, *eventually*, you will give in to temptation and take it to the next step. I heard Kevin tell this to so many people throughout the years that I had no reason to believe he would ever betray our marriage vows. The security of his total fidelity helped me to hold true to my promise of "in sickness and in health."

Some time around 1:30am, Kevin crawled into bed. I had given up shortly past midnight and decided I wasn't going back downstairs to wake him up if he had fallen asleep again. His late nights were taking a toll on me; I was the one who turned the alarm off at 6am every morning, and had to wake him up, get breakfast fixed, and pack his lunch. It was 1:30am and he decided I should wake up because he wanted to *be* with me.

"I'm tired of your 1 o'clock escapades, and you crawling into bed whenever you feel like it and waking me up," I said.

I couldn't believe what came out of his mouth, as I heard him reply, "I don't see anything wrong with 1am, and you should wake up for me whenever I want you to."

I wasn't in a very Christian mood at that point.

"You can kiss my a— and that's as close to sex as you're going to get tonight!" I said angrily.

It was obvious that he had pushed the wrong buttons and wasn't going to get anywhere with me, so Kevin roughly turned over with his back to me.

"Fine then!" he exclaimed.

Needless to say, I couldn't go back to sleep. My insides were all messed up; I felt like screaming and crying at the same time. I spent the next hour quietly praying and asking God what was wrong with Kevin. Tears flowed as I prayed in silence; I was doing my best to put up with Kevin's illness, but this was something different. This wasn't Bi-polar talk, this was just pure meanness towards me, and I couldn't figure out why.

At some point through the night, I fell asleep while praying. The alarm came too quickly, even for a Saturday morning, and I was exhausted. However, I had received something from God during my prayer time. I heard Him tell me, "Don't be afraid to ask Kevin for the truth. There is something he needs to tell you."

I knew I had to do what I was told, even though I might not like what I was going to hear. My mind raced with possibilities, such as online gambling or something addictive like that. Kevin's extra cash always seemed to disappear. Anytime I would question a missing twenty or forty dollars, he would say that someone was always "passing a hat" at work; taking up money for a co-worker in need, or flowers for a funeral, or money for a "feed." I always believed his excuses for the disappearing cash.

I had no way to prepare my ears, heart, and soul for what I was about to hear. The entire eighteen years of my marriage and relationship with Kevin was about to be laid bare before God.

Kevin and I had breakfast and began various household chores. Kasey was going to play at a friend's house, so I took her to see her friend, and came home to a mess. Kevin was supposed to put the laundry in the dryer and finish cleaning the kitchen; however, everything was just like I left it and, once again, he was in the downstairs bathroom.

I began rehearsing all the things I wanted to say to Kevin, hoping I could come up with something that would make him change his lazy behavior. He wasn't lifting a finger to do anything around the house. In fact, earlier that week, I went to Wal-Mart and asked Kevin to simply heat Kasey's dinner while I was gone. When I returned, I found out he had immediately gone downstairs to the bathroom, and never even heated her dinner. Kasey said she knocked on the bathroom door and told him she was hungry, but he wouldn't answer her. He had become so self-absorbed by *something* that he didn't even care if his child was hungry.

I heard Kevin coming up the stairway and I said a quick prayer, asking God to help me face whatever Kevin was going to tell me. I walked back towards our bedroom, and I could hear Kevin coming down the hallway behind me.

"So, do you think you can stay out of the bathroom long enough for us to have a talk?" I asked. "Do you realize how many hours a day you're spending in the bathroom?"

A strange look came across Kevin's face. I couldn't figure out what his expression was telling me.

"Do you need to see a doctor?" I questioned. "Is there some medical condition or problem you don't want to tell me about? Three to four hours a day in the bathroom is ridiculous, Kevin."

Then his expression became clear. Tears rolled down his face as he raised his hands towards heaven and looked upward.

"I am so, so sorry," he began.

I immediately thought, *He must be sick and has been researching what-ever it is, on his phone at night.* I started to move towards him to hug him, but he stopped me.

"No, don't. You don't deserve what I have done to you," he said.

The minute those words came out of his mouth, something moved through me. I stepped back and took hold of a chair, near the foot of our bed. As I grabbed the chair tightly, Kevin fell to his knees, sobbing uncontrollably.

"You're going to hate me forever! I've ruined everything! It's all over," he cried.

Both of my hands gripped the back of the chair, as I stood there unable to feel the floor beneath my feet. Refusing to give in to my legs that were beginning to buckle beneath me, I held tightly to the chair, my hands turning white from my strong grip. Unstoppable tears filled my eyes and fell to the floor. I knew this would be much worse than overcoming one of Kevin's Bi-polar episodes.

Kevin's tears were as thick and heavy as mine. I became his confessor that day, as he unloaded eighteen years of betrayal and deceit, at my feet. He remained in a kneeling position and kept his face covered.

"I have committed adultery all eighteen years of our marriage. I'm hooked on pornography and I am a sex addict," he confessed.

I was truly speechless. The more I listened to his confessions, the more confused and sick I felt. He began to tell me that it started in Hawaii, on our honeymoon.

"I noticed a couple of women in the lobby when we were checking in. I could tell they weren't *guests* at the hotel. When I told you that I was using the hotel lobby bathroom, I was really meeting them," Kevin said.

I just stood there, frozen in disbelief. Why didn't I realize? How could I have been so dumb?

So many things now made sense. When an unexpected letter had come in the mail from the Red Cross, stating that Kevin's blood donation had been rejected, he told me I was reading it all wrong and it was just a *false positive* to Hepatitis B. I believed him, and tried to put the letter out of my mind. Six months later, a second letter came and stated that, due to a second positive test to the core antibodies to Hepatitis B, the Red Cross could no longer accept Kevin's blood donations and his name was being put on a *list*. Even after the second letter, he told me it was nothing for me to concern myself with, and he would get it straightened out. Now I realized that God had allowed me to see those letters, and was trying to let me know Kevin was not only living an immoral life, but was putting my health in jeopardy. As all of this rushed through my mind and I looked at Kevin kneeling before me, a wall went up inside of me I had never felt for him before.

"Hell couldn't be hot enough for you!" I shouted.

I had put up with emotional, verbal, and physical abuse, year after year, because I wanted to honor my marriage vows and take care of Kevin in sickness and in health. He had put me through so much, and I stayed loyal to him, yet all the while he was living a secret life of debauchery and lust, with total disregard for me, and his daughter. Kevin had made himself the king of his own private universe. I felt like a pawn that he had used to provide him with nice homes, luxury cars, and extra cash for his filthy lusts.

The night went from hours of confessions, to Kevin lying prostrate on the floor, begging me to pray the demons out of him.

"I got so bad that I scared myself about how far I was going. I shocked myself over some of the things I got into," Kevin admitted.

"How could you do this to me?" I asked. "Kevin, I've been here for you, year after year. I have stayed up into the wee hours of the morning, holding you and ignoring my own feelings, just to get you through your Bi-polar episodes."

"You have to understand that it had nothing to do with you," he replied. "I love you; I don't love any of them. You're on a pedestal to me. You are the love of my life. After you see enough naked women, they just become bodies and there's nothing personal about it."

"There were many times throughout the years that I wanted to tell you, but I just couldn't," Kevin continued. "I knew what you believed, and I knew adultery was your way out. There were a couple times I almost told you what I was doing. Once was after church, and another time was after we prayed together before bed."

The more I asked Kevin how he could possibly be so cold-hearted and deceitful, the more he beat the floor with his fists, until he finally answered me.

"I wasn't going to give up my sexuality for you or Jesus Christ himself!" Kevin shouted.

A silence filled the room momentarily, as Kevin made his bold statement. I believe he heard his own words and realized the evil that lurked within him. He began to sob uncontrollably. Through his tears, he begged me for help.

"I know I'm asking a lot from you, but I have no one else to ask. Will you please, please, pray for me?" Kevin asked. "I don't want to live like this and I don't want to lose you. I'm asking you as a Christian, if you will lay hands on me and pray the demon or whatever this is, out of me."

I couldn't believe his audacity! Asking for prayer from me, when he had used my faith against me for eighteen years!

"No!" I replied. "You don't realize what you're asking of me. I can't go to my Lord in prayer with un-forgiveness in my heart. In order to pray for you, I have to forgive you! I can't stand you right now. I hate you for what you've done to me!"

My faith and what I claimed to believe was being put to a test. Not only was I being asked to forgive Kevin for unspeakable infidelities, but I also wasn't being given any time to process the information he had unloaded on me. Kevin was asking me to accept his betrayal and immediately offer forgiveness; not only for what he had already confessed, but also for all the things he had not yet had time to confess. I can't explain the power that began to fill our bedroom. Kevin remained prostrate on the floor, his huge sobs watering the carpet beneath him.

"Please, help me! I know how much you love Jesus, and I know you can do this," he cried out. "You are my only hope; there is no one else I can ask. God listens when you pray!"

My throat, my heart, and my body began to ache from the weight of my tears; the tears were heavy and exhausting.

"You don't deserve my prayers!" I yelled angrily.

"No I don't, but *you* deserve to give them," Kevin replied.

I knew I had no choice. Kevin had pushed my faith to limits most people don't face. The evil within him had tried to kill me on numerous occasions, but asking me to pray for him was almost worse than the physical attacks.

It's sometimes easy to look at someone and tell them they're forgiven for a certain indiscretion or action that hurt you, but praying for them takes it to another level. I knew all too well, from dealing with my biological mother, that I could look at Kevin and say I forgave him. Praying for God to help and heal him, and to genuinely ask for forgiveness for my own anger towards Kevin, just wasn't fair. I deserved time to process all of the adultery and terrible sins he had confessed to me. I deserved time to be angry with him. Once again, Kevin was turning the circumstances in his direction. It was all about helping him and ignoring what he had done to me.

I dropped to my knees, and begged, "God help me! I can't stand my husband right now! Help me pray for him. Help me not to hate him!"

I'm not sure how long I prayed, but my eyes and my entire body ached under the weight of the tears. In fact, the word "tears" is too light for what was occurring. It was more than just tears; it was an ache and pain from deep down in my soul. All eighteen years were wasted! I felt like such an idiot. I had given Kevin the best years of my life, believing in a future when his illness could be controlled and our love could be restored, with no more episodes to deal with. How could he betray me?

I remained in prayer, begging for God's help. I wasn't even sure what I wanted help with. Part of me just wanted God to make Kevin hurt as much as he had hurt me, but then there was still a thread of love for Kevin that I couldn't ignore. My prayer was interrupted as I heard Kevin's voice get louder. His sobs were heavy, and I could hear the pain in his voice.

"God help her deal with what I've done to her! Help her God!" he cried.

Kevin was still lying facedown, prostrate on the floor, when he began asking God to help me. Something inside of me heard, "This must be love."

Love seeks not her own; is not easily provoked; Love thinks no evil; Love bears all things, believes all things, hopes all things, and endures all things.

Kevin and I had a love that pushed us to the limits of a Godly love that few people in the world believe truly exists. This was it: true, unconditional love. He was crying out to God for me, and I, for him.

I went to Kevin's side, placed my right hand on his head, and began to pray for him. Despite his confessions of betrayal against me, I couldn't bear to see my husband cry out in pain for his sins. God always forgives, and Kevin's burden would be lighter because of God's love.

I now understood the words he spoke during and after so many terrible, violent Bi-polar episodes. His heavy pain of feeling worthless was because of how deeply he was sinning against not only me, but against God. Kevin had caused his illness to become more severe year after year, with each betrayal. He was in a constant battle against himself. A verse was brought to my mind from Ephesians 6: "*For we wrestle not against flesh and blood, but against principalities, against powers, against the rulers of darkness...*"

The moment I was willing to lay hands on him and pray, the battle against principalities and powers began in our room. Kevin remained prostrate on the floor, as he cried out to God for forgiveness. As he yelled out, confessing unthinkable sins, I continued to lay hands on him, begging Jesus to take the demons from him. Kevin began to heave and said he was going to throw up; I knew it was a demon leaving, so I screamed for it to leave him in the name of Jesus, and by every drop of blood Christ shed on Calvary. The battle continued for hours, as Kevin confessed and I remained in prayer. Some confessions brought images to my mind I knew I would never forget, but I had to put aside human feelings and keep my spirit linked with the Holy Spirit, and continue in prayer. This was no time for *self*.

Several hours passed and Kevin's confessions began to slow, and then he began to pray for me. He prayed that God would heal the pain that he had caused. He prayed for our marriage to be healed, but then he added, "I know it's my fault Lord, and she deserves so much better.

Please just bring her someone that will love her like she deserves, and will be good to our daughter." It was a true, selfless prayer. When he finished, he began to sit up. I knew we were both exhausted, but I told him I didn't think we were done. I could feel there was still something left undone or unsaid.

"I know, I feel it too," he said, "but I have to stop now. I need a break."

We agreed to pray again later that night or the next day.

Our marriage was now changed, and I didn't know what path it would take. I didn't know if I would divorce him, or keep trying to forgive him and trust that he could be faithful. One thing I did know for sure was that only *true* love would cause him to cry out and beg God to help me get over what he had done. Love had shown up through all the pain. As complicated and messed up as it sounds, Kevin and I demonstrated the love found in 1 Corinthians 13 that day.

CHAPTER SIXTEEN

DECEMBER 23rd, 2004

Our relationship was strained, but we continued to communicate, and remained together in the house. This was the worst time of the year Kevin could have picked, to open up about the secret life he had led. Although unintentional, we had not yet resumed prayers from the day of his confessions. I knew *something* still wasn't right; I could feel it when he was near me. Despite all of that, we had to think of our sweet Kasey, and make sure she had a wonderful birthday and happy holidays. After many conversations, I agreed that I would not make any decision about divorce until after the Holiday Season. It was obvious my birthday and our anniversary were already ruined. As difficult as it might be, we had to suppress the realities of our broken marriage, and remain a family until January.

It was December 23rd, 2004, and Kevin was late getting home from work. We had made prior arrangements to spend the evening wrapping all of Kasey's Christmas presents. Kevin said he wouldn't be working overtime and we would have the entire evening to get the wrapping finished. It was approaching 9pm; I hadn't heard anything from Kevin, and I knew he wasn't scheduled for overtime. He should have been home at 6pm to have dinner with Kasey and I, but once again, it was just the two of us.

At approximately 11 o'clock that evening, I heard Kevin coming up the driveway. He stayed in the car for quite a while before coming in the house. Finally, he decided to come inside. I was sitting at the dining room table, wrapping Kasey's Christmas presents. There was no heartfelt apology, just a flimsy excuse for his absence.

"I meant to call," Kevin began, "but there was a supervisor meeting and a feed for the guys, and I just lost track of time."

My gut told me there was a lot more to the story, as to why he was so late. Nevertheless, I didn't want to start anything with him, so I continued wrapping the presents. Kevin sat down at the dining room table and just watched. He didn't offer to help with Kasey's gifts, or even offer to tear a piece of tape. I stayed silent for as long as I could, but finally, I'd had enough.

"Do you think you could show some interest in Kasey's Christmas presents, and at least wrap one of them?" I asked sharply.

Kevin just looked back at me blankly.

"I need to tell you something else," he said.

I didn't want to hear any more of his confessions; I just wanted it to all go away. I wanted to go back to believing that our only problem was his illness, and that if he had just stayed on his medicine, none of the other *things* would have happened. I desperately wanted to believe that he truly loved me, and I wasn't just used. I was trying to decide what to say back to him, when he began talking.

"I just thought you ought to know that I always wondered if Sasha's first child, was mine," he said.

I couldn't believe he was saying this to me, after 18 years! How could he talk about some woman he dated before we met, while I sat there wrapping presents for our precious daughter? The very thought of him having another child sent venom through my core. I glared at him with a mother's vengeance.

"No person better ever walk up to me and try to get half of what Kasey deserves," I said angrily. "She and I are the ones who have suffered through your fits of rage. I think you're just trying to start something anyway, and I don't want to hear it!"

Instead of apologizing for his ignorance in approaching such a subject, he just got up from the table.

"I'll be in our room," he said as he headed down the hall.

I could tell he was upset with himself and knew he had stirred something up inside of me he should have left alone.

It took me about an hour to finish wrapping all of the Christmas presents. I hadn't heard anything from Kevin since he stormed off, and decided to go check on him. I headed down the hallway to our bedroom; when I opened the door, I saw him sitting on the floor in front of his closet. His head was tucked down between his knees, and I could tell he had been crying.

"I wanted to see if you were okay," I said. "I finished wrapping all of Kasey's presents by myself, since you decided to run off and leave everything to me."

The words had barely left my mouth, when Kevin suddenly jumped up from the floor. With fire in his eyes, he swung his large fist at my face. It came across my jaw with such great force that it knocked me backwards onto our bed.

"You will never be able to forgive me!" Kevin screamed as he hit me. "I've messed everything up! You can never love me again!"

I was stunned and in a lot of pain, and I could tell this was the beginning of a terrible episode. While I lay helpless on the bed, still hurting from Kevin's hit, I saw him run to our bathroom and grab a washcloth from our vanity. I will never forget what he did next.

As I tried to raise myself from the bed, Kevin came rushing towards me again. He shoved me backwards and jumped on top of me, using his knees to hold my arms down. He stuffed the washcloth into my mouth, trying to force it down my throat. While he shoved the washcloth with one hand, he used his other hand to pinch my nose shut. Survival instinct kicked in as I fought to draw a breath of air. He continued to press his weight down on me, but I kept fighting. Desperately seeking air, I turned my head from side to side, trying to get the washcloth out of my mouth and free my nose from his strong grip. The whole time I fought, he continued to scream at the top of his lungs, "If I can't have you, no one will!"

I managed to get the washcloth out of my mouth a few times, but each time Kevin would shove it right back in until it felt like it was down my throat. The washcloth had been forced into my mouth so many times that it was ripping my lips open. I could taste the blood as it dripped into my mouth. I simply didn't have the strength to fight against him, especially when he was in a rage this severe. Kevin was a very strong man and he loved lifting weights. Even when he wasn't in a rage, he was much stronger than the average person; certainly not the kind of guy you would want to challenge to a fight. However, when a manic Bi-polar episode was boiling inside of him, he had the strength of a gorilla. A small, 5'3" woman like me was absolutely no match for his power.

My only defense, my only chance for survival, was Jesus. I had my faith, and that was something *no one* could take away from me. Believe me, when you're being suffocated by someone who is bigger and far more powerful than you, that's when you find out how much faith you really have. At that moment, you will find out whether or not you truly believe that Jesus loves you. I was getting tired, and it was becoming harder and harder to get air; I had no choice but to rely on God to renew my strength to fight. As I continued turning my head from side to side, Kevin would occasionally lose his grip on my nose, allowing me to catch a quick breath. I wasn't going down without a fight; if not for myself, then to protect Kasey from her Bi-polar Dad, whose illness was getting worse by the day.

The moments seemed to be passing in slow motion. As I prayed for help and protection, I just kept kicking and fighting to survive. Finally, I rallied all of my strength and rolled over, knocking Kevin off of me momentarily. I quickly reached for the phone and dialed 911, but his hand crushed down on mine and he yanked my arm, causing the phone to fall from my grip. He took hold of the phone cord and ripped it from the wall. Then I noticed Kevin's cell phone and tried to grab for it. Kevin snatched his phone before I could, and held it in front of my face. His face turned blood red and he made a loud Hulk-like scream, and then twisted his cell phone until it broke in half. I had no way of knowing if my call for help had gone any further than our bedroom, but either way, I would continue to fight against his rage.

God would help me. Somehow. Someway.

Perhaps the reality that my 911 attempt might have gone through, and police could show up, was what caused Kevin to loosen his grip on me. The moment I felt his hand loosen around my arm, I pulled away from him as hard as I could and took off running down the hallway. It was late, and all I had on was my nightgown. I had a plan, but I didn't have shoes, gloves, or even a hat, to help me with what I was about to do.

Our area had been hit by a severe snowstorm a couple days earlier, and the entire neighborhood was quiet. Over two feet of snow covered most of the yards, and streets were closed due to the storm. The words of Kevin's psychiatrist rushed through my mind; the doctor had explained the sequence of events, once a Bi-polar has decided on suicide and the murder of his family. Now that I was free from Kevin, all I could think of was getting to Kasey and protecting her from his rage; she was spending the night at her Uncle Mark's, the next street over. I knew that if Kevin killed me, our sweet Kasey would be next. I had no choice but to try and get to her before he did.

Remembering the Bible story of Lot's wife looking back and turning into a pillar of salt, I kept my eyes focused on what was *ahead* of me as I ran. I headed straight down the hallway, towards the kitchen, and mentally mapped out my path to Kasey. I would go through our garage, down the driveway, and then follow the street to Mark's house. The Lord would protect me and get me to Kasey, despite the snow; I knew I had to keep looking ahead and trust God.

There was no time to look for shoes or a coat. I was wearing only a thin gown to keep me warm, and I was barefoot, but I had to keep going. As I approached the back door, an unusual sight was before me. My fur coat, which was always in the closet under a protective cover, was hanging on a small hook beside the back door. Kevin's work boots, which were always in the shoe bin, weren't just by the door, but were actually sitting with toes pointed towards the door. They were unlaced, as if they were waiting for me to take them and run.

I didn't miss a single stride or step. I quickly pulled the coat off the wall with my left hand, jumped straight into Kevin's big work boots, and opened the back door with my right hand. I was prepared to run for my life through two feet of snow, and freezing temperatures. I had to make it.

Following my mental map, I made my way through the garage and down the driveway. As I ran from our house into the snow-covered streets, the air was freezing my throat with each breath I took. I prayed while I ran, literally crying out for the Lord.

"Jesus, help me," I prayed. "Protect my lungs, feet, and hands. Please help me get to Kasey before Kevin tries to hurt her!"

My lungs had not fully recovered from the mold and Histoplasmosis I suffered from earlier in the year. Once this nightmare was over, I was sure I would face pneumonia. I could see each breath I took, and the cold air began to bring pain to my lungs. It was so surreal, running alone down the silent, snow-glistening streets. Each house was dark; neighbors were safely asleep in their beds. If only someone could have heard my cries for help.

My face was burning from the cold, so I tried to keep my head tucked into my coat as I ran. I continued to pray that the snow wouldn't get inside of the oversized boots that were protecting my otherwise bare feet. I curled my fingers tight into my coat pockets. The bitter cold brought thoughts of frostbite for my toes, fingers, and ears. I told myself to stay strong and believe that I would make it through the snow and the freezing cold of the night. After all, I had gotten out of an impossible situation, just moments before; I was alive and running, with no sign of Kevin anywhere.

Our neighborhood was somewhat in the shape of a horseshoe with two middle streets connecting each side; I ran for what seemed like an hour, and I was finally about to make my first turn to head in Kasey's direction. I was almost halfway there. As I paused for a moment to catch my breath, I saw the headlights turn towards me. It was Kevin, in our van. He had found me. I was exhausted, my lungs ached, and I had no more fight left in me. I couldn't outrun a vehicle and there was nowhere to hide. Right there in the snow, I dropped to my knees and began to pray what I thought would be my final prayer.

The van continued towards me, with the headlights glaring at me as I prayed. I'll never forget that prayer.

"Jesus, first of all, thank you for saving me," I began. "I don't know what it feels like to be ran over, but I am about to find out. Please don't let it hurt bad, just let me open my eyes to see you. Please put angels all around Kasey, and don't let Kevin ever hurt her. Now, as you said on the cross, *into Your hands, I commend my spirit.*"

The van skidded to a stop only a foot away from where I was kneeling. Kevin jumped out and ran towards me. He grabbed me by the collar of my coat and dragged me towards the van. He opened the sliding door on the side of the van, and shoved me onto the floorboard between the front and middle seats. I begged him to stop.

"Shut up before someone hears you," he said angrily.

"What does it matter? You're just going to kill me when you get me back to the house," I said. "Just do it here."

When we got back to the house, Kevin pulled me out of the van and dragged me down the hall, to our bedroom. I stayed on my knees and prayed. He couldn't take my faith away from me, and if he wanted to kill me, he would have to do it while I prayed out loud. Kevin began to curse and yell, begging me to "shut up," but I was too close to my Maker and Creator to care what he was yelling about.

As I felt him put the gun to my head, I kept my eyes closed and continued to pray. Kevin tapped the barrel of the gun against the side of my head and started screaming for me to quit praying. He didn't realize that the more he threatened me, the more I would call on my Lord to protect me. I felt the pressure of the gun shift and I realized Kevin was about to pull the trigger. I cried out for the final time, "Jesus please send your Holy Spirit, NOW!"

The words were barely off my lips, when I heard Kevin's knees hit the floor. I opened my eyes, and saw him covering his face with his hands.

"No! No!" he shouted. "No!"

Kevin had laid the gun down when he covered his eyes, and was now lying prostrate on the floor.

"Kimi, get help!" he yelled. "Call for help!"

I scrambled to check the phone cord that Kevin had ripped from the wall earlier. He had yanked it with such force, I figured the adapter was gone, or at least broken. Much to my surprise, it was intact and I was able to plug it back into the outlet. Kevin was still crying, lying facedown on the floor, but I didn't know how much time I had before he changed again. I made the choice to call Kevin's brother, Mark, where Kasey was staying; he was the closest person that could help. Though it was late, Mark answered the phone.

"Help me, Mark!" I said. "Kevin has tried to suffocate me and just had a gun to my head. He's on the floor now, but I don't know how long I have."

We didn't talk long and Mark didn't say much.

"I'll be right there," he said as he hung up the phone.

I prayed that Kevin would stay down until Mark arrived. Soon, I heard a knock at the front door, and I ran to get the first help I had ever received (not including the constant help from the Lord). I let Mark in the front door and he told me he had called Tim, Kevin's other brother. He said that Tim would come help if he could get through the snow, but the roads were bad. As Mark and I stepped from the entry and turned to go down the hall, there was Kevin. He was slowly walking towards us, holding the gun to his head.

"Don't anybody bother me or I swear I'll pull the trigger!" he said.

Mark and I let him pass by us, and he kept the gun to his head as he backed himself through the kitchen and made his way to the basement stairway.

"We're just here to talk to you, if you need to talk about anything," Mark assured him.

Kevin just ranted, "I'm nothing but a screw-up and there's nothing anyone can do for me!"

I seized the opportunity, for the first time in 18 years of marriage, to let Kevin's brother know this was the kind of behavior I had been dealing with all these years.

I looked him in the eyes and said, "Do you see what I've been living with all this time? I'm tired of it, Mark! You need to deal with him and see how you like it!"

Mark had a bewildered look on his face, as if he didn't realize

Kevin had any mental issues. Kevin continued to make his way down the stairs, and once he was in the basement, he ran into the bathroom and slammed the door shut. Mark and I continued down the stairs after Kevin, and approached the bathroom door.

"Do you think he will actually kill himself?" Mark asked.

I told Mark about the time Kevin fired the gun in our closet, and said he was afraid he would go to hell if he killed himself.

"No, I know he won't actually do it. He's just going through one of his episodes, and it will take a lot of talking to get him to come out of it," I replied.

Tim arrived, so I left Kevin in the hands of his two brothers while I took a break. It had already been a terrible night for me. Once again, Kevin was turning things around to make himself the victim and get the attention he craved. I wasn't out of the basement more than five minutes, when Mark yelled, "Can you come talk to him? He won't say a word to either one of us."

After dealing with Kevin for eighteen years, I knew how to talk to him. It had become my life, episode after episode. I felt I deserved an honorary psychiatry degree for everything he had put me through.

I went back down the stairs and talked to Kevin through the bathroom door. It took about an hour before he finally opened the door and shoved the gun out. He immediately closed the door again, but at least he had given up the gun. As Mark and I continued to talk to Kevin, Tim interrupted to let us know he was leaving.

"Well, I guess I'll go. I have to get up early in the morning to drive the church bus."

I couldn't believe what I was hearing from him. My eighteen years of smiling and being nice to Kevin's un-sympathetic, head-in-the-ground family, was coming to an end that night. It was time for them to face what he was.

"So you're just going to leave your mentally ill brother locked in a bathroom, because you're tired and have to get up soon?" I questioned.

"Well, people are counting on me to drive the church bus. I can't just not show up," Tim replied with a dumbfounded expression.

"Why don't you try putting your Christianity in use, right here, for your own brother in need?" I asked, trying to make a point.

My words didn't matter. Tim just rolled his eyes.

"I have to go and get some sleep," he said, as he turned to leave.

"You aren't the only one who's tired!" I yelled after him. "But someone has to help your brother!"

It was no use; he was already going up the stairs and heading out.

Mark stayed until Kevin came out of the bathroom. I told Mark I didn't want Kevin in the house, so Mark said Kevin could sleep on the sofa at his house. Mark promised me that he would keep Kevin on their basement sofa, and not let him anywhere near Kasey. Kevin's mind was in such a bad state, we weren't sure if he even remembered she was spending the night there. I asked Mark to not mention her name in front of him, because it could trigger another episode. I also begged Mark to stay in the room with him, and not let Kevin out of his sight. I tried my best to make Mark understand the danger Kevin could be. I don't know what his family thought Bi-polar disorder was, but whatever they thought was nowhere near the reality of the violence involved.

It took us a while, but we eventually persuaded Kevin to go to Mark's house and get some sleep. I finally crawled into bed around 4am, hoping to get a couple hours of rest. My lips were ripped and bleeding, and my throat was incredibly sore from the nightmare Kevin had put me through. I fell asleep with tear stained cheeks and the painful knowledge that things would never be the same.

The next morning, I decided to give Kevin an ultimatum. He would either have to check himself into the psychiatric ward of the hospital, and tell the doctor what he had done to me; or I was going to contact the Sherriff's Department and press charges against him for attempted murder. Reluctantly, Kevin chose the hospital, and that is where he spent his Christmas.

Kasey and I went to see her Dad in the psychiatric ward of the hospital, on Christmas Day. I tried to prepare my daughter for the unusual hospital room she was about to see. She was brave as the nurse checked my purse, and we entered through the padded hall-way. Kevin saw us approaching and knelt to hug Kasey. It tore at my heart to see where Kevin and I had ended up in our relationship. I saw the shame and sadness in his eyes as he whispered, "Thank You," for bringing Kasey.

We were not allowed to stay long, and when we started to leave, Kevin pulled two candy canes from his shirt pocket. With tears streaming down his face, he knelt before Kasey.

"I know it isn't much," he said, "but it's all I have to give you."

Kasey wrapped her little arms around his neck and kissed him on the cheek as she replied, "I love them. Thank you, Daddy."

Kasey and I left the hospital, and had our first Christmas without Kevin. It was just the two of us.

CHAPTER SEVENTEEN

JANUARY 2005

The New Year arrived without joy or celebration between Kevin and I. It was becoming more difficult to keep up appearances in front of friends and family, especially in front of Kasey.

I never imagined my child would become the product of a broken home. I had tried so hard to hold on to our marriage. Now I wasn't sure about working things out with Kevin. Because of his selfish indulgences, and not letting go of his sins, his mental battle had become more violent than I could continue to face. Our daughter was caught in the middle of seeing our family life totally change. Divorce would mean changing homes and leaving our neighborhood, and her friends. It meant so many things that I never wanted my child to go through.

For eighteen years, I had tried to pretend Kevin was wonderful and life was great, but I was growing tired of the cover and was miserable on the inside. Most people don't *really* want to hear about your inner turmoil or struggles. We are told to act positive, be positive, and stay away from negative people. Unfortunately, life isn't always happy and positive. Sometimes we need a true friend we can tell all of our hurts to; the kind of friend who cries when you cry, and truly loves you for all that you are. How I needed that kind of friend.

Real life taught me that a friend might listen to your troubles for a day or two, rarely for weeks, and certainly not for years. Now I had another issue to face, and no one I could confide in for comfort and advice. To me, divorce seemed almost worse than putting up with Kevin's violence. How could I be sure he wouldn't hurt Kasey and I, even if we were divorced? I wasn't sure I would ever be free from his rage.

I learned to be more and more thankful for my Christian faith. I could pour my heart and tears out in prayer, day or night, and God never let me down. The Bible speaks of a "peace that passes all understanding" and that's what the Lord would send to me during my darkest hours.

Since Kevin's confession on November 13th, 2004, everyday seemed to bring me more pain and tears. Instead of being allowed time to absorb his news of adultery and betrayal, I was in constant danger from his Bi-polar outbursts and increasing violence towards me. I was emotionally exhausted, and another year of living like this was more than I could bear mentally, physically, or spiritually.

Kevin's 39th birthday was on January 9, 2005. It was hard to celebrate, but we went to his parent's house for cake and presents. Sadness could be felt throughout his family. His parents and siblings always thought Kevin and I were the ultimate couple, with a never-ending love. Now the twinkle in our eyes when we looked at each other was gone, and the truth of our troubles was evident.

Kevin was getting weary of staying at his brother's house, but I wasn't comfortable having him home yet. Kevin had been staying at Tim's house since leaving the hospital after Christmas. We were trying to keep the lines of communication open, and let Kasey know that we both loved her, no matter what we decided about our marriage. Kevin called one day from work, and asked if he could stop by on his way home to spend some time with Kasey. I reluctantly agreed to a two-hour visit, but told him I wanted to be in the room with them the entire time. I asked if he had been taking his medication regularly since being released from the hospital, and he assured me he hadn't missed a dose.

When Kasey came home from school, I told her that her Daddy

wanted to come over and see her for a couple hours. She never had an unkind word to say about her Dad or the fact he was staying at her Uncle's house.

"Maybe he'll play Space Invaders with me!" Kasey replied excitedly.

I was in awe of her forgiveness and non-judgmental attitude towards him. She had to visit her Dad in the psychiatric ward of the hospital, behind padded and locked doors, on Christmas day because he tried to suffocate and kill her mother; yet, she had no animosity towards him at all. Kasey's heart was clear and pure. "Jesus forgives, and so should we," she would say.

Kevin arrived later than expected, around 7:30 that evening; Kasey was entertaining herself in her room, watching a movie.

"Kasey's in her room," I said. "You know she starts getting ready for bed around 8 o'clock. What took you so long to get here? You said you were leaving work at 4pm today."

"I guess I just took longer getting cleaned-up than I should have," Kevin replied.

I could feel something was amiss the moment he said those words. My gut told me he had either met up with some woman, or had done something else he didn't want me to know about. True to the routine that brought out his confession, Kevin continued, "I need to use the bathroom, if you don't mind."

I couldn't believe what I was hearing.

"Are you serious?" I asked. "You just got here, and now you want to go to the basement and spend two hours in the bathroom?"

"I promise it isn't like that," Kevin replied. "I drank a large coke on the way over and I really have to go."

"Do what you have to do," I said, "but we're not changing our schedule."

Kevin barely hugged Kasey when he arrived, and I ended up putting her to bed without him spending any quality time with her. I kissed Kasey as I tucked her into bed and told her I was sorry her Daddy hadn't spent any time with her.

"It's okay Mommy," she said.

I gave her a big hug and kiss, and told her it really wasn't okay, but she was precious for saying it.

Kevin finally came upstairs to find me sitting on the sofa, with arms crossed, just waiting for his entrance. I wasn't in a good mood, and this was certainly not the visit he said he wanted, when he called from work earlier that day. He could see I was upset.

"I'm sorry," he said, "but I really did fall asleep on the toilet downstairs."

I immediately rolled my eyes.

"Yeah, sure you did, Kevin," I replied. "It's time for you to leave. I'm tired and this visit was a waste of time."

"It's not late, can't we talk for a while?" Kevin quickly responded.

"I don't see how we're supposed to work anything out, when you just continue your lifestyle of betrayal."

He just denied he was still being unfaithful.

"Is there any hope for us to be a couple again?" he asked.

"Why does the conversation always go back to your questions, instead of you being upright and honest when I ask you something?" I questioned.

Kevin suddenly slammed his hands down on the kitchen counter.

"You're never going to forget what I've done to you!" he screamed. "I can't stand the thought of another man touching you! If I can't have you, no one will!"

Kevin was standing near the stove; he turned and grabbed the two largest knives from the wood block and started coming towards me, with a knife in each hand.

The sofa, where I was seated, was beside the hallway door. Immediately, I jumped to my feet and pulled the door closed behind me, to block the path to Kasey's room. Kevin had the same look in his eyes that I had seen so many times before. It wasn't the Kevin I married, but the demon within him that was coming towards me. A rush of adrenaline surged through my body as I stood straight and tall, and looked him in the eyes.

"You may stab me with those, but I swear I will pull them out of me and put them in you before you ever get to my daughter! So bring it on if you think you're tough enough!" I said. "Jesus, I need you now!"

By that time, Kevin was about three feet in front of me, and the long blades were aimed right at me. Suddenly, his mouth flew open, his eyes widened, and he threw the knives down before running out the front door.

I will never know what Kevin saw that night, but it stopped him in his tracks. Once again, the Lord had come to my rescue.

As soon as I saw the knives fall, and Kevin turn towards the front door, I quickly opened the hallway door, then shut and locked it behind me. I glanced at Kasey asleep in her bed, as I raced to my bedroom to get my handgun. Kevin could change in an instant, and I didn't know if he would try breaking the door down or bust through a window. I just knew I had to get to Kasey.

My heart was pounding up into my throat, as I entered Kasey's room. I could barely catch my breath; the reality of almost being stabbed by two huge knives was beginning to sink in. Kasey heard me come in.

"Are you okay, Mommy?" she asked.

Although my heart was pounding so loud that I was sure she could hear it, I tried to be soft and calm as I leaned over to give her a kiss.

"Everything is fine sweetie," I said. "Daddy just left and I'm going to sit here by your bed for a while, if you don't care."

In a half-asleep voice, she replied, "That's fine Mommy. Sleep good."

I had to smile. She was so innocent and sweet. Little did she know that I had just stood between her and knives… but she didn't need to know. My job was to protect her, and with God's help, I was going to do just that. I sat beside her bed through the rest of the night.

Kevin's boss ordered a mandatory electrical supervisor weekend of meetings, out of town, for late January. Supervisors and their spouses were to arrive before 6pm on Friday, and be prepared for a social meet-and-greet. Saturday was lined with meetings, followed by a steak dinner that evening for the employees and their spouses. Sunday was to consist of a brief meeting after breakfast, and then dismissal for everyone to return home.

On Saturday, I spent most of the day wandering around the hotel, going in and out of various shops on the lobby level. Kevin stressed that we had to be ready for dinner at 6pm, so I watched my time closely. No one at Kevin's workplace knew anything about our troubles, and we were trying to keep it that way. I had agreed to attend the weekend meeting with Kevin, so his co-workers wouldn't suspect a problem between us.

Kevin and I were a few minutes early for dinner and we found ourselves talking with one of his supervisors. Mr. Dane was nice, and I knew Kevin thought highly of him. More and more of his co-workers began to fill the dining space, which had been reserved for the employees who were attending the weekend meetings. It was a nice dinner; I thought we did a wonderful job of smiling and socializing with Kevin's bosses and co-workers.

After dinner, I asked Kevin if he wanted to walk around the hotel lobby, and he said that would be nice. We made small talk and tried to pretend the tension wasn't there. Our walk wasn't long, which was fine. I knew Kevin had to be up early to meet his co-workers for breakfast before his final meeting. Breakfast wasn't scheduled as mandatory, but it was an unspoken rule that a supervisor should be present for any and all meetings, whether social or work-related.

While we were walking around the lobby, I could tell something was bothering Kevin, but I couldn't imagine he would have an episode with all of his co-workers in their rooms, just up and down the hallway from ours.

Once inside the room, I asked, "What's bothering you Kevin?"

He turned to me with tears in his eyes.

"I saw how all the guys looked at you. I've been such an idiot."

I tried to stop the conversation from going further, but it was too late; he was on a roll. Kevin began his episode by talking about how beautiful I was, how he had screwed everything up, and kept on messing up. With each negative comment he made, I tried to counter with something positive, in an effort to diffuse what I feared was about to happen. Unfortunately, it didn't work. After a few minutes, he began pacing like a caged animal; then he grabbed my purse and started going through it.

"What are you looking for?" I asked.

"I want the car keys," he replied. "I need to go for a drive."

"You certainly do not need to go for a drive, or even leave this room right now," I said sternly.

Kevin had a crazed look in his eyes. He was still pacing back and forth, as he frantically tried to dig for the keys in my purse. I tried to reason with him once more.

"Kevin, you need to calm down. All of your bosses are down this hallway. Do you want to get fired?"

"Fine!" he said. "If I can't go out the door, I will just jump out the window."

He hurried to the window and tried to pull-up the sash. I rushed over and tried to stop him.

"Kevin, look down there," I said. "We are on the fourth floor! What do you think you're doing?"

Kevin grabbed me, picked me up completely off the floor, and threw me into the wall. I hit with a loud thud, but I couldn't think about the pain; I had to keep him in the room. He managed to find the car keys, so a battle ensued as I tried to take the keys from his hand. In an effort to keep him from leaving, I blocked the door with my body and held tightly to the doorknob. Kevin began hitting my arm and tried jerking me away from the door. As he was beating my arm, to loosen my grip on the doorknob, I managed to get the keys from him and I threw them across the room.

Kevin was yelling that he was nothing but a screw-up, and he just needed to get out of the room. I continued to try and talk him down. Once again, he grabbed me and threw me into the wall, screaming for me to let him leave. I knew I had no choice but to try and close myself up in the room with him somehow. If I let Kevin out of the room, he could hurt himself or possibly someone else.

As my body hit the wall once more, I noticed Kevin's silk ties; one was on the bed and there were at least three more within my reach. I remembered studying textiles during my interior design studies, and I knew that if I could tie the silk tight enough, I could "lock" us up in the room. There was a wall-mounted coatrack right beside the door; I knew I had enough ties to reach between the door handle and the coatrack. Even if it didn't work, it would buy some time; hopefully, Kevin would stop and come to his senses.

Kevin began hitting himself and knocked himself to the ground. I looked at him, then at the door, and rushed to tie the first tie; I knotted the other ties to each other, and bolted towards the door. Kevin must have thought I was trying to leave, when I headed for the door. He lunged towards me and knocked me into the door. Ignoring the pain, I tied the tie tight around the door handle and reached up to the coatrack. Kevin finally figured out what I was doing.

"Do you think you can keep me in this room?" he asked angrily.

"Between me and Jesus, yes! I'm sure going to try!" I replied. "You are not fit to leave this room. You could hurt yourself or someone else!"

While Kevin made fun of me and tried to knock my hands away from the rack, I tied the tie tight to the coatrack. I had managed to "tie us in." I had no idea what he would do to me, but I couldn't let him loose on someone else. Kevin must have realized how crazy the situation was because he began pounding his head into the floor. He was showing himself no mercy. He continued to hit his head over and over. I couldn't stand to watch it. I begged him to stop, but he just kept screaming that he was no good.

Kevin finally stopped.

"Oh... Oh, I think I really did it this time," he said.

"What do you mean?" I asked.

Kevin looked up at me, and I couldn't believe what I saw. His eyes were rattling back and forth, repeatedly, like something from a cartoon.

"I think I'm going to throw up," he said.

"You've really hurt yourself this time, Kevin! Let me call for a doctor," I replied.

"Don't you dare call a doctor!" he said forcefully. "I'll be fine."

"Kevin, your eyes are going back and forth!" I responded. "Something isn't right!"

"I probably just gave myself a concussion. It wouldn't be my first."

216

Again, I tried asking him if I could call a doctor, but I finally gave up. I was sore from being thrown into walls and being hit.

"Kevin, you have to know what you want. I'll call a doctor if you want me to. Otherwise, I'll just try to stay awake and keep you from falling asleep," I said.

Kevin agreed that he probably shouldn't go to sleep, and said he would call his supervisor around 6am and tell him he needed to go home because of a stomach virus or something.

The hours passed slowly as Kevin continued to throw up. When things began to calm down, I couldn't help but cry. I was exhausted. I had barricaded myself in a room with a mad man, and after all the years of putting up with Kevin's Bi-polar fits, he had seriously messed up his head this time. What if he had done so much damage that he couldn't work any more? It seemed like every time I believed things could get better, Kevin only made our situation worse.

Kevin was so sick, but I didn't know what to do for him. His eyes continued to race back and forth, nonstop. I had no way of knowing if he would die right there in the hotel room, so I laid hands on him and lifted him up in prayer. Despite everything he put me through, somewhere inside of him was the sweet Kevin who had asked me to marry him. I stayed by his side and continued to pray for him, until 6am, when he called his boss to tell him he was sick, and couldn't attend the morning meeting.

Kevin sat on the floor and rested with his back against the bed, as I packed our belongings and loaded the car. While I prepared for our departure, Kevin stayed in the room, careful not to be seen by anyone. I managed to get Kevin to the car without running into anyone we knew. As we made the two-and-a-half hour drive back home, Kevin barely spoke. I tried to keep talking so he would stay awake.

Once back home, I told Kevin that I was taking him to our house because he didn't need to be by himself. He said he didn't want his family to know about his possible concussion, unless it got worse.

Kasey was at her Grandma's house, so I called and talked to her. I told her that Daddy wasn't feeling well and I needed her to stay at her Grandma's one more night. She was her usual, sweet self.

"Okay Mommy," she said. "Tell Daddy I hope he feels better."

When I told Kevin what she had said, tears rolled down his face.

"I really messed everything up," he cried.

Kevin wasn't any better Monday morning; I called him in sick on Tuesday as well. I begged him to let me take him to the doctor, but he reminded me of a car crash he was in when he was only 19. He said he had been diagnosed with a severe concussion, but checked himself out of the hospital, the following day. Kevin reasoned that a concussion must not be that serious, if you can leave the hospital and drive yourself home. I wasn't going to argue with him, but told him I would help him if I could.

"You deserve better than what I've put you through, Kimi," he said.

His attitude was different when he said those words to me. There was pure sincerity and unselfish love in his voice. He said he was going to his brother's house because I deserved some time to myself. I asked him to call me if he needed anything.

Something had to change, but our love for one another was so strong that neither one of us could bear the thought of saying goodbye. January had been a difficult month, and I couldn't imagine what would happen in February, but I knew God would help us both through whatever was ahead.

CHAPTER EIGHTEEN

FEBRUARY 5ᵗʰ, 2005

It was February 4ᵗʰ, 2005, and Kevin called to ask me if we could talk after he got off work at 11pm. I told him I was actually thinking of driving to the mall, and would consider meeting him. The mall closed at 9pm, but I knew I could grab a late dinner and kill time until 11pm. Kevin had been staying at his brother's house, most nights. We had a lot to discuss so, like it or not, I knew I needed to meet him.

I told Kevin I agreed we needed some face-to-face time, to discuss what we should do about our marriage. Kasey was spending the night with her Grandma Martha, so I would be free to meet with Kevin that evening.

It was about 1pm when Kevin called me; I said I would follow him to work, so I would know where he parked. I was very firm with Kevin about his car being in the same location in the parking lot, after work. I reminded him he had promised not to leave work anymore to meet with *anyone*. Kevin assured me his car would be in the same spot after work.

I followed him to the parking lot, which was massive due to the workforce size at the factory. I pulled into a vacant spot behind his car, and watched as he took his lunch box, coat, and other necessities from the trunk. He was about to lock the car, when I stepped out of our van.

"Just a minute," I said. "There's one more thing I have to check."

"What do you need to check?" Kevin asked.

Using my car key, I turned the car on to see the current mileage and wrote the number down.

"Yeah, I finally figured out you were smart enough to get the same space some nights," I told him. "But, I've been checking the mileage and I know you've been meeting someone."

Kevin stared at me, like the proverbial kid with their hand in the cookie jar. I explained that I had been following him to work for weeks, and gathering information; I checked his mileage in the parking lot, and checked it again when he got back home. He looked stunned and ashamed.

There was silence for a few minutes, as I just stared at Kevin with the "gotcha" look on my face.

"Now do you see why I seem cold towards you?" I asked. "You promised to behave, and yet it looks like you're still hooked on your women and secret lifestyle."

"I didn't know you were checking mileage," Kevin said shamefully. "I should've known you were smart enough to keep checking."

"Yes," I continued, "and that's another reason why we need to talk. Your eyes tell me you still love me, but your actions are not proving it."

"I have to get to work, but I'll be in the parking lot at 11 o'clock to follow you back to the house," Kevin said; then he headed off to work.

As crazy as it sounds, I missed Kevin's hugs and the love I thought we shared. I'm not sure what I hoped would become of our talk but I wanted my husband back. I had learned to deal with and accept his Bi-polar fits, but the secret life he had created was making his episodes more violent and dangerous for both of us. I knew that down deep in his heart, he wanted to be a good Christian husband, but temptations were overloading his mind. When he gave in to temptation, it only fueled his episodes. His mind was truly like Jekyll and Hyde, and he was losing the battle. Despite advice from counselors and friends, I couldn't bring myself to call a lawyer. I just couldn't let go. Kevin and I had even discussed living in separate houses, side-by-side. I could be next door to help him, but Kasey and I would be safe from his episodes of rage.

I found myself in constant prayer, asking God, "What do I do?"

I felt trapped in a hopeless situation. If I left Kevin, I would constantly worry about his condition, but I also knew that he would come after me. On many occasions, Kevin said he couldn't stand the thought of another man touching me. I knew exactly what he meant by that. Divorcing Kevin and marrying someone else wasn't an option I could even consider.

On the other hand, Kevin's episodes were becoming so violent; eventually, one of us wasn't going to make it out alive. Daily, my mind raced with questions of what to do. I had to protect Kasey, which meant me staying alive to keep Kevin from hurting her. On an ordinary day, I knew he would never hurt her, but his Bi-polar Disorder made him a danger to us.

The past couple months had worn me out, physically and mentally. I still had bruises from being thrown around the hotel room in January. Kevin had not recovered from the beating he gave his head. I knew he had a serious concussion. It had been a couple weeks since he beat his head into the concrete floor, but his eyes were still shaking back and forth, and he was unable to focus. I didn't know what was going to happen to either one of us, but I knew we needed God's help and divine intervention.

While waiting for Kevin to get off work, I spent time going in and out of various stores at the mall. The bookstore was quite helpful in passing the time. I read books about Bi-polar Disorder, as well as one about forgiveness. Finally, the announcement came across the speakers, saying the mall would be closing in fifteen minutes. I gathered my shopping bags and headed for the parking lot. I drove to a restaurant on the east side of town, which put me closer to Kevin's work. I wasn't particularly interested in food, but I had to kill some time and there were limited options that time of night.

The time seemed to creep by. It had been a long day and I was getting tired. I prayed that Kevin would stay "nice" because I was too tired to put up with anything. I sent Kevin a text and reminded him I would meet him in the parking lot at exactly 11pm; I emphasized that I wanted to find his car in the same spot when I arrived. He sent a text back and said he was going to take a shower after work, but would text me as soon as he was headed for the parking lot. Instead of texting back again, I called and left him a voicemail.

"That's fine, just make sure you are taking me seriously," I said. "I want your car in the *same* space where you left it, Kevin. With the same mileage."

Kevin didn't call or text back, and my gut told me I was going to be disappointed at 11pm.

At 10:45pm, I paid for my food and walked to the van. I was approximately 15 minutes from the factory, so I knew I would arrive at exactly 11 o'clock. If Kevin wasn't out of the building yet, I would just wait in the parking lot. I had only been driving for about five minutes, when my phone rang. It was Kevin.

"I got off work a little early," Kevin said. "I'll just meet you at the end of the road, by the highway."

"Don't you dare!" I immediately replied. "You agreed to be in that parking lot where I left you, and I expect to find you there!"

"Well, I've already left the parking lot and I'm headed towards the highway," Kevin responded.

I was livid. I knew exactly why he didn't want us to meet in the parking lot. Kevin was trying to cover his tracks. He probably lost his parking space when he left work to meet someone. I couldn't believe I had waited for him all day, only to be disappointed once again. When were the lies going to stop? When was he going to change?

"There's no point in talking to you because you're just full of lies and deceit," I said.

"Just let me explain, please. I do love you and we really need to talk," Kevin quickly responded.

"I want you to put your phone in the holder on your dash, so I can see it while we drive," I demanded. "Keep it on so I can talk to you the entire trip back home."

"I can put my phone in the holder where you can see it, but we don't have to talk all the way," Kevin said.

I remembered Kevin had a Bluetooth device for his ear, not to mention his degrees in electronics and electrical engineering.

"You're not going to be talking to some other woman while I'm following you," I said sternly.

"What makes you think I could even do that?" Kevin asked, with a slight laugh.

"Seriously, Kevin, I'm way beyond gullible, thanks to what you've turned me into. I never dreamed that I would need to learn so many ways to catch a lying cheat of a husband."

"I'll talk to you the entire way home, if it will prove to you that I'm not talking to anyone else," Kevin said.

I said okay, but told him I wasn't sure about us talking at the house, like we had planned.

Kevin and I talked constantly as we drove. However, I questioned Kevin about the phone going silent several times. Kevin denied that he was muting me to take another call, but I could tell his phone was going mute. When we first started the drive home, I could hear music playing in the background, which is what I should have heard. However, the more we talked, the more silence came across the phone. I began to time the moments of silence and quit asking Kevin about it. I knew what was happening and I was ready to confront him. Kasey and I didn't deserve what he was doing to our family. Things were going to change, or I was done with him.

We couldn't figure out where to stop along the way, so I told Kevin he could come to the house. My mind was racing with all the things I wanted to say to him, but another part of me just wanted everything to go away, and for our love to be restored. I missed Kevin so much. I didn't want to be divorced and a single mother. I missed him being beside me at night, and laying my head on his chest as we fell asleep. Only God could fix the mess we were in.

Neither one of us could totally let go. Kevin may have spent years committing adultery, but I was the one he loved, not them. I was furious over his deceit and betrayal, but my heart melted when I saw him and my body ached to feel his arms around me.

We arrived at the house and Kevin quickly jumped out of his car to open my door for me. I used to think it was so sweet, but now I thought, *That's the least he can do.* Kevin helped carry my shopping bags inside and made small talk about my time at the mall. He wanted to know where I went, and even asked if I saw anyone I knew. I couldn't believe he was questioning me!

"I don't think you're in a position to ask me about anywhere I've been," I said boldly.

"I'm sorry," Kevin apologized. "I didn't mean anything by it, I was just making conversation."

Kevin began telling me how much he missed me and how sorry he was about the mess he had made of everything. The more he talked, the more my heart went out to him. He began to cry.

"Do you believe Jesus really forgives everything we do wrong?" he asked.

"I absolutely believe he does." I answered. "That was the whole purpose for Calvary."

"I wish I had your faith," Kevin replied.

"Don't say that. You have faith, you just have to stay focused on Jesus and quit letting the devil tempt you," I said.

I don't know if you call it the Holy Spirit or what, but the conversation led us to kiss; before we knew it, our love felt new and perfect. I looked deeply into Kevin's eyes.

"With all the Christian faith that is in me, I forgive you for everything. If Jesus could die for my sins, then I can forgive you for everything you've done to me," I said.

Kevin kissed me passionately, saying he was sorry. We melted in each other's arms and our marriage bed was restored. It was more beautiful than words could explain. I will always be grateful to God for the spirit of love he poured out for us, one last time.

It was about 2:30am when Kevin began to change. It started with little comments like, "I'm so stupid," and, "I can't believe I almost lost you." The conversation took a turn for the worst when he asked if he could move all of his things back home.

"Are you taking your medication?" I asked. "I want proof that you're taking your medication seriously, before you move back in."

I could tell something was on Kevin's mind, but I wasn't quite sure what he was thinking.

"Would you have remarried if we hadn't made it?" Kevin asked.

"Well," I began, "I would hope that I wouldn't have to be alone forever. Yes, I would want a husband. After all, you wanted women even when you had a wife, didn't you?"

Kevin glared at me with a look I had only seen once before in eighteen years of marriage; the last time I saw that look in his eyes was when he tried to suffocate me. Immediately, I knew I was in trouble. Kevin let out a Hulk-like scream and began to beat his chest.

"NO!" he shouted.

I jumped from our bed, and ran to our master bathroom; I slammed the door shut and locked it as quickly as I could.

I couldn't see Kevin, but I soon heard him; he began banging his fists on the bathroom door.

"No!" He screamed. "No one will ever have you! Never!"

As Kevin's fists pounded on the solid wood door, he shouted "Never!" over and over. Luckily, I had hidden a small 25 caliber, pearl-handled gun in the bottom of a tissue box, in our bathroom, after the December episode. I grabbed the gun from its hiding place, braced myself against the vanity, and pointed the gun at the door. Kevin was hitting the door with such force that it was bowing inward, and the frame was starting to come loose. There was nowhere for me to run; the bathroom didn't have a window, which is what prompted me to hide a gun in the tissue box, in case I ever became *trapped* in there.

After Kevin's episode in December, I had strategically hid various weapons in each room of the house. As I stood braced against the vanity, with my gun aimed at the door, it happened; Kevin busted the door off the frame, and it came crashing down into the bathroom. He was standing before me with my black revolver. I had hidden it between the mattresses, and couldn't believe he found it. There we stood, guns pointed at each other, and each of us ready to pull the trigger. Kevin's face was blood red and every vein in his upper body looked like it would burst open. I saw the demonic look in his eyes, and tried to reason with him.

"Stop it Kevin!" I shouted. "It's me! Stop and think!"

I had always been able to talk Kevin down from a manic state, but he looked worse than I had ever seen. Kevin's eyes didn't even look like him, and they were rattling back and forth. Suddenly, I thought of how he had beat his head into the concrete floor less than two weeks earlier; I realized I was in serious trouble. Something had snapped in him. While I was trying to talk to him, he reached over and grabbed for my gun.

Kevin and I struggled in the bathroom doorway. He tried to take my gun from me, and I struggled to keep my only means for survival. Unfortunately, Kevin won that battle. As he ripped the gun from my hand, I shoved myself past him and ran for the phone by the bed. I quickly picked up the phone and dialed 911, but Kevin was right behind me and snatched the phone away. As he snatched the phone from my hand I shouted, "My husband is a Bi-polar, I need help!"

For a second, I thought I heard someone on the other end of the line, but I had no way to know if my cry for help was heard. After all, no one showed up to help me when I dialed 911 in December, so why should I expect help this time?

Kevin slammed the phone back down and I tried to take off running. I kept telling Kevin to calm down, but he wasn't making any sense.

"It's all over! It will never be the same!" he shouted.

Kevin and I struggled from the side of the bed, where the phone was, to the foot of the bed. I fought to keep him from getting a complete hold on me and managed to yank away from him and run towards the hall.

"Stop!" Kevin yelled after me.

Suddenly, there was a gunshot. If the bullet hit me, I didn't feel it.

"Jesus, help me!" I screamed.

After a few more steps, I heard another gunshot behind me. I just kept yelling for God's help. Once again, the gun rang out. Three shots had been fired as I ran from him. I kept going forward and never looked back.

"I need your help, Lord!" I cried out.

Less than two months earlier, I ran the same path, to get away from him. This time there were no shoes to jump into and no coat to grab, but I knew the Lord would supply all of my needs, even if it meant I had to run out into the cold, barefoot and uncovered. I knew the Bible promised, in Jesus' own words, "*I will never leave nor forsake you.*" So, I kept running. I was directly beside the wall phone in the kitchen, when it rang. The timing was almost comical, but I knew it was God's timing. I stopped running and answered the phone.

"Hello?"

"Ma'am, this is the State Police. We are at your front door," a voice replied. "Can you get to the door?"

I couldn't believe my ears. Someone was actually there to help me.

"Yes, I can," I answered.

The phone was at the end of the kitchen, only a few steps from the front entry. As I hung up the phone, Kevin ran past me.

"You've done it now!" he shouted.

I had no idea what he was talking about. Kevin ran towards the garage door, which was beside the basement stairs. I figured he was going outside to jump in his car and take off. The only other option was for him to run into the basement.

Quickly, I went to the front door and let the Troopers inside.

"Where is he, ma'am?" they asked as they entered the house.

"He just took off towards the door," I said, pointing towards the garage door.

I followed the two Troopers into the kitchen, and all three of us saw Kevin run downstairs, into the basement.

Just like the December episode, I heard Kevin slam the bathroom door shut.

Immediately, I told the Troopers, "He just locked himself in the basement bathroom."

"How do you know where he is?" they asked curiously.

"I just heard him shut the door. He did the exact same thing back in December," I answered.

While I tried to explain what had happened in December, more officers showed up at the house. Two Deputies with the Sheriff's

Department had arrived, in addition to the two State Troopers who were already there. The two Troopers commented that it was dark and they couldn't see anything down the stairway, so they asked me to draw a diagram of the basement. As I was drawing the basement layout for them, I heard one of the troopers say he was going out to his car. When he came back into the house, he was carrying a shotgun.

"I need to go downstairs and talk to Kevin. He's a Bi-polar and he's having a bad episode. He just needs his medication and rest," I tried to explain.

The officers asked me to draw a diagram of the basement at least three or four more times. I was beginning to think they were just giving me busy work. Soon, my house was flooded with officers. One officer asked me to explain what a typical episode was like.

"Just tell me about some of Kevin's most recent episodes, so we can better understand where his mind is and what he might do," he said.

"Kevin won't hurt anyone," I assured them.

I described the most recent episodes and tried to explain to the officers that I had dealt with Kevin for eighteen years, and he needed to talk to me. I could hear him asking for me.

"Just let me talk to my wife!" Kevin yelled repeatedly.

The more he yelled for me, the more the officers talked amongst themselves. From the kitchen, I tried to yell back to Kevin, hoping he could hear me.

"I'm here Kevin!" I shouted.

The Troopers seemed angry that I was talking to my husband.

"Ma'am, if you don't sit down and be quiet, we're going to ask you to leave the room," they said.

I could tell they had absolutely no idea how to deal with Kevin.

"Can I please call his doctor?" I asked.

"No Ma'am, we're handing this. Now please sit down and be quiet."

Kevin had been yelling for me constantly, and it was breaking my heart. He was counting on me to be there for him, but I couldn't get to him, or to the basement, to let him know I hadn't abandoned him.

Finally, Kevin had enough.

"If you don't let me talk to my wife, I'm going to kill myself!" he screamed.

"Please let me talk to him," I begged the officer's. "He will listen to me!"

"No, we're handling this!" they abruptly responded.

From what I could see, they weren't handling anything. There were two State Troopers blocking the stairway, one standing on each side of the doorway that led to the basement. They were in the same position, since their arrival, 20 minutes earlier. They stood there with their guns aimed at the basement. Two county deputies were behind them, along with a third State Trooper, who they all called the *negotiator*. The so-called negotiator didn't know a thing about talking to a Bi-polar, I was sure of that, and he certainly wasn't doing any negotiating. The two troopers standing in the doorway kept complaining about how dark the stairway and basement landing were. I heard them both say they couldn't see anything. The light bulb in the stairway had gone out a few days earlier, and we had not yet replaced it.

Kevin began to count down from ten. I continued to plead with the officers; I needed to talk to Kevin. They just kept telling me, "No." Suddenly, we heard shots; three gunshots rang out from the basement, followed by total silence. I watched as the State Troopers and Sheriff's Deputies looked at each other, unsure of what to do next.

"Kevin? Are you there? Say something to us Kevin," the negotiator yelled.

There was no response. My heart started to race. I had to get to my husband.

"Is he okay?" I asked frantically.

"That's what we're trying to find out, ma'am," an officer replied.

Finally, one of the officers spoke up.

"Let her say something. Maybe he will respond to her."

The officers allowed me to yell to Kevin, but I was instructed not to start a conversation with him.

"Kevin?" I called out.

"I'm here," Kevin finally replied.

The moment Kevin spoke, I was told that I needed to move to the end of the kitchen. In other words, they wanted me out of their way.

"Kevin, why don't you come on out so we can talk to you," the negotiator said. "Just come on out of the bathroom."

"What if I told you that I can't get out?" Kevin replied.

"Could he have locked himself in the bathroom?" an officer asked me.

"No," I answered. "The door locks from the inside. I've been trying to tell you he isn't thinking straight. He doesn't know how to turn the doorknob, to get out. He needs his medicine and rest."

It was obvious that none of the officers had any concern about Kevin's illness. They had no desire to call a doctor or get medicine to him. They continued to yell, telling Kevin to come out of the bathroom. That was all their "negotiating" consisted of. Their badges were apparently the only credentials necessary, to determine what Kevin needed. I believe they were actually scared of him. I had faced Kevin all by myself, for eighteen years. Here were five officers, holding guns, wearing bulletproof vests, scared of one man, locked in a basement bathroom.

Kevin began beating on the bathroom door. I knew the sound well, because I'd heard him do the same thing to our master bathroom door about 30 minutes before.

"He's trying to beat the door down because he can't think correctly, and turn the knob," I told the officers.

One of them wanted to see the bathroom door Kevin had knocked down. I told him our room was at the end of the hallway. The officer was coming back into the kitchen when there was a loud bang in the basement. Every single one of the officers jumped and gripped their guns a little tighter.

"He just knocked the door down," I announced.

"Kevin, is everything all right?" the negotiator called out.

"Can I get some pants?" Kevin asked.

An officer turned towards me and gave me a strange look.

"Does he not have any pants on?"

"No, his jeans are in our bedroom," I said. "He just has his underwear on."

I was asked to get Kevin's jeans and bring them to the kitchen.

"Can I get some jeans please?" Kevin asked again.

The officer nodded to me and I tossed him Kevin's black jeans.

"Okay, Kevin. Just push your guns to the foot of the steps where we can see them, and I 'll throw your jeans to you," the officer said.

I heard Kevin say something, but I couldn't quite understand what he said.

Then I heard the officer say, "Okay, that's good Kevin. Now here come your jeans." He tossed the jeans down the stairway, and another officer asked, "Can you see him?"

There was some quiet talk amongst the officers. I felt they were trying to decide what to do next. Kevin hadn't said anything since his jeans were tossed to him. About five minutes passed, and it sounded like he was coming up the stairs. I heard a couple of thuds and wondered what Kevin had thrown at the officers. Suddenly, there were gunshots. I heard three shots, followed by a loud boom; it sounded like someone was falling down or hitting a wall.

An officer rushed over to me. "I need you to step out on the porch with me," he said.

"What happened?" I asked.

"I'm not sure, but I need you to stay outside on the porch."

Within minutes, my home and front yard was flooded with officers and EMT's. There was a lot of activity with officers and EMT's rushing in and out of the house. No one would tell me anything about what was going on, though.

"Is there someone I can call to come be with you?" an officer asked.

I thought it was a strange question, considering that I had asked to call Kevin's doctor several times already.

"No, I don't need anyone," I answered.

For eighteen years, I had dealt with Kevin, and no one ever showed up to help me. I was starting to get angry. No one would tell me why I had to stand on a cold porch in February, while a bunch of officer's were in my warm house thinking they knew how to handle Kevin. I didn't know what the gunshots were for, where they came from, or anything. The officer persisted and said he needed to call a family member to come be with me. I said that, if he insisted, he could call my brother, Lucas, and his wife, Bobbie. I still had no idea why he wanted to call someone. I figured Kevin and I would go to the hospital and he would be admitted, just like in December. I didn't need to talk to family; I knew this routine better than anyone.

As I stood on the porch, getting angrier by the minute at the lack of communication, several EMT's rolled a stretcher out the front door. It was Kevin! They wheeled him past me, but Kevin didn't say a word. I thought the least he could've done was say, "I'm sorry for all this mess." His foot was sticking out from the sheet, and I saw blood on it. I thought, *well, he must have shot his foot.*

The EMT's were putting Kevin in the ambulance when my sister-in-law, Bobbie, showed up. She was actually very kind to me. Bobbie put her arm around me and asked if I was okay. I wasn't sure how I was, because I didn't know what was going on. Bobbie asked me to come over and sit with her on the sofa; she said Lucas was on his way. Within a matter of minutes, Lucas arrived. Bobbie and I continued asking the officers how Kevin was doing, but no one would answer. When I asked an officer if I could go to the hospital to be with Kevin, I was told "No." An investigator was on his way from the State Police Post about 30 miles away; I was instructed to stay at my house because he needed to ask me some questions.

I couldn't believe the officers wouldn't let me go to the hospital; Kevin didn't have his wallet, insurance card or anything with him. Bobbie, Lucas, and I just sat on the sofa, watching officers come and go from the basement, and walk back and forth down the hallway to my bedroom. We couldn't get an answer out of any of them.

After about 20 minutes, the investigating Lieutenant showed up and asked me to have a seat at my dining room table, and answer a *few* questions. The Lieutenant questioned me about Kevin's *entire* life; he wanted me to start from the moment I met Kevin, and tell him about every episode I could think of. I did my best to answer all of his questions, but I didn't understand what past episodes had to do with tonight. Each episode was different; the point was that Kevin was a Bi-polar, and I needed to get to the hospital with his insurance card and medicine.

I explained that Kevin had been at work since 3pm the afternoon before, and I'd followed him back home when he got off work at 11pm. I told the Lieutenant that Kevin was tired, and I knew he hadn't taken his medicine since we got to the house. The Lieutenant asked question after question about Kevin's illness. He wanted to know if Kevin had ever tried to commit suicide. I told him about the time Kevin said he was too afraid to kill himself because he thought he would go to Hell.

Another officer interrupted and asked to speak with the Lieutenant. The Lieutenant excused himself briefly; I sat quietly and looked around at the other officer's hovering around the room. Soon, the Lieutenant returned and began questioning me again.

"Can I please go to the hospital and see Kevin?" I begged.

There was momentary silence. The officers glanced at each other, then an officer placed his hand on my shoulder.

"Ma'am, Kevin is deceased," he said.

"No!" I screamed, as I jumped up from my chair.

I stepped towards the kitchen island, and immediately fell to my knees. I cried out in prayer, "God, Jesus, please let Kevin into heaven! He didn't mean to shoot himself! He didn't mean it! He wasn't think-ing straight, please! Please!"

Tears flowed like heavy streams of water. I could hardly breathe. It couldn't be true! My mind was rushing through the events since the officers arrived. He couldn't be dead! As I lamented, an officer interrupted me.

"He didn't shoot himself. We shot him."

My mouth dropped open in shock.

"Why?" I asked. "Why would you shoot him? I heard him coming up the steps! He did everything you said! You even threw his jeans down the steps for him."

Officers questioned me again, about what happened before their arrival. Little did I know, the officers were protecting themselves and preparing for a possible legal battle. They already had an advantage over me because of all the questions they made me answer. I had spent over an hour answering the Lieutenant's questions, without any of them telling me what happened to Kevin. During what felt like an *interrogation*, I had repeatedly asked to go to the hospital to see him. The police should have told me they shot him! They never should have asked me to talk about my husband and his illness. I had been set-up, and it was too late.

After hours of questioning, I was instructed to leave my house, so the police could continue their investigation. I asked if I could go to my bathroom to get make-up and clothes, but I was sternly told, "No!" An officer said he would get what I needed and bring it to me. When I asked if I could get my purse from my van, I was told, "No," again. The officer said Bobbie could go to my van, but I couldn't.

My Dad's wise words echoed in my head, *Always be aware of your surroundings.* I looked around to observe what I could about the scene. Kevin's work boots were lying by the garage door, at the top of the stairs, and there was a shotgun shell lying beside them. I desperately wanted to see the stairwell and the basement, but I was told very strongly that I wasn't allowed near the scene.

Bobbie tried to support me, and helped gather some things I needed.

"Kimi will be at our house if you need to ask her anymore questions," she told the officers.

"We will call and let you know when Mrs. Burghess can go to the hospital to see her husband," an officer replied.

Bobbie made sure they had the correct phone number, and she walked me to their van. I couldn't do anything but cry. How was I going to tell Kasey that her Dad was dead? Our evening was going perfectly. Kevin and I had felt such love for each other, and now he was gone. It just couldn't be real. I felt so numb.

CHAPTER NINETEEN

THE FINAL GOODBYE

It was 2:35am on February 5, 2005, when I made the fatal 911 call, and around 2:50am when the first two officers arrived. Kevin was shot at 3:45am with a .12-gauge/00 shotgun and .40-caliber handgun.

According to the Medical Examiner's report, "Kevin died of multiple gunshot wounds to the upper torso at 0345 hours." The M.E. marked it as homicide. After reviewing all of the EMT reports, it was certain that Kevin died instantly. The EMT's were never able to get a pulse; there was no sign of life when they got to Kevin, or anytime after.

The State Police had the EMT's remove Kevin's body from the basement before the Medical Examiner could arrive on the scene. No one was allowed to give me any information. I wasn't told about Kevin's death until around 4:50am, over an hour after he was killed. The State Police put me through a battery of questions until almost 6am. I was then told to leave my house and go with my brother and sister-in-law, so the police could finish their investigation. They also instructed me not to go to the hospital until they called me, because they had some *things to do* before I would be allowed to see him.

The phone rang at about 7am; it was the hospital. Kevin's sister and older brother, Mark, were there asking to sign for his body. The hospital wanted to know if I would allow them to sign.

"No!" I answered immediately. "I will sign for my husband's body."

I had no idea how they found out what happened or why they were allowed to see Kevin before I was. He was *my* husband, and I had been waiting for hours to see him. I was told I couldn't go to the hospital until the State Police told me it was okay to go. Something was definitely wrong. Lucas quickly started his truck and drove me to the hospital, but Kevin's brother and sister were gone when we arrived. They didn't even wait to see me or speak to me. I had been in their family for eighteen years and taken care of Kevin through countless Bi-polar episodes, even at the expense of my own safety, and this was how they repaid me? It clearly wasn't going to be pleasant, but I still had to go to Kevin's parents' house and tell Kasey about her Dad.

Lucas and I arrived at the hospital and were led into an exam room, where I saw Kevin laying on a stretcher. He was covered with a white sheet from his neck down. I leaned over and kissed his forehead; he was so cold. A State Trooper was in the room, as if he was guarding the body. I wasn't allowed to be alone with Kevin, which made me very suspicious. *Why is there an officer in here?* I thought to myself. *I should be allowed to say goodbye to my husband in private... Is there something they aren't telling me?*

An officer told me an autopsy would be performed; then I was led to a desk and asked to sign some papers. Lucas and I were back at his house by 8:00am. Bobbie asked me when I wanted to talk to Kasey, and I said I was ready whenever Lucas felt like driving me over there. At approximately 8:30am, my brother drove me to Martha's.

I knocked on the door, and was greeted with a very cold hello.

"Is Kasey awake?" I asked. "I need to talk to her."

Lucas and I were told to wait in the living room and they would bring Kasey to me. They treated me more like a stranger than an in-law who had been part of their family for 18 years.

"They need to watch the attitude," Lucas said sternly.

I appreciated his concern. I had gone without sleep for over 24 hours, and was mentally and physically exhausted. I heard my daughter's voice, and I dropped to my knees as she came towards me for a hug. I sat her down and looked her in the eyes as I said, "I am so sorry

Kasey. Your Daddy is gone. The police shot him."

Kasey patted my shoulder and leaned forward to give me a hug. "It's okay Mommy," she replied. "We're safe now."

I was so proud of her maturity and strength.

Unfortunately, I still had to talk to Kevin's Mom; she was in a hospital bed, in the den. Martha had a rare blood cancer that was incurable. I didn't want to face her, but I knew I had to. Lucas followed me into the den. Martha was already crying, and my heart broke for her. I didn't know what to say except, "I am so sorry." She was kind and told me it wasn't my fault.

We talked briefly; I told her Kevin had been off his medication and had gotten progressively more violent since November. Martha said she was sorry for how her son had treated me. I appreciated her candor, but I couldn't help but think that her apology was 18 years past due. Maybe if someone other than me had encouraged Kevin to stay on his medication, it wouldn't have come to this. Now Kevin was gone, and I was widowed at age 41 with a 12-year-old daughter to rear by myself. I still had two parents in a nursing home, both with Alzheimer's disease, and I wasn't sure how I was going to manage everything on my own. Thoughts were flooding through my mind, when Lucas said, "We have to get back soon. An officer is coming to the house to talk to you."

Lucas said he wasn't sure why, but the State Police wanted to conduct a gunshot residue test on my hands. I told Martha good-bye, and she said Kasey could stay at her house, as long as I needed. I mentioned that Kasey didn't need to come home until we could get some *things* cleaned-up. Those words were as hard for me to say, as they were for Kevin's mother to hear. My entire life was wrapped up in Kevin; I had no idea how to unwrap myself from him, and I didn't want to. All I could think was, *This can't be real. There must be some kind of mistake. This didn't really happen, did it?*

An officer arrived at Lucas and Bobbie's around 11am. I tried to talk to him, but he was short with his answers, borderline rude. I asked why the state police were testing *my* hands, but he didn't want to answer. So I decided to reciprocate his unkind attitude and said,

"You're the ones who shot Kevin, not me!"

The officer was a little friendlier after he completed his test. He said my hands were negative for gunshot residue, and even said he was sorry for my loss. However, he left without telling me why my hands were tested.

Later, I found out that all the bullets fired from the gun when Kevin was locked in the basement bathroom were accounted for. However, there was a missing bullet. Out of the three shots Kevin fired at me before the police arrived, only two bullets could be found. An officer informed me they searched everywhere it could be, but it was nowhere to be found. I thought of the story in the Bible, when the apostle Paul was bitten by a poisonous snake. Paul shook the snake off, and miraculously wasn't harmed from the bite. Could it be? I would never know, but it didn't matter because I knew God could have miraculously removed *it* from me, if that was His plan.

My preacher came over to Lucas and Bobbie's to check on me. It was a nice visit and I certainly needed the prayer. Shortly after my pastor left, an officer called and said I was allowed to return to my house.

Lucas and Bobbie drove me back home and walked through the house with me. There were no police when we arrived. We walked down the hall towards my bedroom, and found a huge area of carpet cut out. My dresser drawers and closets had been ransacked; even the bathroom cabinets were left open from an obvious search. Thankfully, we had thought to bring a camera. I wasn't ready to approach the basement, so Bobbie took pictures of the remaining scene for me. She said we needed to call professionals to clean the carpet before Kasey saw it. I asked if she would take care of all the details for me; she kindly agreed to make the phone calls and arrangements.

During the entire ordeal, Bobbie was a huge help to me. She even helped hide me from multiple camera crews that were camped out on my front lawn. The news had spread across the entire state, and into several surrounding states.

Friends of my parents, who lived two hours away, called because they saw the story on the news. Calls of concern began to pour in, and friends began to show up at my house. Bobbie continued to help answer phone calls and greet visitors. I just needed rest. I couldn't even process Kevin being gone, much less tell people why.

I didn't know what was being said on TV or to the press; little did I know, the State Police had manipulated the story. They over-exaggerated the time line and events, to cover for the two officers who killed Kevin. They even used information I gave them about past episodes. They tried their best to make Kevin look like a mad man who shot up our house and threatened them while they were trying to help. I learned the hard way; the so-called "facts" given to the media, by police, should not be considered reliable or accurate in an officer-involved shooting. I was too dazed from the events to realize I should have spoken to the media myself. I should have given them the correct time line, and information about how the entire episode *actually* played out.

The State Police told the media they tried to talk to Kevin all night long, for hours, but he wouldn't co-operate or give up his weapons. They said he came up the steps pointing a gun at them, and they had to shoot him because they feared for their lives. The *truth* was (and is verified by the 500+ page police investigative report), they were at my house for less than one hour, before they shot and killed him. Not to mention, Kevin was locked in the basement bathroom for the majority of that time. He never shot a gun at anyone while the police were there. Each first responder that arrived on the scene admitted no weapons were found near Kevin's body, and there was nothing in his hands. The only so-called weapon found lying around, were the work boots Kevin threw at the two officers' right before they opened fire on him. (According to both of their depositions, given to my lawyer, one of the State Trooper's had thrown Kevin's work boots down the stairs, because they couldn't get a response from him.)

I provided Kevin with the most beautiful funeral I possibly could. I chose the casket, guest book, and everything else I thought he would like. On our wedding day, I had promised to love him in sickness and in health, for better or worse. I had fulfilled my promise not only to him, but to God as well.

I spared no expense on his funeral, and stayed with him every step of the way, up until the moment he was lowered into the ground. As the men lowered Kevin down into his grave, I waited patiently.

"Is there anything else I can do?" I asked.

One of the men looked up at me with sympathy and kindness, in his eyes.

"No ma'am, you have done all you could possibly do," he answered.

"Then I have seen him through to the end," I replied.

I think I saw a tear in his eye, as he nodded in agreement.

As I stood up from my chair and walked away from Kevin's grave, I focused my eyes on Kasey. I didn't know what lay ahead for she and I, but I knew God had released me from a life of fear and abuse. I had honored my marriage vows, and the Lord saw me through the many difficult years. He didn't leave me or forsake me, when I cried out for help.

Being a widow and single mother scared me, but God makes no mistakes. God knows our strengths and weaknesses, and the plans he has for us. A new chapter was beginning for my daughter and I. We would face our days with prayer, rely on the Lord to carry us through the difficult times, and trust that he would bless us for our faithfulness.

Despite the things I believe the officer's did wrong that fatal night, I know mistakes can be made, and there are many good police officer's who would never want to see a wrongful shooting covered up. In fact, the two deputies who were standing directly behind the State Troopers that shot Kevin, both quit their jobs with the Sheriff's department, after the incident in our home. They must have seen something they didn't agree with, and didn't want to be part of.

I will always believe the first noise I heard was one of Kevin's work boots hitting the officer who was holding the handgun. Being hit by the boot caused him to react by firing his weapon; the other officer reacted accordingly to his partner, and pulled the trigger to his shotgun....

There is one very important thing I will always be grateful for. A kind-hearted officer, who had been near the steps when it all happened, said, "I need to tell you something." I asked him what it was and he said, "When the bullets hit him and he began to fall, he cried out, 'Jesus Save Me!' Those were his last words." I smiled and said, "Thank you for telling me."(I didn't have to worry about my Kevin anymore; he was okay now.)

My faith is not based on feelings or emotions; it is secure because I have witnessed the amazing power of God. I have seen countless miracles happen before my eyes. There is no other name greater than the name of Jesus. There is no other name a person can cry out to, during their most difficult moments, who will show up to fight your battles for you. There is truly *something* about that name.

Through all the things I've witnessed in my life, and all the life-threatening moments I survived, one thing I know with unwavering certainty is this: **God is REAL!**

My Personal Observations
of Bi-polar Disorder

1. If you have a friend or family member who suffers from this illness, they will need your forgiveness and patience through each episode, and for the remainder of their life.

2. No matter what they say or do to you, please remember they have a mental illness.

   For example: I had a friend whose husband was diabetic. He had to take insulin twice daily. When his blood sugar was "off" he would sometimes cuss at her or tell her she was stupid. He would act totally out of character, due to his medical condition. Once his blood sugar was back in normal range, he was himself again. Naturally, she would forgive and forget all that he said or did during those times, because his behavior was due to his illness.

   Why do we not give our loved ones who suffer from a mental illness, such as Bi-polar Disorder, the same empathy and forgiveness? It's an illness they cannot control on their own.

3. Doctors never told me about things that go along with Bi-polar Disorder such as: grandiose behaviors, like taking extreme

chances or believing they have super-human abilities; going days without sleep; becoming easily addicted to things like gambling, drugs, alcohol, and pornography; spending money excessively. A Bi-polar also tends to be hypersexual (which can lead to perversions as well).

Doctors also didn't warn me about the violence involved with the illness. I was never told that Kevin could turn on me in a violent rage, and that my life could be in danger. The only thing the doctors wanted to say was that the word, Bi-polar, meant he could go from happy to sad, without provocation. The brain has a chemical imbalance, which causes abnormal emotional responses. This is part of my reason for writing this book. My husband wanted me to tell the truth about what life is *really* like, when you live with a person who has Bi-polar Disorder.

4. You will need to maintain a selfless, thick-skinned attitude, with your loved one who is a Bi-polar. Be strong with them, try to monitor their medications, and help them remember to take their medicine daily. A Bi-polar will most likely quit their medication, at some point, because they think they're feeling better. This is not a "feel better" illness; it is a LIFETIME illness, which will always require medication. You will need the patience of Job, and it will not be easy, but remember that this person needs you. A Bi-polar needs someone in their life who understands their illness, and will continue to love them despite what they might say or do.

5. Take this illness seriously. I have heard of family members who make fun of a loved one who is diagnosed as Bi-polar. Please do not call them "crazy" and make derogatory remarks towards them. Would you make fun of a person who was just diagnosed with brain cancer, or some other life-threatening illness? Of course not. Your loved one is not responsible for their condition, and they did not cause their disorder. No person should be made fun of or demeaned because they have an illness, of any kind.

6. As much as I do not like what happened to my husband, do not hesitate to **call 911** if your loved one becomes violent in a life-threatening way, to you or someone else.

7. I must put a warning here: Police are usually not trained to deal with mental illness. They will treat the person like someone who is on drugs, or someone who is simply violent and out of control. I hope the day will come, when police are trained to treat a person with a mental illness differently than a gang member or some other type of unlawful citizen. I pray they will learn to Taser a Bi-polar instead of shooting them. They should at least call the person's doctor, during the episode, and get a professional medical opinion on how to handle the situation.

> In the example of my friend, whose husband was diabetic: if it had been her husband out of control on Feb. 5th, and she told the police he was diabetic, they would have called a doctor, given him insulin, and he would have survived.

8. The words *Bi-polar* and *Mental Illness* often scare people, even police and first responders. Educate yourself on this disorder; learn all that you can about how to deal with the person when they are in a manic state. It may not be *your* loved one, with Bi-polar Disorder, you encounter one day that puts you in a difficult situation. Learn how to talk to the person and diffuse whatever negative actions, or violent actions, they may be spiraling towards. (Do NOT believe that *Bi-polar* means just depression!)

I am not a doctor, but I have 18 years of experience in dealing with extremely difficult situations. Always remain calm with the person. If you can walk away and get help, then do so. If you are trapped, then use *wise* words to diffuse the situation, and pray.

9. On a legal note: It is very difficult to bring an officer-involved shooting before a judge and get anywhere with a lawsuit against *any* division of Law Enforcement. I spent almost a year

reading and re-reading the 500+ page police report; I practically had every detail memorized. I had pictures and undeniable proof of errors; there were inconsistencies in what various officers stated during their depositions versus their statements in the police report.

Despite my evidence, I could not get a judge to allow a jury trial. During my final attempt, the judge I stood before said, *"I don't care what your pictures or your papers say. I have known both of these officer's for years, and if they say they feared for their lives, then that is good enough for me. Case closed!"* The gavel slammed down, and I was told I could leave the courtroom.

Just because you file a lawsuit does not mean you will get a trial, or get to say anything in court. I did not realize how "closed" and inaccessible the judicial system was to citizens, until this happened to me.

10. If the worst case happens, and your loved one is killed, insurance can be another very difficult obstacle. My husband was the sole source of income for our family. I had closed my gift shop to take care of my parents, who both had Alzheimer's. The officer's not only took a husband and a dad, but they took away our income when they killed him.

    Kevin had Accidental Death Insurance through the aluminum factory he worked for. Insurance took an automatic premium payment from each of his paychecks, for several years. When I tried to submit a claim for his accidental death, I was denied. The insurance company said they did not pay, when death resulted from a Bi-polar or mental issue. I told them they knew he was a Bi-polar when they were taking his premiums out of each paycheck, and when he received the insurance. I was told that if I could prove in court that the officer's were at fault, then they would re-consider. Of course, I never was allowed a trial, to prove anything. My daughter and I never received his Accidental Death Insurance.

11. The last issue I would like to bring awareness to, is the reaction of friends and family after the initial shock, and after the funeral has passed. Grief is difficult, and we often find ourselves not knowing what to say to the family that lost a loved one. In the case of my husband, we had tried to keep his illness as private as possible. After his death, there was total confusion, disbelief, and awkwardness amongst many friends and relatives.

My daughter and I had hundreds of people come to the funeral home and offer their love and support; however, it was the aftershock we were not prepared for. Weeks and months after his death, people began to talk and gossip with one another. Slowly, we became isolated and alone. My daughter would come home from school crying because of the mean things that were being said to her. Kids she once called "friend" were making fun of her "crazy Dad" and saying that she was crazy like him. It was obvious they had heard conversations about Bi-polar Disorder from the mouths of their parents. I assured her she had nothing to worry about, and she would not have to be in school with those kids when she started 7th grade, after summer break.

My daughter and I went to the courthouse and both had legal name changes. I returned to my maiden name, and my daughter took my maiden name, as her last name, and she chose to change her first and middle name as well. We moved from the house where Kevin was killed, and I purchased a home that would place her in a different school district. The challenges of our new life, alone, were beginning, and they were neither easy nor pleasant.

It is my prayer that no one goes through the rejection by family and friends, like we did. I hope with each passing year, more people will be open and honest about their struggles with Bi-polar Disorder; so both they and their families receive support. We would have appreciated (and desperately needed) hugs and words of encouragement, rather than sneers and whispers. Church youth leaders should be there for kids who lose a parent. They shouldn't just give them a business card and say, "Call me if you need anything." After this happened to my daughter, she tossed his card aside and said, "I can tell he really cares my Dad is dead!"

Please be the person who cares about and checks on children and families who have lost someone in a violent way, due to mental illness. You probably have *no idea* what they have experienced; just know they need love and friendship, not gossip.

My Personal Observations
of Alzheimer's' Disease

1. My first indication of a problem came after a missed lunch date. My Mom called me one evening, and asked if I wanted to have lunch with her the next day. I happily said I would love to. We lived approximately 20 miles apart; she would have about a thirty-minute drive into town, to meet me. I was at the restaurant at 11am, our agreed upon meeting time. I sat there almost two hours. I finally went home, so I could call her and see if everything was okay. (This was before the popularity of cell phones.) When she answered the phone and I asked her what happened, she became indignant and defensive. She responded with, "I don't know what the big deal is...it wasn't like we had to meet." This was totally out of character; I could tell she didn't really know what I was talking about, and didn't even remember we had talked the night before. (Alzheimer's may cause their personality to become the total opposite of how they conducted themselves before the illness.)

2. When you begin to suspect your loved one's memory loss is more than ordinary forgetfulness, it may be helpful to keep detailed notes. I began to journal the times of my parent's calls and unexpected visits to my gift shop. I made notes each time

they called me in the evening, asking me to take them to a doctor appointment the next day, or meet for lunch. I paid special attention to what they said they had done the day before, and who they claimed to have seen or spoken to. Without them realizing, I found that a lot of their days were "made-up." With just a few phone calls, I found out that people my parents claimed to have seen, had not heard from them in quite awhile. The more I observed, the more I realized something was definitely wrong.

Be diligent in staying in touch with your loved one, on a daily basis. They will be more confused in the evenings, and as the illness progresses, they will have difficulty distinguishing between day and night. Wandering is also common. Be alert!

3. There will be friends and family members who argue with you about your concerns of Alzheimer's or dementia. It can be very difficult to admit that your once vibrant, intelligent loved one is on a downward spiral to total memory loss. Your detailed notes, and confirmation from their doctor, may help friends and family accept the diagnosis easier. In the case of my parents, it was a very difficult road of acceptance by people.

    Prepare yourself for a certain amount of negative criticism and well-meaning advice from people who tell you how wrong you are. I was not able to convince family members of my parents' illness, despite a letter from their family doctor and a diagnosis from a geriatric specialist. Remember that *time* will tell the truth! As the illness progresses, it will become undeniable.

4. The specialist who confirmed both of my parents were in the first stages of Alzheimer's, told me the average life span is seven to ten years, once diagnosed. The specialist diagnosed both of them in 1998, and they both died in 2008. (10 years)

5. Difficult decisions will need to be made concerning such things as: how to take care of them at home or make arrangements for

them elsewhere; when to take away their car keys; how to legally protect their assets; who will be their power of attorney; when to remove items from their home, and prepare for a sale.

(Note: You can have a dual power of attorney, as well as having the estate checking account set-up to require two signatures.)

6. When it comes time to remove personal belongings from their home, I would suggest taking pictures of all items, and keep an extremely detailed list of who is to receive the items.

> *For example: One evening, I received a call from an older gentleman I had known from church, all of my life. He said, "I wanted you to know that your Dad wants me to have his antique violins. I went to visit him and we started talking about music, and he told me he would love for me to have all three violins." I was shocked! I replied, "Ed, my Dad would never give those violins to anyone other than my brother and I. You know he's been diagnosed with Alzheimer's and doesn't know what he is saying." He replied, "Well, I just wanted you to know he said I could have them."*

I will never know what became of those violins or many of my parents belongings. On various occasions, I found where the garage had been cleaned-out, as well as closets, drawers, etc. It was useless to ask my Mom or Dad about the missing items. They would tell me *they* had decided to clean things out. In reality, someone saw an opportunity to relieve them of valuable items, by convincing my parents they were there to *help*. My advice is to take valuable items out of their home, as soon as possible, so that non-family members can't help "clean things out" for them.

7. The most valuable advice I can give you in regards to this illness is to be extremely patient. No matter how many times your loved one asks the same question, try to keep a pleasant

tone and answer again and again, if need be. This will be one of the first indications there is a problem. They may ask you the same question five or six times during a single phone call. Remember, they're not trying to irritate you. They deserve your love and patience.

Do unto others as you would have them do unto you.

8. Being a caregiver can be stressful for you, as well as your family. Take care of yourself by getting plenty rest and proper nutrition. You cannot take care of your loved one if you become ill. Ask friends and other family members to fill the role as caregiver, at least once a week.

    This time in your life will pass, and it will become a memory. Make it a memory you can be proud of; knowing that you did the absolute best you could for your loved one.

CPSIA information can be obtained
at www.ICGtesting.com
Printed in the USA
FFOW03n1935221217
44123461-43445FF

9 781478 764410